Untold:
Northeastern Ontario's Military Past

VOLUME 1, 1662–WORLD WAR I

Copyright © 2018 by Dieter K. Buse and Graeme S. Mount

Library and Archives Canada Cataloguing in Publication

Buse, Dieter K. (Dieter Kurt), 1941-, author
    Untold : Northeastern Ontario's military past / Dieter K. Buse and Graeme S. Mount.

Contents: Volume 1. 1662-World War 1
Issued in print and electronic formats.
ISBN 978-0-9958235-0-1 (v. 1 : softcover).--ISBN 978-1-988989-05-1 (v. 1 : PDF)

    1. Ontario, Northern--History, Military. 2. Ontario, Northern--Biography.
I. Mount, Graeme S. (Graeme Stewart), 1939-, author II. Title.

FC3094.4.B87 2018   971.3'13   C2018-905097-7

Printed and bound in Canada on 100% recycled paper.

Book and Cover design: Olivier Lasser (depositphotos/ philipimage)
Dieter K. Buse photo credit: Judith M. Buse

The production of this book was made possible through the generous assistance of the Canada Council of the Arts and the Ontario Arts Council.

Published by:
Latitude 46 Publishing
info@latitude46publishing.com
Latitude46publishing.com

Dieter K. Buse
and Graeme S. Mount

Untold:
Northeastern Ontario's Military Past

VOLUME 1, 1662–WORLD WAR I

46

Sudbury: Latitude 46, 2018

Table of Contents

Introduction

William Merrifield (Regimental Number 8000) volunteered with 126 other Sault Ste. Marie men as soon as World War I broke out. Formerly of Sudbury, he left Northeastern Ontario to serve in Europe for more than four years. Twice, he spent weeks in hospital with what was known in the military as a "self-inflicted wound," venereal disease (one in five soldiers had VD). Merrifield won the Military Medal while working as a stretcher bearer on 6–7 November 1917 at the Battle of Passchendaele. His platoon raced through a heavy artillery barrage to reach the wounded, and despite being hit, Merrifield ignored his own wounds to treat five fallen soldiers and send them back to the aid station. He carried on with his platoon through the battle, and it was not until the next day that he was "forced to go out" to have his injuries treated. A year later, his heroism would again be recognized at Abancourt, where he won the Victoria Cross. Thereafter, various places sought to claim this hero as their own.

George Gibb (754325), a Scottish blacksmith from Echo Bay, enlisted with the local battalion, the 119th Algoma Overseas,[1] on 5 January 1916. He assigned $20 of his $30 monthly pay to his mother in Bar River. After training at Camp Borden and in England at Camp Witley, he was transferred out of the local battalion, first to the 8th Reserve Battalion, then to the 58th, arriving in France on 11 May 1918. Like one-tenth of those recruited, Gibb was killed. He died instantly, shot in the head by a machine gun, on 29 September 1918 at Cambrai, France.

Frank Lavalley (754529) was a 27-year-old Ojibwa sailor with ties to both Cape Croker and Wikwemikong. He enlisted in the 119th Algoma (Overseas) Battalion on 4 January 1916 at Manitowaning, on Manitoulin Island. His medical history describes him as a relatively tall man at 5 feet 8 inches, and "Strong Robust." Lavalley took machine gun training after being transferred to the 52th Battalion, and became a member of the 1st Canadian Motor Machine Gun Brigade. He died on 2 September 1918 in the last push to end the war, when his unit was involved in action on the road between Arras and Cambrai, France: "After having engaged the enemy, and whilst the car was being turned, it was struck by enemy shell fire, and Private Lavalley was instantly killed."[2]

On the home front, on 16 December 1918, the *Porcupine Advance* announced, "Timmins Red Cross Doing Good Work." It listed "Mrs. Simms, 2 pair socks; Mrs. Seeds, 4 pair socks; Mrs. Studor, 2 pair socks, 35 pillow slips …" continuing on for a half page. The mothers, aunts, and sisters of servicemen had their own role in the war and after it.

These are the kinds of stories that are explored in this book, demonstrating that Northeasterners fully participated in Canada's major conflicts, and developed local ways to remember those who served. Here we begin to tell the largely unknown military history of Northeastern Ontario. In researching and writing it, we have had the pleasure of visiting Legion halls and people's living rooms as they shared stories, photographs, documents, and evidence. In our quest for knowledge, librarians and archivists have gone far beyond the call of duty. We have read thousands of soldiers' service files, researched newspapers, and examined cenotaphs, yet we have only scratched the surface of involvement in and contributions to wars by people of the Northeast.

"Northeastern Ontario" comprises the territory of the six districts of Algoma, Cochrane, Manitoulin, Nipissing, Sudbury, and Temiskaming, or the area defined by Mattawa in the southeast to Moose Factory in the northeast, to White River in the northwest and Sault Ste. Marie in the southwest, including Manitoulin Island (see fig. 1).[3] In the late 19th and early 20th centuries, the area was called New Ontario.[4]

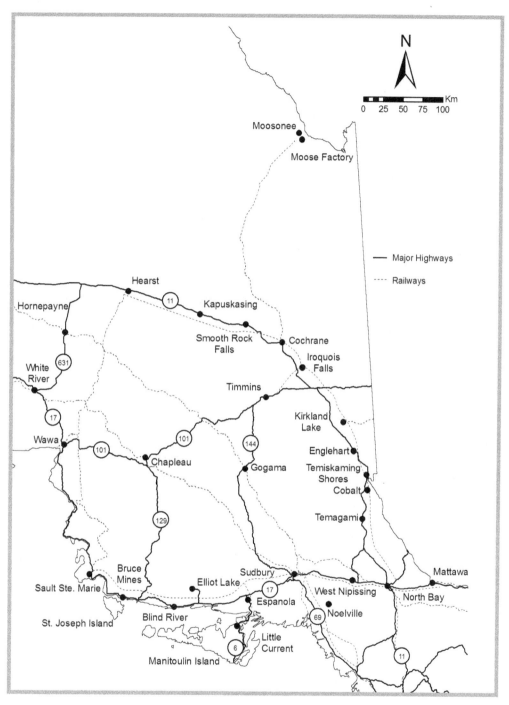

Map of Northeastern Ontario

Although many think of Northeastern Ontario as marginal—a place of few people and many resources—a closer look suggests that it has always been central to the country's development. For much of its history, Northeastern Ontario has been seen as a place to "pass through" en route to somewhere else. During the days of fur trading and exploration, its rivers and lakes (the Ottawa and Mattawa rivers, Trout Lake, Lake Nipissing, the French River, Lake Huron, and St. Marys River) provided the main thoroughfares to what became the Canadian West. The search for the Northwest Passage brought expeditions led by Henry Hudson and Thomas James to the northern bays that bear their names. The westward military and mounted police expeditions of 1870 and 1885 could pass through the region only because of what happened around Sault Ste. Marie during the War of 1812. During World War I, the region served as a place for troop trains from the west to rest and refuel as they passed through. Following completion of the Trans Canada highways (between 1923 and 1970; Ontario Highways 11 and 17), it continued to be seen as an area to pass through.

However, for much of this history, we contend, what is now Northeastern Ontario frequently served as a place important in its own right, though its contributions have been just as repeatedly overlooked or forgotten. The struggle between the French and British empires was played out strategically here. Lumber and minerals extracted from the region often bolstered Canada's economy. Early in the twentieth century, silver from Cobalt decisively reduced Ontario's debt. And during World War I, battalions of men raised in Northern hamlets, towns, and cities served in the Canadian Expeditionary Force fighting in Belgium and France.

The resourceful people of the region and their experience of warfare—local, national, and international—are the focus of this account. Northeasterners—men and women, young and middle-aged, English- and French-speaking, Cree, Anishinabek, or immigrants and their offspring—fought in as many wars as other Canadians, and their families suffered and contributed as much. Their stories remain relatively unknown. Increasingly, historical reassessments illustrate how many Indigenous snipers and soldiers decisively affected the battles of

World War I.[5] Yet their contributions and the war's impact are acknowledged primarily in historical novels, such as Joseph Boyden's *Three Day Road.* What of those Cree who canoed or walked 300 kilometres from Moose Factory to Cochrane to enlist? Did the women and children of Northeastern Ontario not experience shortages of food and coal on the home front? Did ethnic groups not repeatedly struggle with divided loyalties between their old and new homelands during war? If this book provides answers to such questions, it will have served the purpose of showing that Northeastern Ontario was more than a place to pass through. It also served as a source of men, women, and wartime support during the conflicts that have shaped the country.

The reasons for creating this book include the lack of attention nearly all Canadian military histories have given to the contributions, sacrifices, and involvement of men and women from Northeastern Ontario. Two examples of typical military history reveal the problem:

A recent, well-illustrated book about World War I war monuments in Canada offers not one example from Northeastern Ontario, despite some of the earliest and most impressive monuments having being built in the region.[6]

Much has been written about the so-called Mad Fourth Battalion at the Battle of Ypres in 1915, acknowledging the "Brantford Boys" but not the northerners who fought in the same battalion and who suffered similar casualties.[7]

Part of the problem is that although the volunteers and conscripts from Northeastern Ontario might have been recruited locally, the region's units and individuals often fought within battalions identified with more populated areas of southern Ontario.[8]

Wars are usually fought by countries, but Canada is diverse and regionally distinct. This is reflected in the historical and military accounts that often focus on major population centres. Yet soldiers were recruited locally; they had local as well national ties, and they identified with their kin and comrades from their home regions. Their different frames of reference are revealed in the way they described wartime experiences and the way they later commemorated the wars. This book adds the contributions, sacrifices, exploits, and experiences of the people from Northeastern Ontario to the existing accounts. Despite the blemishes, reservations, and problems that appear in the stories below, Northeasterners can be proud of their military past. They were intensively involved in the wars they fought, and most thought their cause important and just.

Readers may want to further pursue the histories of the individual soldiers who appear in this book. Service files are available at Library and Archives Canada. Regimental numbers (given in parentheses after soldiers' names) can be entered at the Library and Archives Canada website (www.bac-lac.gc.ca) in relevant databases, such as "South African War," or "Soldiers of the First World War," where soldiers' attestation (sign-up) forms can be retrieved. As of 2018, the complete service file, including medical history, for World War I soldiers can be viewed and downloaded.[9]

Part 1 of this volume relates the participation in and contribution to warfare by Northeasterners. Part 2 illustrates their diverse experiences of warfare on both the home and the fighting fronts. Part 3 looks at the ways that military struggles and personal losses are remembered publicly and privately. This volume highlights the period up to and including World War I; a second volume will address World War II and later conflicts. Blank pages at the end of each of the three parts of this book will allow readers to add the stories of their family members and fit their own histories into the larger context. In this way, the stories told here can be supplemented by the personal narratives and other untold stories.

Part 1: The Wars

CHAPTER 1

Warfare in Northeastern Ontario and Contributions to Warfare Elsewhere

Early Indigenous Warfare

Although many kinship tribes populated the northeast, two main groups dominated: the Anishinabek (who include the Ojibwa, Algonquin, and Odawa, among others) in the south and Mushkegowuk (Cree) in the north.[10] Hurons and Iroquois from farther south often intruded upon the region during periods of warfare, which was waged over territory and in retaliation for damages and deaths in previous conflicts. As it was in Europe, warfare became one path to social status in Indigenous societies, as an arena where men could demonstrate their skill, courage, strength, and resilience. According to one summary of warfare in Aboriginal societies, at times "war was a persistent reality."[11] At other times, peace developed, as illustrated by the rival early 17th-century co-existing confederacies of Iroquois and Hurons.

Little of the military history of Indigenous people has been researched and published. Information recorded by settlers and their descendants tells of intertribal conflict, but often these accounts served settler-society interests. For instance, the pamphlet *Warriors of the Ojibway Country* (1908) positions the 97th Algonquin Rifles, a militia unit formed in Sault Ste. Marie, as the heirs of Algonquin "Braves" defending their territory from "the Docotas on the west and Iroquois on the east."[12] The pamphlet tells of a 1662 battle between Algonquins and Iroquois, who had intruded north to the St. Marys Rapids, known as Baw-a-ting (now Sault Ste. Marie). According to this account, the Algonquins fell upon the Iroquois camp west of the rapids at Gros Cap (just west of the Sault), taking their enemies by surprise and killing all but two, who were tortured and sent back to their people as a warning against future intrusions.[13]

While the military history of the Anishinabek and Mushegowuk is yet to be written, it has been well established that Europeans encouraged tribal conflicts over territory, especially over areas with fur, fish, and game, as they began to infringe on Indigenous trading areas and searched for allies in their imperial conquest of the continent. Indigenous people also often fought as allies in French and English conflicts over trade and sovereignty, and their European allies acknowledged their skills at fighting in small groups on difficult terrain.

Northeastern Ontario experienced a long period of displacement of Indigenous and fur-trading societies with the subsequent marginalization and destruction of Indigenous cultures by colonizing settlers. Places and people changed as colonists infringed on Indigenous territories and created new identities during the 19th and 20th centuries.[14] More needs to be learned about the way that process was carried out, but settlers slowly submerged the traditions of the Indigenous people. Still, Indigenous cultures persist, and some World War I Indigenous participants referred to their own warrior tradition as a reason for their enlistment. The cenotaph at Wikwemikong (unceded Indigenous territory) on Manitoulin Island tellingly states, "We are the Warriors of this village who served and fought for peace and freedom. To you we pass on the eagle feather. A symbol of honor and compassion, so that you may carry on the tradition of the Warrior, whenever and wherever you are called."

The Imperial Ambitions of England and France

European great power rivalry often caused tensions in Northeastern Ontario. Between 1610 and 1631, Henry Hudson and Thomas James sailed west in the service of England, in search of the Northwest Passage, a water route from England to Asia. They discovered that the waters now bearing their surnames were not the Pacific Ocean, nor even a strait, but bays. During a horrendous winter in 1631–32 on Charlton Island, about 100 kilometres northeast of what is now Moose Factory, James decided that if a water route existed across North America to Asia, it was too far north to be useful. For a generation, the English avoided the area.

Then, in the early 1660s, Médard Chouart des Groseilliers and Pierre-Esprit Radisson, two explorers/fur traders, travelled north from New France to Hudsons Bay in search of furs. They returned to Québec City with such wonderful pelts that the colonial governor confiscated them on a technicality. Furious at what they considered robbery, Radisson and Groseilliers travelled to negotiate with the rival English in London in 1665. They won the support of Prince Rupert, uncle of King Charles II (1660–85), for a new venture. In 1670, the king chartered the Hudson's Bay Company (HBC), and the following year the company established Rupert House, its first fur-trading outpost in the area, which is now Waskaganish on James Bay's Quebec shore. Moose Factory, the second outpost created to draw the fur trade from the French in the south, was established on an island near the mouth of the Moose River in 1673.[15] This commercial rivalry between Britain and France sometimes led to conflict. For instance, in 1686, a French overland expedition led by Pierre de Troyes captured Moose Factory and renamed it St. Louis. It would be returned to the British by the Treaty of Utrecht in 1713, but not manned until the 1730s.

Around the globe from 1688 to 1815, Great Britain was frequently at war with France. Like two bull moose circling each other, they tried to gain control over territory by much huffing and bluffing. Louis XIV, the ambitious King of France (1643–1715), hoped to expand his empire beyond the St. Lawrence Valley, while the English Crown laid claim to what it called Rupert's Land—all waters flowing into Hudson Bay. Although religion intensified the animosity between English and French, it had limited significance in these essentially territorial battles, and the sparring continued even during the reign of England's last Roman Catholic king, James II (1685–88). Few physical battles took place in Northeastern Ontario; the competition mostly involved forays into each other's territories and claims about who had trading rights and sovereignty over rich lands.

One European dynastic struggle had important implications for the residents of what is Northeastern Ontario. At the end of the War of the Spanish Succession (1700–13), in the Treaty of Utrecht, France dropped its claims to all territory north of the Arctic/Atlantic watershed that runs through Northeastern Ontario; the watershed became the boundary between Britain and France. Given the pretence that the lands were empty, the Europeans involved in the disputes did not consider Indigenous interests. Then, in 1763, after two more lengthy wars, the French ceded all lands of the North American mainland to Britain. Until 1912, the watershed marked the northern limits of Ontario, and it continues to serve as an ecclesiastical boundary. To its north are the Roman Catholic Diocese of Hearst and the Anglican Diocese of Moosonee. To its south are the Roman Catholic Diocese of Sault Ste. Marie and Anglican Diocese of Algoma. These conflicts show that, as early as the 18th century, distant wars influenced the social fabric of Northeastern Ontario in terms of which religion and language would dominate.

Challenges from the United States: The War of 1812 and the Fenians

Negotiations and warfare, most of which occurred elsewhere, determined Canada's borders and its trading routes in Northeastern Ontario. The Treaty of Paris of 1783, whereby the British accepted the independence of the United States, established the Great Lakes and their connecting waterways as the boundary between the United States and British North America. Again British negotiators had not consulted Indigenous people, despite the fact that the outcome affected them most directly. One of the issues driving the American rebellion had been the colonists' desire to settle the lands between the Appalachian Mountains and the Mississippi River. The Treaty of Paris clearly declared such lands south of the Great Lakes to be part of the United States, land where Americans of European extraction could live. As a result, war between American settlers and the Indigenous tribes became a strong probability. Britain feared that such conflicts could spill over the border into British North America if, for instance, Indigenous people attacked American settlers, and then fled to British territory. If the US Army pursued its enemies into British North American territory, it could lead to war. Hence, the British government decided to delay implementation of the boundary agreement, and British soldiers remained at their posts south of the Great Lakes. One of those posts, Fort Mackinac on Mackinac Island, located just east of the Strait of Mackinac in Lake Huron, strategically overlooked the links between lakes Huron and Michigan (see fig. 1.1).

Figure 1.1. Map of area around Sault Ste. Marie, showing waterways and contested territory. (Courtesy of the Geological Survey of Canada, 1901)

Events in Europe once again intervened.[16] War broke out between Britain and France in 1793. Jay's Treaty, signed in 1794, handed over Fort Mackinac to the Americans, postponing conflict between Britain and the United States for a generation and leaving Britain free to focus on the war in Europe. In 1796, the British Army left Fort Mackinac, which became an outpost of the US Army. The British built Fort St. Joseph (now a National Historic Site), on the southernmost tip of St. Joseph Island, near the mouth of the St. Marys River. At the same time, employees of the North West Company, most of them Métis, relocated from Sault Ste. Marie in what is now Michigan to the Canadian side of the St. Marys River, where they continued to call their community Sault Ste. Marie. Fort St. Joseph and the North West Company canoe canal at Sault Ste. Marie served as vital links for explorers and the fur trade, then a pillar of the Canadian economy. Water provided the only transportation from Montreal to western Canada: up the Ottawa River to Mattawa, up the Mattawa River to Trout Lake, across a short portage, down LaVase Creek and across Lake Nipissing, down the French River to Lake Huron, and along the northern shoreline to Sault Ste. Marie, defended by Fort St. Joseph.

Jay's Treaty bought time, but did not resolve all the issues between Britain and the United States. During the war with France, the British Navy prevented American trading ships from reaching continental Europe to supply Emperor Napoleon's France, and British ships also forced US seamen into the British Navy. Hence, in 1812 President James Madison asked Congress to declare war on the United Kingdom. The War of 1812 lasted until December 1814.

British North America was the battleground, largely because of its accessibility to US forces. Most of the fighting, but not all of it, took place in what is now southern Ontario.[17] Sir Isaac Brock, the administrator of Upper Canada (since the Lieutenant-Governor was absent), notified the garrison at Fort St. Joseph of the outbreak of war before the Americans at Fort Mackinac received the news. In the pre-dawn darkness of 17 July 1812, 34 British privates, four corporals, two sergeants, an ensign, and two lieutenants of the 10th Royal Veteran Battalion, accompanied by some 200 French Canadian fur traders (a rough militia) and about 400 Odawa, Ojibwa, Menominee, and Winnebago warriors, crossed Lake Huron and landed on Mackinac Island, where they captured the fort and its surprised American soldiers.[18]

The garrison from Fort St. Joseph remained on Mackinac Island for the duration of the war. In 1814, it successfully resisted when the United States tried to retake the island, and also thwarted an attempt by the US schooners *Tigress* and *Scorpion* to stop the British from sending supplies to Mackinac Island. British forces captured both ships in early September by a surprise attack. American soldiers did, nevertheless, destroy Fort St. Joseph during the war, as well as the Canadian canal at Sault Ste. Marie, which the North West Company had constructed to enable its canoes to bypass rapids on the St. Marys River between Lake Superior and Lake Huron. The events in Northeastern Ontario proved crucial. Control of Fort Mackinac guaranteed the British and Canadian control of the upper Great Lakes, and thus of the route to the west. This provided a bargaining chip against pressure for northward boundary adjustments at the talks in Ghent, Belgium, at the end of the war.[19]

The Rebellions of 1837 also heightened tensions with the United States. By the 1830s, most adult white males could vote in Upper Canada, but the legislative assembly's influence was limited because the legislative council, appointed by the Lieutenant-Governor, rejected most of the assembly's proposed legislation. A small and wealthy élite thus held power disproportionate to its numbers. In 1837, rebellion broke out in Upper Canada, and when they lost, some rebels fled to the United States. By then, the Hudson's Bay Company had purchased the North West Company. The HBC factor at Sault Ste. Marie, William Nourie, cultivated friendly relations with his counterpart across the river, Gabriel Franchère of the American Fur Company, and he learned that US citizens sympathetic to the rebel cause planned an attack. In the aftermath of the War of 1812, with many Anglo-American issues still unresolved, the US government had built forts along the border, including Fort Brady in Sault Ste. Marie. In 1838, the commander at Fort Brady was Colonel George Croghan, leader of the forces who had tried and failed to retake Mackinac Island in 1814. Artillery shots aimed at the Canadian Sault rang out from Fort Brady on 12 September 1838, but amounted to little: after Croghan's departure, authorities at Fort Brady expressed regret for the incident.[20] Because of ongoing concerns about US aggression, as well as Britain's decision to move its troops to other parts of the empire, the

Legislature of the Province of Canada (present-day Quebec and Ontario south of the Arctic–Atlantic watershed) passed militia acts affecting all males from 16 to 60. While few operational militia companies came into being, there was one at the Canadian Sault in 1849.

A few decades later, the Fenian crisis again brought the threat of violence to Northeastern Ontario. The Fenians were Irish Americans (also known as the Irish Brotherhood) fighting for Ireland's independence. In 1800, an act of the British Parliament had made Ireland an integral part of the United Kingdom, but Ireland's Roman Catholics saw themselves as a conquered people and their island as occupied territory. Many wanted full independence. Meanwhile, a famine between 1845 and 1852 forced mass emigration. The Irish blamed British misrule, with reason: while multitudes of Irish starved, British authorities exported food from Ireland.[21] Hundreds of thousands of angry Irish émigrés migrated to the northern United States, arriving just as north–south tensions were escalating. During the US Civil War, the British professed neutrality (and in fact favoured the secessionist slave states in the south) in a war that many regarded as a battle between good and evil.[22] Many Irish Americans fought for the North, gaining military experience—and some put that experience to use shortly after the war.

Fenians could not strike at Britain from the United States, but British North America lay within walking distance. In 1866, they launched a series of raids across the international border into the Maritimes and what is now southern Ontario.[23] Sault Ste. Marie too had a scare. Rumours of American invasion had led to the formation of a local Sault militia company in 1861, as well as companies at Bruce Mines (to protect its copper mines) and Thessalon. By 1862, a small company drilled at the school house in Sault Ste. Marie, and a battery with canon was organized. When a merchant named O'Neill from Sault Ste. Marie, Michigan, warned that 400 Fenians were assembling in Marquette and planning to attack, the Sault militia mobilized, patrolling the border for 13 days from 6 to 19 June 1866. No incursions took place,[24] but some militia members, being seasoned troops, prepared to defend Sault Ste. Marie and surrounding area. While standing guard, they discovered a barrel of communion wine deposited by an itinerant priest, and a boisterous party ensued.

The Red River Rebellion, though it took place in Manitoba, also affected Northeastern Ontario. Troops and militia were sent west under Colonel Garnet Wolseley to suppress the rebellion. Because the Americans refused to allow Canadian military goods or personnel to pass through the canal on the US side of the St Marys River between lakes Huron and Superior, Canada's first prime minister, Sir John A. Macdonald, announced the construction of a large, new canal at the Canadian Sault (see fig. 1.2). Though it did not become operational until 1895, the canal's necessity illustrates how the region was affected by military events occurring elsewhere.[25] The existence of the Soo locks (the world's first electrically operated canal and now a Canadian National Historic site) demonstrated that Northeastern Ontario was key to westward travel, security, trade, and expansion for Canada.

Figure 1.2. Construction of the Sault Canal. (Courtesy of Parks Canada)

The British and US governments resolved their serious differences in 1871, most of them connected to Britain's alleged support for the Confederacy during the US Civil War. The British had decided that a land war against the US had become unthinkable and that the cost of empire was becoming too high. They wanted to transfer British soldiers to other parts of the empire (India, Africa), or Europe (where Germany, having unified in 1871, was quickly industrializing and developing into a potential rival). Having decided to withdraw its soldiers from Canada, the British government sought to resolve the issues that inflamed Anglo-American relations and, to that end, negotiated the 1871 Treaty of Washington. Only since then has it been appropriate to speak of an undefended border between Canada and the United States.

Though no war threatened, a short-lived militia existed at Sault Ste. Marie from 1887 to 1896.[26] In seeking funding, political leaders from northwestern Ontario and the Sault argued that transportation, such as the canal and the new transcontinental railway, needed protection and that large numbers of foreign workers might create labour unrest. However, the 96th "District of Algoma" Battalion of Rifles militia unit (see fig. 1.3) lasted only nine years, mainly because of insufficient funds, lack of interest and manpower, and an inability to organize training over such a large area.

Figure 1.3. The cap badge of the 96th "District of Algoma" Battalion of Rifles militia. (Courtesy of Phil Miller, Sault Ste. Marie)

The South African War

The next important British imperialist venture, the South African War (or Anglo-Boer War, 1899–1902), drew volunteers from Northeastern Ontario.[27] The British Empire fought the settlers of Dutch and French Huguenot extraction (collectively Boers) who had settled near the Cape of Good Hope in the 17th century. During the Napoleonic Wars, the British had captured the militarily strategic cape from the Dutch. Almost a century later, the British fought the Boers for control of diamond and gold territory in southern Africa. During the war, the British set up the world's second concentration camps (the Spanish had first used them in Cuba) and caused the deaths of 28,000 civilians, mostly by starvation.

At the beginning of the war, Canada's prime minister, Sir Wilfrid Laurier (1896–1911), faced a dilemma. Canada, under the British North America Act, was legally at war whenever the United Kingdom fought. However, the government of Canada could decide the extent of its contribution. Many French Canadians sympathized with the Boers, whom they regarded as fellow victims of British imperialism. However, Canadians of British extraction enthusiastically supported the British cause. Despite the absence of British soldiers, some Canadians took pride in their status as British subjects living in a mighty empire, in whose expansion they gloried.[28] Some shared the typical racial attitudes of the day. James Orr, publisher and principal editor of the *Sudbury Journal*, strongly supported "Anglo-Saxon" imperialism and ignored all its shortcomings, such as the assumption that white people had the right to govern all others. "The Anglo-Saxon race," he wrote in an editorial of 9 November 1899, "[must] civilize the waste places of the world, bring up the dependent races, educate them to the standard of manhood and liberty that we ourselves enjoy." Laurier resolved the matter by allowing those who wanted to fight in South Africa to go as part of the British army, and 8,372 men volunteered.[29] The Canadian troops served in their own Canadian units within the British army.

The number of those who participated from Northeastern Ontario is not clear but, according to contemporary newspapers, Sault Ste. Marie responded positively three times to calls for volunteers, and nine went from North Bay. Among those were Richard Pringle (7312), a time keeper/coachman from Sault Ste. Marie. His attestation form and discharge document (figs. 1.4, 1.5) indicate that he served as a bugler in the 2nd Battalion of the Canadian Mounted Rifles for 12 months before returning to work. The estimate of his health and deportment (see fig. 1.5) illustrates assumptions about the type of men wanted.

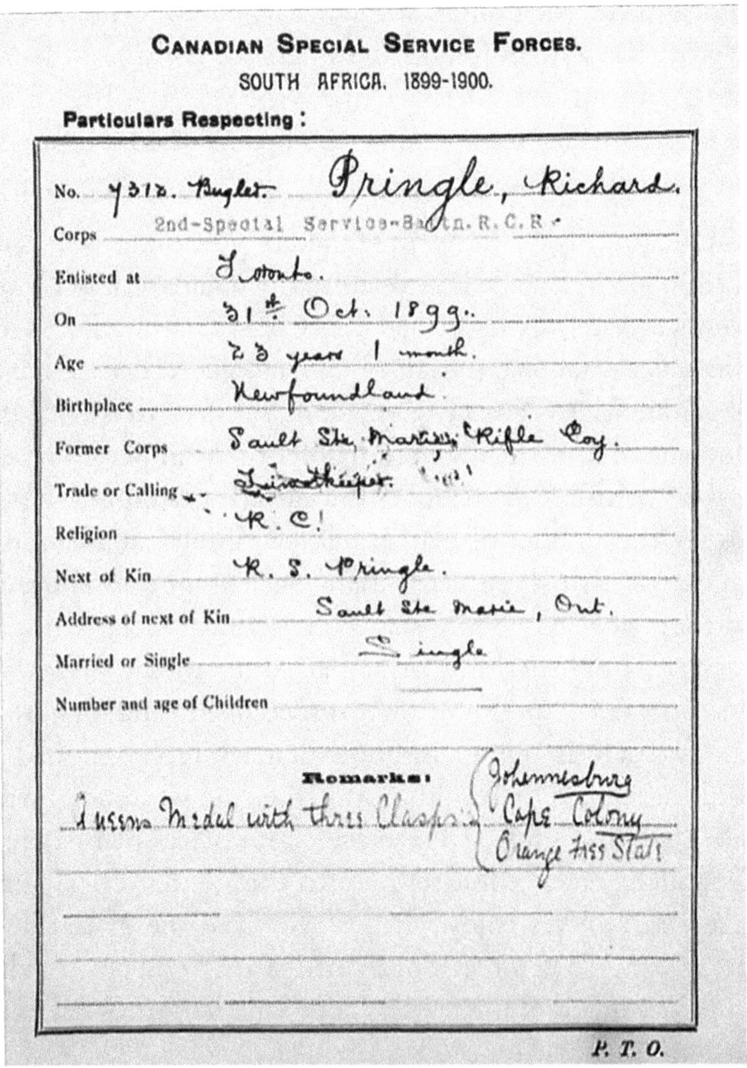

CANADIAN SPECIAL SERVICE FORCES.

SOUTH AFRICA. 1899-1900.

Particulars Respecting:

No. 7312. Bugler. Pringle, Richard.

Corps 2nd-Special Service-Battn. R.C.R.

Enlisted at Toronto.

On 31st Oct. 1899.

Age 23 years 1 month.

Birthplace Newfoundland.

Former Corps Sault Ste. Marie Rifle Coy.

Trade or Calling Timekeeper.

Religion R.C.

Next of Kin R. S. Pringle.

Address of next of Kin Sault Ste Marie, Ont.

Married or Single Single

Number and age of Children

Remarks:

Queens Medal with three Clasps: Johannesburg, Cape Colony, Orange Free State

P. T. O.

Figure 1.4. Attestation form for Richard Pringle (7312) of Sault Ste. Marie, who served in the South African War. Note the list of medals at the bottom of the form, added after the war. (Courtesy of Library and Archives Canada)

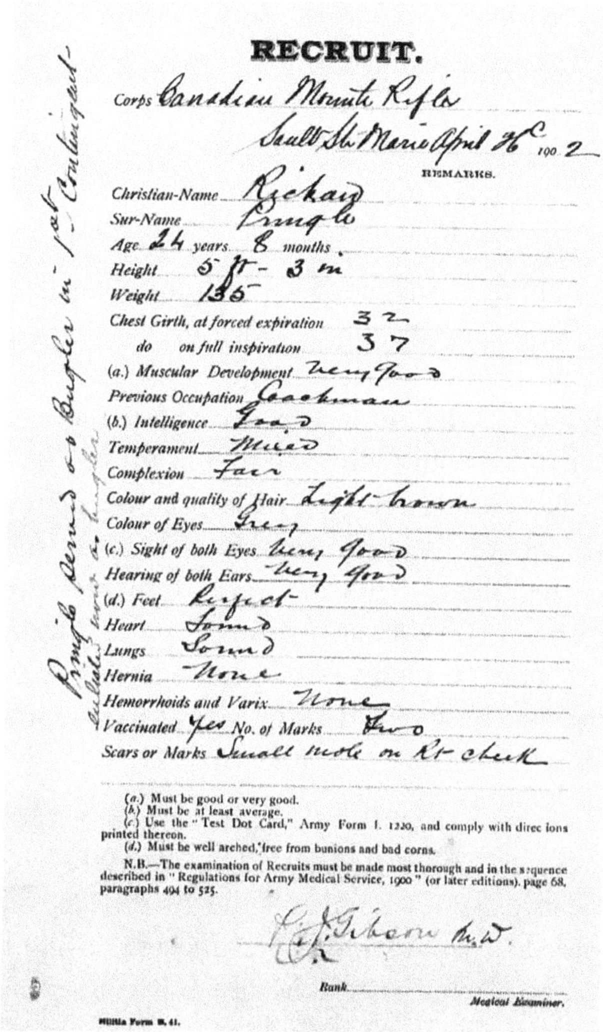

RECRUIT.

Corps Canadian Mounted Rifles

Sault Ste Marie April 16th 1902

REMARKS.

Christian-Name Richard
Sur-Name Pringle
Age 24 years 8 months
Height 5 ft - 3 in
Weight 135
Chest Girth, at forced expiration 32
do on full inspiration 37
(a.) Muscular Development Very Good
Previous Occupation Coachman
(b.) Intelligence Good
Temperament Mixed
Complexion Fair
Colour and quality of Hair Light brown
Colour of Eyes Grey
(c.) Sight of both Eyes Very Good
Hearing of both Ears Very Good
(d.) Feet Perfect
Heart Sound
Lungs Sound
Hernia None
Hemorrhoids and Varix None
Vaccinated Yes No. of Marks Two
Scars or Marks Small mole on Rt cheek

(a.) Must be good or very good.
(b.) Must be at least average.
(c.) Use the "Test Dot Card," Army Form I. 1220, and comply with direc ions printed thereon.
(d.) Must be well arched, free from bunions and bad corns.

N.B.—The examination of Recruits must be made most thorough and in the sequence described in "Regulations for Army Medical Service, 1900" (or later editions), page 68, paragraphs 494 to 525.

Rank.............................
Medical Examiner.

Militia Form B. 41.

Figure 1.5. Discharge form for Richard Pringle (7312). Note the attention to his physical and mental fitness for service. (Courtesy of Library and Archives Canada)

Like Pringle, mineral prospector Corporal Frank Leach (182) enlisted from Sault Ste. Marie. During the war he served, according to his service file, in the "F[iel]d Intelligence Dep[artmen]t" trying to find out who supported the Boers. After the war, he worked for the Canadian Pacific Railway (CPR) as an engineer. Another volunteer, F.E. Lea (317), gave his mother in Toronto as next of kin and enlisted in Guelph, but in

1901 he enquired with the military authorities from Copper Cliff about the medals he had not received. He worked as a metal assayer. By contrast, Dr. James Henderson (43), later a druggist in Warren, east of Sudbury, served in a field hospital in South Africa, though in 1900 he was still a medical student. Like Lea, in 1905 he too wanted acknowledgement in the form of a medal, which he hinted that everyone else had received.

Information about residents of what is now Northeastern Ontario who may have fought in the South African War remains somewhat unreliable. The cenotaph in Warren names a Darrel Warren as a veteran of that war. The files on the South African War at Library and Archives Canada confirm that such an individual fought in that war, but show no association with Warren, Ontario. A local history of the town of Capreol claims that Frank Dennie "served in the Boer War in 1898 in the Lord Strathcona Horse regiment,"[30] but the war did not start until 1899, and that regiment formed in 1900, specifically for the South African War. No service record could be found for anyone with his or a similar name. Even his descendants admit he had a strong urge to invent whatever story served his purposes.[31]

The Canadian canal at Sault Ste. Marie was a security concern during the South African War.[32] Alerted early in January 1900 by Great Britain's vice-consul in Seattle, James Laidlaw—the British consul at Portland, Oregon—discovered that residents of Seattle were raising funds to assist the Boers, and that a man named Magee was raising military forces. Laidlaw took the matter seriously enough to ask the vice-consul at Seattle to maintain close surveillance, and Clayton Pickersgill, the British consul general in San Francisco, engaged the consulate general's law firm, to employ Agent X, an amateur detective. Agent X remained so mysterious that Pickersgill did not learn for months that he dealt with a woman.

With a willingness to take considerable risks in return for expenses plus $120 per month, X won the confidence of the conspirators. On 28 March 1900, X reported that she had interviewed a fanatically anti-British Irish-American named Donovan, who had spent four weeks in Esquimalt planning an attack on Canada. Donovan remains thoroughly mysterious. Even X did not know his real identity. After a projected attack on Esquimalt and Lachine failed to materialize, on 19 June 1900,

Donovan told X of plans to dynamite the Lachine Canal at Montreal and the Sault Ste. Marie Canal on the Canadian side of the St. Marys River. Irish agents, subsequently arrested, had already attacked the Welland Canal. Lachine would be first, Donovan said, and three men had already gone to Montreal to do the job. The men slated for Sault Ste. Marie had already been chosen.

The Dominion Police, a federal force later absorbed into the Royal Canadian Mounted Police (RCMP), took these threats seriously. On 11 July 1900, Colonel Arthur Percy Sherwood explained that he needed $26,000 to hire men to guard Canada's most strategic canals: 21 at Welland, 5 at Sault Ste. Marie, 16 at Lachine, 4 at Soulanges (near Montreal), and 16 at Cornwall. Terrorist plots against Canadian targets appear to have stopped about the middle of 1900, however, presumably because British and Canadian intelligence proved adequate.

During the South African War, Northeastern Ontario's local militia organizations became permanent and better organized. Established by 1900, the 97th Algonquin Rifles regiment consisted of four companies of 20 to 50 men each, with A Company in the Sault and Bruce Mines, B at Sudbury (initially formed in 1896), C at Thessalon (1899), and D at Sturgeon Falls; later E at Massey, F at Gore Bay (formed in 1892), and H at New Liskeard. They all became part of the 97th.[33] The militia pay lists of their annual training camps indicate that just before World War I small groups of men received basic instructions in drill, shooting, and operating as a unit, while officers learned history and management. At least 14 officers and 246 men underwent training in 1908; the numbers remained stable with slight increases until 1914.[34]

Militias and regular troops in New Ontario usually served under officers who saw themselves as prominent social leaders, which they undoubtedly were as lawyers, businessmen, and wealthy landowners. Occasionally, the state employed the militia to deny social rights and contain unrest from the lower classes. That aspect of military life first appeared in Northeastern Ontario during riots at Sault Ste. Marie in 1903. In 1903, when the resource and financial empire of F.H. Clergue collapsed, more than 3,500 lumbermen and mine workers (nearly a third of the work force of the Sault area) went on strike and threatened to riot to obtain their unpaid wages.[35] The authorities summoned the militia to guard buildings until regular troops could arrive from Toronto. The troop presence contained the violence, but the workers never received their wages.

The headquarters of the 97th Algonquin Rifles militia shifted to Sudbury in 1908. Perhaps because of that move, at Sault Ste. Marie Colonel Sydney Penhorwood organized the 51st Soo Rifles militia in 1913. Meanwhile, in North Bay a militia started in 1902; Company G of the 23rd Regiment numbered 35 men by 1909; the regiment was headquartered in Parry Sound. These militias provided the main recruiting base at the start of World War I. Most places in Northeastern Ontario had only recently been established, so the fact that there were at least nine companies of militia of approximately 30 to 50 men each demonstrates that the military history of the region has been more continuous and more significant than acknowledged. For example, by 20 August 1914, 16 days after World War I started, Sault Ste. Marie sent 127 volunteers recruited through its militia (fig. 1.6). Similar numbers were recruited through the other New Ontario militia units identified above.

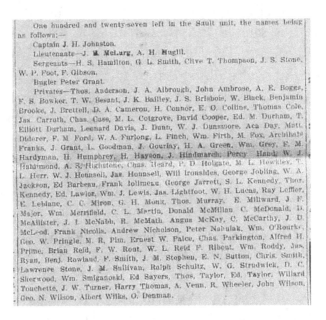

Figure 1.6. List of Sault Ste. Marie area volunteers
for the Canadian Expeditionary Force on Day 16 of World War I.
(Courtesy Sault Star, a division of Postmedia Network Inc.)

Until the Great War broke out in 1914, warfare and military matters remained an undercurrent involving a small number of men in Northeastern Ontario. The South African War produced much pro-British rhetoric, but daily existence in the region continued to be dominated by mining boom-and-bust cycles, railway building, and the search for new farmland. Indigenous warrior traditions had mostly been marginalized. The struggles of the so-called Great Powers over three centuries had significantly reshaped the boundaries, languages, and peoples of Northeastern Ontario. The threats from the United States inspired militia building and the South African conflict consolidated it. That generally peaceful dominion would be shattered in 1914.

Notes

Notes

CHAPTER 2

The World-Shattering War: The Northeast Marches Along, 1914–16

World War I shattered lives and families in Northeastern Ontario as the area contributed heavily to the war effort. The extent of Northeasterners' activities and sacrifices generally has not been researched and explained. However, a review of the conflict can reveal the extent of Northeastern Ontario's participation by noting their presence at every major battle.

Almost all observers agree that World War I was a tragedy for both Canada and the globe. It differed from World War II, when leaders who would appropriately be charged with war crimes, Adolf Hitler and his fellow Nazis, threatened the world. The first war resulted from mistakes rather than crimes. Unlike World War II, it left the world worse than it had been, with influenza pandemics, political destabilization, and a political and economic climate that resulted in fascism, the spread of communism, and a great depression barely a decade later. Historical overviews have summarized the causes of the war as the system of international alliances, which drew allied countries into each other's conflicts, and the imperialist and territorial ambitions of European states. Once the declarations of war and the process of mobilization began, most European countries, including Britain (which had strategic interests in the Low Countries and feared German control over the continent) participated.

Unresolved pre-war issues created tension in Europe. The German annexation of the French province of Alsace-Lorraine at the end of the Franco-Prussian War (1870–71) led French governments to assume that Germany was their principal foreign enemy and that war against Germany was highly probable. In 1894, France and Russia had concluded a military alliance clearly aimed against Germany. Not unreasonably, German strategists prepared for a war on two fronts, against France and Russia simultaneously. Germany's Schlieffen Plan envisioned a rapid defeat of France before Russia could undertake serious action, but the plan required the German army to travel through Belgium, despite the small country's neutrality. Britain also regarded Germany as a threat, since, throughout the reign of Kaiser Wilhelm II (1888–1918), Germany had been building up its navy.

In the Balkans, relations were increasingly tense. In violation of treaty commitments dating from 1878, the Austro-Hungarian Empire annexed the Ottoman province of Bosnia-Herzegovina in 1908. This thwarted the ambitions of Serbian rulers, who wanted to incorporate the Slavs of the Balkan Peninsula into a united country (this would happen in 1918, with the creation of Yugoslavia). Serbia's ally, Russia, recently defeated in the Russo-Japanese War of 1904–1905, took no action. However, on 28 June 1914, a Serb terrorist assassinated the heir to the Austro-Hungarian throne, and the Austro-Hungarian government threatened to invade Serbia. This time Russia insisted that it would support the Serbs, and the German government said that it would support the Austro-Hungarian Empire to punish Serbia. Assuming that war against Russia would also involve war against France, Germany activated the Schlieffen Plan, and German forces entered Belgium. Evidence has surfaced that the British government had decided to assist France and Russia before the German invasion of Belgium, but the fate of Belgium made it possible to sell the war to the general public.[36] Once Britain declared war, Canada was again automatically involved, though Canadians could decide on the extent of their commitment.

The diplomatic manoeuvring resulted in two camps: the Allies (primarily Britain and France with their colonies [including Canada], Russia, Serbia, and later Italy) against the Central Powers (primarily Germany, Austro-Hungary, and the Ottoman Empire). Both sides whipped up much hysteria (with epithets like "Huns," "baby-killers," and "God punish England") and used drastic tactics, including food blockades, use of poisonous gas, and submarine warfare. In what became nearly total war, civilians and industries actively participated in supporting and supplying the troops. Though political leaders feared a long war and military leaders prepared for one, the public was encouraged to believe the war would be short and victory easy.

About 620,000 Canadians enlisted or were conscripted. Of the men and women who served in the Canadian Expeditionary Force (those who went overseas), 60,661 were killed and 172,000 wounded; about 4,000 became prisoners of war (POWs).[37] More than two-thirds of those who first enlisted were British born.[38] They died in a war only indirectly connected to Canada. Since autocratic Russia was allied with Britain and France, the claims about fighting for liberty and freedom served propaganda and rallying cries as much as reality.

The soldiers recruited from Northeastern Ontario fought in most of the major battles, though often the units with which they started were broken up to provide support to those whose ranks had been thinned by trench warfare and artillery fire. At first, volunteers were recruited by the regional militia units, the 97th Algonquin Rifles or the 51st Soo Rifles; however, these men often ended in different units, such as the 2nd, 4th, 10th, or 15th (which included the 48th Highlanders) battalions, and many served in the 8th Reserve Battalion. Nearly all of these battalions are identified with southern Ontario. As the war continued, local battalions were raised by community leaders rather than the militias. No typical pattern or experience predominated for the soldiers aside from being organized in local units; learning discipline, marching as a unit, and shooting at Valcartier, Quebec (later at Camp

Borden and Niagara); being shipped overseas; and undergoing more training in trench warfare in England before being sent to Belgium or France. Edwin Durham[39] (7954) of Sault Ste. Marie summarized: "My experience of the war follows the Second Battalion in the 1st Contingent which went over … We wintered on Salisbury Plains doing war training and building camps."[40] This soldier, like many from the 51st Soo Rifles militia, had been placed in a battalion identified with central Ontario. Already by 4 November 1914, the *Sudbury Star* noted the pattern of deployment with the headline "97th Men Scattered." It detailed, "Almost Wherever You Look One Can Find New Ontario Men," then pointed out that about 140 of the Sudbury volunteers had been drafted into the 48th Highlanders and about 20 into the 4th, and that "the rest are in Bermuda [where they replaced British soldiers]." The article listed men from Engelhart serving with ammunition columns, some from New Liskeard in Bermuda, and some from Haileybury in the military police. The officers from the 97th Algonquin Rifles militia, who came from Sudbury, Cobalt, New Liskeard, Haileybury, and Elk Lake, served in diverse units, including the 48th, the 5th Royal Highlanders, and 15th Royal Nova Scotia.[41] Typical might be Bruce Allen (27864) of Copper Cliff, who had been with the 97th Algonquin Rifles and enlisted in August 1914, then was transferred to the 48th Highlanders (identified with Toronto) in September and by the end of the next month served with the 4th Battalion. When he died on 15 August 1917, he was a member of the 15th Battalion.

Similarly, the 1915 nominal roll for the 2nd Battalion shows 53 men from Northeastern Ontario out of 116 soldiers in its Company D (see fig. 2.1). Most of the 53 were soldiers from Sault Ste. Marie, including Steelton, plus one each from Creighton Mine (near Sudbury), Richards Landing (on St. Joseph Island), and Thessalon.

No.	Rank	Name	Former Unit	Next of Kin	Address	Country	Place	Date
7960	Private	Day, Aca.	R.C.G.A.	Day, Alex.	Wiarton, Ont.	Canada	Valcartier	Sept. 22
7961	Private	Dunsmore, Wm. John K.	L.O.R.G. & I.Y.	Dunsmore, Wm.	Carscube, Maryhill, Glasgow, Scot.	Scotland	Valcartier	Sept. 22
7962	Private	Furlong, Wm. Andrew	Nil	Furlong, Mrs. Julia.	Creighton Mine, Ont.	Canada	Valcartier	Sept. 22
7963	Private	Furber, Allan	Nil	Little, Mrs. James.	Cobourg, Ont.	Canada	Valcartier	Sept. 22
7964	Private	Finch, Llewellyn	1st S.W. Borderers	Finch, J. F.	Baglan Britain Ferry, Glam'shire, S. Wales	England	Valcartier	Sept. 22
7965	Private	Firth, William	Nil	Firth, Edward	619 Cranmore Cres., Belfast, Ire.	Ireland	Valcartier	Sept. 22
7966	Private	Fox, Michael	Nil	Fox, Mrs. Michael	Sheenboro, P.Q.	Canada	Valcartier	Sept. 22
7967	Private	Franks, Archibald Geo.	Nil	Franks, George	908 Easterday Ave., Sault St. Marie, Mich., U.S.A.	England	Valcartier	Sept. 22
7968	Private	Grant, John	Nil	Grant, Mrs. John	75 Albert St., Sault Ste. Marie, Ont.	Scotland	Valcartier	Sept. 23
7969	Private	Gray, William	R.F.A.	Gray, Mrs. Henry	3 Queen's Rd, Aberdeen, Scot.	Scotland	Valcartier	Sept. 22
7970	Private	Grant, Peter	Nil	Grant, Mrs. John	75 Albert St., Sault Ste. Marie, Ont.	England	Valcartier	Sept. 23
7971	Private	Goodman, Thomas H.	7th Worcestershire	Goodman, Thomas	84 Baxter Ave., Kidderminster, Eng.	England	Valcartier	Sept. 23
7972	Private	Gourlay, John	Nil	Gourlay, Mrs. John	32 Ferris Ave., Sault Ste. Marie, Ont.	Scotland	Valcartier	Sept. 22
7973	Private	Green, Herbert Allan	Nil	Green, Henry	College Farm, Impington, Cambs, Eng.	England	Valcartier	Sept. 22
7974	Private	Hardyman, Ferdinand Napier	Nil	Hardyman, L. F.	Garden River, Ont.	Canada	Valcartier	Sept. 23
7975	Private	Humphries, Harry	97th Regt.	Humphries, Rev. H. B.	Thessalon, Ont.	England	Valcartier	Sept. 22
7976	Private	Huyson, Herbert		Particulars will be furnished when available.				
7977	Private	Hand, Percival Alex.		Hand, T. A.	115 Kohler St., Sault Ste. Marie, Ont.	Canada	Valcartier	Sept. 22
7978	Private	Hallimond, William John	Nil	Hallimond, Rev. J. G.	227 Bowery, New York, N.Y.	England	Valcartier	Sept. 22
7979	Private	Hindmarch, John	Nil	Hindmarch, Mrs. Margaret	Manor House, Preston, N. Shields, Eng.	England	Valcartier	Sept. 22
7980	Private	Highstone, Albert S.	Nil	Highstone, Mrs. M. L.	371 Albert St., Sault Ste. Marie, Ont.	U.S.A.	Valcartier	Sept. 22
7981	Private	Hughes, Ellis Duncan	Nil	Hughes, Mrs. Elizabeth	31 Byford St., Liverpool, Eng.	England	Valcartier	Sept. 23
7982	Private	Heard, Charles	Nil	Brown, Mrs. Annie	Haliburton, Ont.	Canada	Valcartier	Sept. 23
7983	Private	Holgate, Bert Peter	Nil	Holgate, Henry	413 Sault Ste. Marie, Ont.	England	Valcartier	Sept. 22
7984	Private	Herr, Philip Leslie	U.S. Cavalry	Herr, P. P.	Minnie, Arizona, U.S.A.	Canada	Valcartier	Sept. 22
7985	Private	Hounsell, James	Nil	Hounsell, John	Steelton, Ont.	Canada	Valcartier	Sept. 22
7986	Private	Hounsell, Wilbert	Nil	Hounsell, John	Steelton, Ont.	Canada	Valcartier	Sept. 22
7987	Private	Ironsides, Wilcox J. S	Nil	Ironsides, Mrs. Ross	223 McGregor Ave., Sault Ste. Marie, Ont.	Canada	Valcartier	Sept. 23
7988	Private	Jackson, Wilfred	Nil	Jackson, Mrs. Turner	275 Northern Rd, Sault Ste. Marie, Ont.	Canada	Valcartier	Sept. 23
7989	Private	Jarrett, George	H.O.R.L.R.	Jarrett, Mrs. George	549 Bush St., Steelton, Ont.	England	Valcartier	Sept. 23
7990	Private	Jarbeau, Eddy	Nil	Jarbeau, Miss Eva	c/o. Gideon Jarbeau, Haileybury, Ont.	Canada	Valcartier	Sept. 22
8040	Bugler	Johnston, Thomas	97th Regt.	Johnston, Mrs. Thos.	112 Pim St., Sault Ste. Marie, Ont.	Canada	Valcartier	Sept. 22
7991	Private	Kennedy, Stuart	C.E.	Kennedy, Jno. Wm.	Apple Hill, Ont.	Canada	Valcartier	Sept. 22
7992	Private	Kennedy, Thomas		Kennedy, Edward	492 North St., Sault Ste. Marie, Ont.	Canada	Valcartier	Sept. 22
7993	Private	Leffler, Raymond Douglas	Nil	Leffler, Mrs. Henry	13 St. Thomas St., Sault Ste. Marie, Ont.	Canada	Valcartier	Sept. 23
7994	Private	Lightfoot, James Daniel	Nil	Lightfoot, John	157 Cathcart St., Sault Ste. Marie, Ont.	England	Valcartier	Sept. 22
7995	Private	Lucas, William H.	Nil	Lucas, Mrs. Emily	314 Albert St., Sault Ste. Marie, Ont.	England	Valcartier	Sept. 22
8041	Private	Malone, Edward	43rd Regt.	Malone, John William	Almonte, Ont.	Canada	Valcartier	Sept. 22
7996	Private	Miron, Charles C.	Nil	Miron, Mrs. R.	622 Bay St., Sault Ste. Marie, Ont.	Canada	Valcartier	Sept. 23
7997	Private	Monk, George Henry	23rd Bat.	Monk, Mrs. Catherine Ann	699 King Edward Ave., Ottawa, Ont.	England	Valcartier	Sept. 23
7998	Private	Murray, Thomas	Nil	Murray, Mrs. Colin	62 Wright St., St. John, N.B.	Canada	Valcartier	Sept. 23
7999	Private	Major, Franklin John	Nil	Major, John	Steelton, Ont.	Canada	Valcartier	Sept. 22
8000	Private	Merrifield, William	97th Regt.	Merrifield, Wm.	Aylmer Road, Ottawa, Ont.	England	Valcartier	Sept. 23
8001	Private	Martin, Charles L.	1st R.C.F.A.	Martin, Mrs. E.	646 Hartington Road, Chatham, Kent, Eng.	England	Valcartier	Sept. 23
8002	Private	MacMillan, Donald	1st Batt. Q.O.C.H.	MacMillan, Miss Mary	39 Old Dunbarton Rd, Overnewton, Glasgow, Scot.	Scotland	Valcartier	Sept. 22
8003	Private	MacNab, John J.	29th Horse.	MacNab, Mrs. W. H	Richards Landing, Ont.	Canada	Valcartier	Sept. 22
8004	Private	McDonald, Charles S.	4th Seaforth Highlanders.	McDonald, Rev. Angus J.	Killeman Manse, Ross-shire, Scot.	Scotland	Valcartier	Sept. 22
8005	Private	MacAllister, David	A. & S. Highlanders.	MacAllister, Mrs. David	192 Woodward Ave., Sault Ste. Marie, Ont.	Scotland	Valcartier	Sept. 22
8006	Private	McLeod, John Donald	3rd Seaforth Highlanders	McDonald, Mrs. Murdoch	South Brager, Lewis, Ross-shire, Scot.	Scotland	Valcartier	Sept. 22
8007	Private	McCarthy, John Carl	Nil	McCarthy, David	32 Fisher St., Toronto, Ont.	Canada	Valcartier	Sept. 22
8008	Private	McKay, Angus	33rd Regt.	Marten, James	131 North Bruce St., Sault Ste. Marie, Ont.	Canada	Valcartier	Sept. 22
8009	Private	Munroe, James	R.C.R.	Munroe, James	290 East Ave., Hamilton, Ont.	Canada	Valcartier	Sept. 23
8010	Private	Mahulak, Peter.		Particulars will be furnished when available.				
8011	Private	Nicholls, Frank W. R.	Nil	Nicholls, Wm. L.	176 Pim St., Sault Ste. Marie, Ont.	Canada	Valcartier	Sept. 23
8012	Private	Nicholson, Andrew		Nicholson, Miss Margaret	Blind River, Ont.	Scotland	Valcartier	Sept. 22
8013	Private	O'Rourke, William.	Black Watch Regt.	O'Rourke, Thomas	Seaforth, Ont.	Canada	Valcartier	Sept. 22
8014	Private	Pringle, George William	Nil	Laidlaw, Mrs. Eliza	34 Athol St., Dunston, Eng.	England	Valcartier	Sept. 23
8015	Private	Pim, Michael R.	Nil	Pim, Mrs. Margaret	87 Brock St., Sault Ste. Marie, Ont.	England	Valcartier	Sept. 22
8016	Private	Partington, Charles Edward	U.S. Artillery	Van Dusen, Mrs	110 York Place, Chicago, Ill., U.S.A.	England	Valcartier	Sept. 22
8017	Private	Pomroy, Harold	Nil	Pomroy, Wm.	Hemel-Hempstead, Herts, Eng.	England	Valcartier	Sept. 22

Figure 2.1. A page from the Nominal Roll of D Company, 2nd Battalion.
(Canadian Expeditionary Force, *Second Battalion: Nominal Roll of Officers, Non-Commissioned Officers, and Men*, [Ottawa: Minister of Militia and Defence, 1915], 13)

Northeasterners of British background enthusiastically went to war in August 1914. The requested quotas of soldiers were oversubscribed in Sault Ste. Marie (127 men) and Sudbury (over 250).[42] All had to sign an attestation paper after being found medically fit (fig. 2.2). Unlike the evaluation of the South African War recruits, in World War I, men's character received little attention in this declaration of loyalty and commitment to serve.

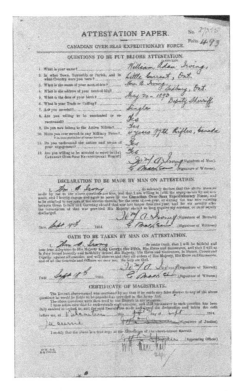

Figure 2.2. Attestation papers of William Adam Irving (27355). Typically, this soldier served with the 97th Algonquin Rifles militia and was placed with the 15th Battalion. (Courtesy of Library and Archives Canada)

Battles Involving Soldiers from Northeastern Ontario

The large war monument in North Bay lists the World War I battlefronts of France and Belgium where young men from Northeastern Ontario died or suffered: Amiens, Armentières, Arras, Beaumetz, Bourlon Wood, Cambrai, Courcelette, Festubert, Givenchy, Hooge, the Somme, Passchendaele, Sanctuary Wood, St. Eloi, St. Julien, St. Quentin, Vimy, and Ypres (fig. 2.3). At these places in northeastern France and in Belgium on Europe's western front, millions of young men died as opposing armies attempted to push forward. Hundreds of kilometres of trenches, sometimes three or four rows deep and intersecting, criss-crossed the landscape from Belgium to Switzerland. Like heads butting a wall, dug-in armies tossed men at immobile foes while both sides lived half underground in dugouts. Trench warfare turned out to be horrible. In letters home men could only offer the expression "hell" for mud, bombardment, flying and rotting flesh, homeless civilians, and lost comrades. The following pages will provide a short overview of the general situation, the flying corps, and the numbers who served and died from the region, and then review the battles chronologically, with attention to the soldiers of Northeastern Ontario.

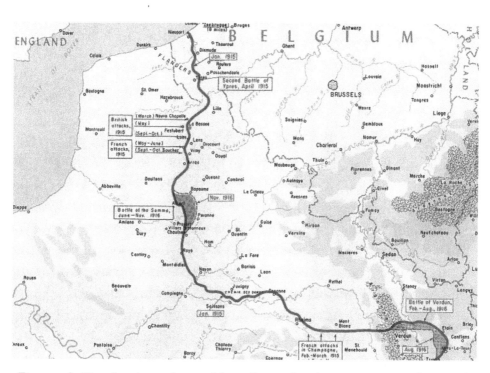

Figure 2.3. Map showing stalemated front line and major engagements of 1915–16.
(Courtesy of the USMA, Department of History,
www.gwpda.org/maps/westpoint/WWOne11.gif)

Young men from Northeastern Ontario participated on many fronts. The region sent more than 400 volunteers among the First Contingent (later called the First Division) of nearly 30,000 Canadian soldiers in 17 battalions. That contingent, plus the Princess Patricia's Canadian Light Infantry (Princess Pats, or PPCLI), sailed for England in October 1914, and a Second Contingent (Division) of about 25,000 followed in February 1915. By the end of 1915, about 115,000 Canadians were overseas, and 165,000 followed them in 1916. Aside from the Princess Pats, who went to France on 21 December 1914, the first battalions of Canadian soldiers arrived in France and Belgium in March 1915, although a few Canadian soldiers had arrived earlier with British troops. At least five of the battalions and the Princess Pats included men from Northeastern Ontario.

Most of the Canadians who enlisted fought in the trenches or provided support, but about 22,000 joined the British Royal Flying Corps, because Canada then had no air branch.[43] These men are hard to trace because their service records are embedded in British files, but some examples exist. Austin Blackie (1003045), a university student from Spring Bay on Manitoulin Island, served first in the 227th (the Men of the North, from Algoma and Manitoulin) Battalion. Born on 17 November 1894, he enlisted on 10 April 1916. He would be discharged in December 1916 due to pneumonia. He reenlisted (490930) in March 1917 but was discharged on 5 May "to join RFC [Royal Flying Corps]." He died in a collision of two training planes: "both spun to the ground probably during photography."[44] In contrast, Lieutenant Edgar Meath Martyn, a contractor from North Bay, died on 15 May 1918 in air combat. Canada's *Circumstances of Death Registers* say simply "Killed in Action."[45] Martyn enlisted in April 1916 and survived numerous battles before joining the British flying corps early in 1918. Shortly before noon on 15 May, three German warplanes shot down the aircraft carrying Lieutenant Martyn and his British co-aviator.

During the last years of the war, recruitment for the air service increased. For example, the *Porcupine Advance*, on 19 September 1917, announced that five Timmins-area men had left to join the aviation corps; it had earlier noted the need for thousands of mechanics to service aircraft.[46] By then the British were training hundreds of airmen in southern Ontario. Most of the men from Northeastern Ontario who went overseas served in the army, however, though many worked in subunits such as the Canadian Forestry Corps. The latter included many Indigenous soldiers recruited through a special "Indian draft" in July 1917.

The population from which soldiers could be drawn was limited because Northern Ontario's resource towns were small, and its farms, mines, lumber mills, and railways had only employed increasing numbers since the 1880s. According to the Census of 1911, the last before the war, the population of Northeastern Ontario's districts was 147,510. This was a low figure because until 1912 the Arctic–Atlantic watershed marked the northern boundary of Ontario. The region's population was distributed over three districts: Algoma West, 28,752; Algoma East (including Manitoulin and part of what is now Sudbury District), 44,628; Nipissing, 74,130. Places such as Cochrane and Timmins fell within the Northwest Territories. Ontario expanded to its present northern limits in 1912, between the census and the war. Based on service files that recorded soldiers' birthplaces and residence at enlistment, about 5,000 young men went overseas during World War I from what is now Northeastern Ontario; this total includes Cree and Anishinabek. On a per capita basis, this is similar to the number of per capita enlistees for Canada as a whole.[47] Many places in Canada make claims about having some of the highest recruitment rates. For example, Brantford, Ontario (1911 population: 27,500; with Brant county over 44,000), estimates that 12.7% of the total population enlisted.[48] By late 1916, a small railway and lumbering community such as Chapleau (population in 1911: 1,305) had contributed 182 soldiers or 13.9% of the population.[49] In the lumbering town of Blind River, 259 men who were born or lived there enlisted: 11.5% of its population of 2,558. The larger centre of North Bay, with 7,737 inhabitants, had 825 enlistees or 10.6% of the population. Since many men of the North enlisted in southern cities or the training centre at Valcartier, Northeastern Ontario probably contributed more than its share of personnel.[50]

Canadian soldiers on the ground fought well, despite the appalling conditions, cumbersome equipment, and inefficient rifles. The Ross rifle, though highly accurate, tended to jam in wet and rough conditions, so that Canadian soldiers resorted to picking up guns from fallen British soldiers. The Oliver kit had poor webbing and proved difficult to carry. Steel helmets only became the norm in 1916. Poorly sewn boots disintegrated in mud. These problems persisted until well into 1916.

Despite such hindrances, Colonel G.W.L. Nicholson, official historian of the Canadian Expeditionary Force and its role in World War I, praised Canadian efforts at their first major engagement, the

Battles of Ypres, Belgium, fought between 22 April and 31 May 1915. The battle has been controversial because the Germans employed poisonous gas. Though the French had used debilitating gas without much impact in September 1914 to stop the German advance on Paris, and the Germans had used it unsuccessfully on the eastern front in November 1914, Ypres gained notoriety because the Germans twice unleashed asphyxiating gas, on 22 April and 24 April. The German forces hoped to capture St. Julien, a small village near Ypres (fig. 2.4).

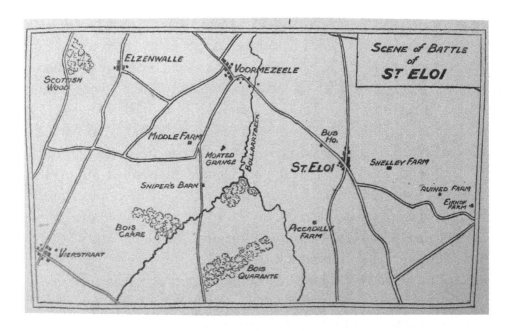

Figure 2.4. The Battle of St. Eloi. Note St. Julien, centre right.
(Reproduced from *Canada in the Great War*
[Toronto: United Publishers of Canada, 1919], 3:76.)

At Ypres and St. Julien, Canadian soldiers fought as part of the British Expeditionary Force, under British command. The Canadian units included the Princess Pats (identified with Ottawa), and the 2nd (identified as an eastern Ontario regiment), the 4th (identified with central Ontario), the 10th, and the 15th (including the 48th Highlanders, identified with Toronto) battalions. All contained soldiers from Northeastern Ontario, including some who later would become famous: boxer and prospector

Jack Munroe (1769) of Elk Lake was a member of the Princess Pats, and William Merrifield (8000) of Sault Ste. Marie, who would win a Victoria Cross, served with the 4th. Despite shallow trenches and a lack of sandbags, the Canadians managed to retain their positions. According to historian Tim Cook, some of the Canadian soldiers suffered such damage to their lungs or psychological anguish that the army sent them back to Canada. Some 1,410 became prisoners of war (POWs), and of those roughly half had been wounded at the front, 87 of them so badly that they died as POWs.[51]

Yet the POW situation might not have been as grim as Cook suggests. Nearly all prisoners of war did survive and, aside from food shortages shared by their Germans captors, were treated as well as could be expected given the emotions of total warfare. Two robins do not make a spring, but they provide a hint: one 2nd Battalion soldier from Sault Ste. Marie, Edwin T. Durham (7954), among the wounded and captured at Ypres, has left extensive memoirs of his three years in captivity.[52] His memoirs emphasize the special medical care he immediately received when captured. His photo collection documents drama groups, choirs, visits to nearby towns, and language lessons. Donald Cameron (7948), also of the Sault and with the 2nd Battalion (identified with eastern Ontario), shared Durham's fate, though he was sent to a different POW camp in southwest Germany. He escaped in June 1918 and proved strong enough to walk to the neutral Netherlands despite having flat feet and being on the edge of starvation.[53]

At Ypres, in return for a small piece of land, the British Army had sacrificed 59,275 Allied soldiers; only a couple of dozen died from gas warfare.[54] Canadian casualties other than those in the Princess Patricia Canadian Light Infantry "numbered 208 officers and 5828 other ranks." PPCLI casualties added an additional 678.[55] (The term *casualties* includes the wounded and those taken prisoner, as well as those killed.) All the main units of the Canadian corps included soldiers from Northeastern Ontario. One of those, Enos Grant (11484) from New Liskeard, wrote home on 8 May 1915:

> Well, we got in a scrap with the Germans at last, on the 23rd of April ... They got a lot of us Canadians, but I think they got it as hard as we did, if

not harder. But we didn't have any chance for we had to advance about half a mile over open country ... But just wait until we get a chance at them again ... When we were advancing to the German trenches, after the French had retreated, bullets were flying all around me. Many of our men fell around me ... the only thing I regret is that I couldn't get a chance to bayonet some of them ...[56]

Grant, who was part of a large group from the New Liskeard area serving in the 4th Battalion, later lost his enthusiasm and his life. An officer from New Liskeard, Lieutenant Alfred Morgan, wrote about the battle on April 24:

Yesterday afternoon, the French gave away again and the Germans got in behind the Canadians, and our men had to cut their way out ... The Canadian [First] Division has gained undying honor ... [I] caught sight of Smith, whose mother, Mrs. Gains used to keep a restaurant in New Liskeard, who came with the 97th from Porcupine ... [and saw] Green, of Dane [near Kirkland Lake], another 97th man ... [Later] we met a tall unshaven soldier of the 10th Battalion who told us that all that was left of our Battalion (10th) was about 100 men [out of 800].[57]

Another description of Ypres came from Cyril MacDonald (5713), a signaller who worked as a clerk in Copper Cliff before the war. The *Sudbury Star* published his letter on 15 June 1915:

Scarcely daring to draw a full breath, with eyes straining even through the powerful prism binoculars, I watched, those rushes [of soldiers] ever drawing nearer to that fateful ridge. And every time a rush commenced not all would go forward, for some still, silent forms told that many had "fought the last fight." Occasionally, one who was wounded could be seen crawling back, while regardless of life and limb, steadily coming behind, worked the heroic stretcher bearers.

Once I thought that a whole bunch were wiped out, when two "Jack Johnsons" [very large artillery shells] literally blotted out a field; but when the dense black smoke cleared, I saw that they had taken a left incline into a swampy hollow. Then the light grew bad, so we started to go in. We met a "Jack" carrying a pal and relieved him, and went back and carried in another wounded man.

One thing I saw that night that very much impressed me was the sight of a soldier stopping behind a tree and lighting his pipe, after which he ran to catch up to the rest. I can just imagine how he appreciated that smoke. I myself lost three pipes in the scrap, one of which came from a dead man's kit.

The service files of many soldiers read like that of Lewin Bass (27793), a 22-year-old labourer from Thornloe who had been with the 97th Algonquin militia and transferred to the 15th Battalion: "29/4/15 … now for official purposes presumed that he died on or since 24/4/15."

A veteran of the Ypres campaign, Major Victor Odlum, stated, "We just did not know how to get out [of the situation]."[58] Whatever the reason, the Canadian soldiers made an impressive defence. Their effort helped Belgian, British, Canadian, and French morale, and "it blocked a German advance to the Channel ports … [It also] maintained the threat of an Allied drive toward Lille [in German-occupied France] and Brussels [the Belgian capital, also under German control]."[59] Given that the battalions involved were associated with southern, eastern, and central Ontario, the contributions of soldiers and units from Northeastern Ontario went unacknowledged. For instance, most of the 127 men of the 51st Soo Rifles who left Sault Ste. Marie on 20 August 1914, trained at Valcartier, and shipped overseas in October ended up in the 2nd, 19th (identified with western Ontario), and 37th battalions. Many served at Ypres. One of the early Sudbury recruits in August 1914, James Ault (27158), was placed with the 15th Battalion, 48th Highlanders. He went through Ypres without a scratch though he later spent 15 days in hospital with a sprained knee. He had been a plumber in civilian life and attached to the 97th Algonquin Rifles militia.[60]

Ypres was not the only test for soldiers from Northeastern Ontario. The monument at North Bay lists both Festubert and Givenchy as battle zones, although casualties of men from Northeastern Ontario appear fewer than elsewhere. Lieutenant Alfred Norton Morgan, a lawyer and popular officer from New Liskeard who had served in the 97th Algonquin Rifles militia, was killed in action on 24 May 1915. He was with the 10th Battalion. One historian writing of these early battles at Ypres, St. Julien, Givenchy, and Festubert, stated that in late April and early May, Canadian soldiers experienced 8,500 casualties within ten days. Approximately two-thirds to three-quarters of the soldiers in some 1,000-man infantry battalions could no longer fight. The Battle of Festubert became a slaughterhouse that Cook describes as "the most callous sacrifice of Canadian lives."[61] Yet it depended on where the soldiers were on the line. One soldier from Haileybury, Angus McLean (47910), noted the luck of rotations to the front trenches: "they put us in the first line right off the bat, but it was quiet while we were in. We put in four days in the firing line and have eight days to put in here in reserve ... We haven't seen any Germans yet ... Our trenches are only three hundred yards from them."[62] Also unscathed thus far were two soldiers who had worked underground in Copper Cliff as pipefitters, J.B. Lowes (58014) and Sydney Rhodes (57096). They had been members of the 97th Algonquin Rifles militia and found training in England hard, but, Lowes wrote, "appreciate it now that we are on the firing line." Lowes wrote to another band member about the noise: "We both thought we were on the 9th level [of the mine] when the blasting gang was down."[63]

Luck ended for some in the spring of 1916. Young Canadians died in horrendous numbers at St. Eloi, as they did in many of the places fought over near Ypres.[64] Casualties included Percy Don Jacobi (57864), who was born on 28 March 1888 at Gore Bay. This electrician enlisted at Timmins on 12 November 1914, and declared his father, Don H. Jacobi of Haileybury, where both lived, as his next of kin. He was "Killed in Action at the trenches while serving with the 20th Battalion at St. Eloi 24 October 1915."[65] The battle at St. Eloi changed little. Both the British and the Germans laid landmines around the village, which lay between Givenchy and Ypres. On 27 March 1916, the British detonated so many of mines that they were heard in Folkstone, England. German and British soldiers rushed into the muddy mess that resulted, and the 2nd Canadian Division moved to assist the 3rd British Division. In their first combat experience, the Canadian soldiers proved "ill-prepared and untrained for what awaited them."[66] Major General Richard Turner, a merchant from Quebec City and veteran of the South African War (where he had won a Victoria Cross), questioned the need for holding the artillery-shell craters that were at stake. In the narrow salient where the fighting occurred, German soldiers could shoot at the Canadians from three sides (fig. 2.5). Superior officers overruled Turner.[67] Pandemonium resulted. The Canadians could not distinguish their own lines from those of the enemies, and dead bodies lay everywhere. The German army captured the craters. Aware of the hopelessness of the situation, General Edwin Alderson, another Canadian who had fought in South Africa, ordered a retreat.

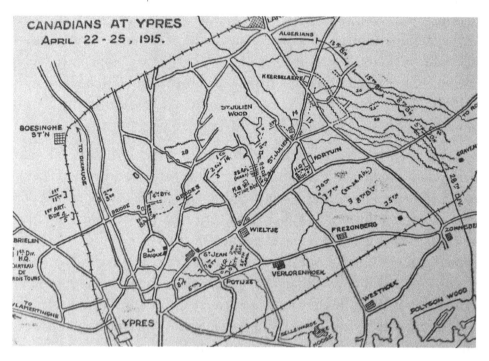

Figure 2.5. The Battle of Ypres. The German lines were east of the village
with an observation point at Eikof farm.
(Reproduced from *Canada in the Great War*
[Toronto: United Publishers of Canada, 1919], 3:239.)

The horror continued over the next two weeks as Allied and German soldiers killed and wounded each other, with little to show for the efforts of either side. Several problems exacerbated the situation. The Canadian officers chose not to use all available manpower but to save some for battles planned along the Somme River. This meant that exhausted front-line soldiers, cold and wet, had to maintain the trenches in wooded areas near St. Eloi. On 3–4 June 1915, the Canadians launched a counterattack. Their British commander, Sir Julian Byng, insisted that they recapture what they had lost earlier, near Mount Sorrel. Failure to do so would have left the Germans in a position to push forward from the trenches they had captured, occupy the Ypres salient, and cut through the British Army to divide its forces on either side of the salient. Though the German lines were exposed and vulnerable, the Canadian artillery failed to locate them and the number of attackers proved insufficient. Cook describes the attack of 3 June as a failure.[68] He estimates that the Canadians suffered 9,000 casualties (deaths, serious injuries, and men captured) at Mount Sorrel.[69]Among those who died were Joseph Gallagher (472167) of Gore Bay; George Hawkins (193352), a fisherman from Blind River; and Charles Chambers (452956), an engineer from Sault Ste. Marie. At one point, the German army stood only three kilometres from Ypres.[70]

The nightmare continued when, on 6 June, the 28th Battalion surrounded Hooge, a Belgian village. That afternoon, the Germans detonated mines that killed, wounded, or led to the capture of 300 of the unit's 650 soldiers. The Germans captured the remains of Hooge, but the surviving Canadians fared better than they might have and retained some of their ground. For the next week, as the winds blew and the rains pelted, the Canadians bombarded German enemy forces, and in an attack on 13 June they managed to recapture most of the land they had lost. Superior air power was decisive in the Allied effort.[71] However, again after many casualties, the ground held by each side had hardly changed. Among those who fought in this battle was Lieutenant Elliott Durham of Sault Ste. Marie (brother of Edwin), who had been placed in the 2nd Battalion. Durham received a gunshot wound to his back. According to his service file, he would be in and out of hospitals until August 1916 and would be shot again the following March. Despite the wounds, Durham survived the war. His example again illustrates the way someone who enlisted with the 51st Soo Rifles ended in a battalion associated with eastern Ontario, thereby making it difficult to quantify Northeastern Ontario's full contributions to the war effort.

At the end of 1915, the war that many had thought would lead to a swift victory continued and kept devouring men. Canadian battalions, with men from Northeastern Ontario among them, had begun to make their mark on the battlefields of Belgium and France, despite the challenges they faced from the terrain, their equipment, and the enemy. More challenges but also victories lay ahead.

Notes

Notes

CHAPTER 3

The World-Shattering War: Costly Contributions, 1916–19

As the destruction continued on the military front, raising regional battalions became more important to the war effort. Four battalions provided crucial manpower from Northeastern Ontario. The 119th, 159th, 227th, and 228th battalions fulfilled their quota of 800 to 1,000 recruits each, though it took longer to bring the 227th and 228th to a full complement. Ads appeared in local newspapers calling for recruits (fig. 3.1).

By March 1916, the 119th Algoma Battalion achieved full strength. Initial training, in particular marching in unison to learn discipline and group cooperation, took place in 14 local detachments, including Thessalon, Bruce Mines, Sault Ste. Marie, Blind River, Massey, Webbwood, Gore Bay, and Little Current. Starting in May 1916, training at Camp Niagara (at Niagara-on-the-Lake) included route marches and drill. The battalion gained the nickname "Algoma Roughnecks." The journey to England began on 27 July by train to Halifax, where the battalion boarded

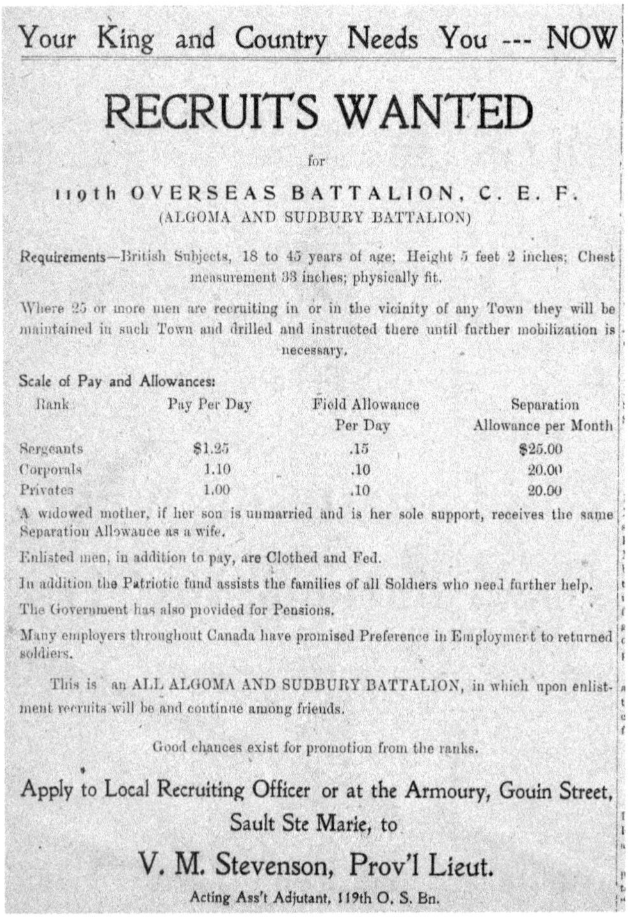

Your King and Country Needs You --- NOW

RECRUITS WANTED

for

119th OVERSEAS BATTALION, C. E. F.

(ALGOMA AND SUDBURY BATTALION)

Requirements—British Subjects, 18 to 45 years of age; Height 5 feet 2 inches; Chest measurement 33 inches; physically fit.

Where 25 or more men are recruiting in or in the vicinity of any Town they will be maintained in such Town and drilled and instructed there until further mobilization is necessary.

Scale of Pay and Allowances:

Rank	Pay Per Day	Field Allowance Per Day	Separation Allowance per Month
Sergeants	$1.25	.15	$25.00
Corporals	1.10	.10	20.00
Privates	1.00	.10	20.00

A widowed mother, if her son is unmarried and is her sole support, receives the same Separation Allowance as a wife.

Enlisted men, in addition to pay, are Clothed and Fed.

In addition the Patriotic fund assists the families of all Soldiers who need further help.

The Government has also provided for Pensions.

Many employers throughout Canada have promised Preference in Employment to returned soldiers.

This is an ALL ALGOMA AND SUDBURY BATTALION, in which upon enlistment recruits will be and continue among friends.

Good chances exist for promotion from the ranks.

Apply to Local Recruiting Officer or at the Armoury, Gouin Street, Sault Ste Marie, to

V. M. Stevenson, Prov'l Lieut.

Acting Ass't Adjutant, 119th O. S. Bn.

Figure 3.1. Advertisements such as this one, which appeared in the *Manitoulin Expositor* on 23 December 1915, emphasized the fact that men enlisting in local battalions would serve together in the war. However, they were often transferred to other battalions after training.

the ship *Metagama*, which arrived on 16 August. The battalion remained in England at Camp Witley for more training but soon began to supply reserve manpower to fill holes in the depleted ranks at the front. Training included more drill and learning trenching, range shooting, bivouacking in the countryside, and bayonet practice. Diversions involved athletic competitions, a visit by the Canadian prime minister, and a hypnotist for entertainment (fig. 3.2). The battalion remained in England and continued to supply reserves to fill units at the front, until, in February 1918, it was disbanded and absorbed into the 8th Reserve.

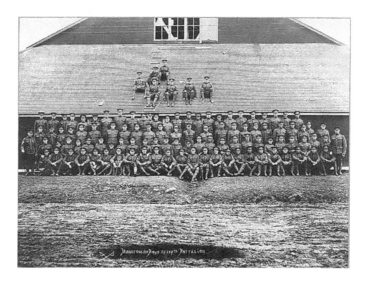

Figure 3.2. War Diary, 119th Battalion. "Battalion Routine"
meant drill, shooting, marches, bayonet, and trenching practice.
Note the prime minister's visit and the hypnotist on 9 April 2017.
(Courtesy of Library and Archives Canada).

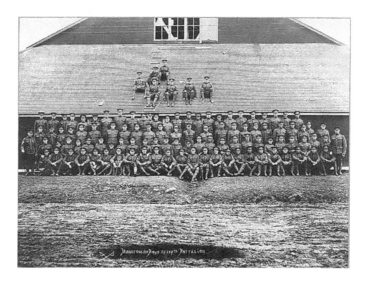

Figure 3.3. The Manitoulin Boys of 119th Battalion, 1916.
The photo is part of the battalion's war diary.
(Courtesy of War Diaries collection, MIKAN no. 3192668,
Library and Archives Canada).

Small towns in Northeastern Ontario made large contributions to the 119th Algoma Roughnecks. Massey, for example, contributed at least 48 men to its platoon. Tekummah, a small farming community on Manitoulin, sent at least 25 on the *Metagama*, including seven from two generations of the Kay family. A photo of the "Manitoulin boys of the 119th Battalion" depicted 101 men (fig. 3.3). Despite the high numbers from small communities, the war behemoth wanted more.

By early 1916, many men of service age had become disillusioned with the war. The long lists of deaths, published daily, raised questions about the war's purpose. Doing one's bit seemed to amount to dying in a foreign land, and fewer were motivated to volunteer out of patriotism, the need for a job, or a desire for adventure. Recruiters resorted to shame, encouraging women to berate supposed slackers. Recruitment drives replaced volunteering. After the 119th Algoma Battalion was raised through volunteers from the Sudbury, Sault Ste. Marie, and Manitoulin districts, organized recruitment for the 227th (Men of the North, also known as the Hunters and Fishermen) Battalion was authorized in early 1916. Simultaneously, after the 159th Algonquins of Sudbury and Nipissing districts had been raised, the 228th (Northern Fusiliers) was authorized to begin recruiting from North Bay and further north. Recruiting officers went to towns and villages, giving speeches about the need to be patriotic. On 21 April 1916, "a huge patriotic meeting was held in Chapleau to hear Colonel [Charles Hugh Lepailleur] Jones [in charge of 51st Soo Rifles militia] … At this same meeting the Chapleau Citizens Recruiting Committee was formed" comprised of pastors, judges, and local leaders.[72] In May, a recruiting office for the 227th Battalion opened under Lieutenant William Augustus Lyness, the former police chief of Chapleau. The local newspaper "chastised the ladies for not encouraging their husbands, sweethearts and brothers to enlist." By 15 June, 50 recruits had been found, including, in the language of the day, "an Indian Chief and four of his braves."[73] Similar recruiting efforts, backed by newspapers extolling the war effort, took place as far north as James Bay. The 159th and 227th underwent basic training at Camp Borden before going overseas (fig 3.4), where men were transferred to reserve battalions, no longer identified with their origins.

Figure 3.4. Camp Borden, 1916. Note the 159th Battalion's tents at the top left, and those of the 227th on the right. (Reproduced courtesy of Dave Deloye)

In the meantime, the attrition at the front continued, in particular at the River Somme. Sir Douglas Haig, British commander-in-chief during the Somme campaign (1 July to 19 November 1916), considered it a huge success, even though the results fell well short of his goal—victory in 1916. One of the objectives at the Somme was to divert the German army from the French fortress of Verdun, where the French and German armies had been fighting since February. Haig wrote, "Verdun had been relieved; the main German forces had been held on the Western front; and the enemy's strength had been very considerably worn down. Any one of these three results is in itself sufficient to justify the Somme battle."[74] His opinion, however, is hardly universal: in 1952, the editor of Haig's papers wrote that the "failure to gain much ground and the heavy losses suffered by the Allied forces ... [rendered it] a costly failure."[75] He also thought that the Battles of the Somme took a heavier toll on the Australian, British, Canadian, French, and New Zealand forces than on the Germans. In one notorious incident, on a single day, close to 800 Newfoundlanders advanced towards German positions; only 68 reported for roll call the following day.[76]

The toll on Northeastern soldiers was lower but was also less visible because they were scattered among units associated with other Ontario regions. Robert Bell (409320) recorded his ordeal in a letter home, printed in the *Sudbury Star* on 28 October 1916:

> I was only eight days at the Somme from Ypres. I was wounded on the 20th of September and in the hospital on the 23rd, which is pretty quick work. It was a surprise attack and we were pulling it off early in the morning, about five o'clock. Fritz' [German] trench, a strong point, was about two hundred yards off. A continual rain for two days had mixed things up a little and we could scarcely get through the mud and water and a kit of 27 pounds, and a rifle made it all the heavier. No. 3 section of the bombers [grenade throwers], the one I am in, had to stay in our trenches (shell holes) … Our fellows stood their ground in the captured trench, but daylight was upon them … and they had run out of bombs … I grabbed a box of twelve bombs and beat it over the open ground … the hail of lead was terrible … I was running double when I came to a shell hole. I jumped in for a second and looked back for the others, but I was all alone. I beat it again. I had taken only a couple of steps when one bullet went through my steel helmet. It dazed me but there was no scratch. A second after I felt a burning sensation in my shoulder and the power left my arm … I was feeling faint through loss of blood and was out of wind … The Red Cross men were so busy that I would have to wait too long to be dressed, so I only had the blood stopped and started for the ambulance with my pal.

Bell, born in England in 1893, had enlisted at Niagara on 18 August 1915. He had been a member of the 97th Algonquin Rifles militia but trained with the 37th Battalion and then was transferred into the 43rd Battalion. After recovering from his shoulder wound, he served with 5th Army Troops Company France (attached to Canadian headquarters, perhaps because he had been wounded). After the war he returned to work as an electrical engineer at Inco. Similarly, James Ault (27158), a pipe fitter from Copper Cliff, who had also been a member of the 97th Algonquin Rifles, enlisted on 10 August 1914, served with the 15th Battalion, 48th Highlanders, and was first wounded in August 1915. Regarding the Somme, his medical file states, "accident 7.9.16 buried and blown out of dugout. Lost consciousness. Pain in back and leg muscles." The file offers a few more details—"Sep 7/16 Somme buried by shell explosion"—and lists the series of English hospitals where he was treated, until December 1916. Ault made it back to Canada with some hearing problems, but many did not survive the Somme.

The Battles of the Somme took place at or near Amiens, Arras, Courcelette, and the road between Amiens and Cambrai. The Allied offensive began in the summer of 1916, and Canadians became actively involved in September. When the Battle of Flers-Courcelette (15–22 September 1916, named for two French villages) began on 15 September 1916, many of the Canadians were too angry to take prisoners and killed Germans who attempted to surrender.[77] With assistance from tanks, Canadian soldiers managed to capture both Courcelette village, which burned during its liberation, and Flers. On 26 September, one kilometre to the northwest of Courcelette, the Canadians launched another offensive to oust German forces from Thiepval Ridge. Historian Tim Cook considers that battle a "partial victory" but notes that the two campaigns, Flers-Courcelette and Thiepval Ridge, came at a cost of 10,000 Canadian casualties (those killed, wounded, or taken prisoner).[78] Fighting alongside the British near Courcelette were the 1st and 2nd Canadian Divisions of the Canadian Corps. One participant was Matthew Green (454376) from Rutherglen, age 22, who served with the 20th Battalion, part of the 4th Brigade of the 2nd Canadian Division, charged with the capture of Courcelette's sugar factory.[79] The 4th Brigade *did* capture the factory, but Green did not live to celebrate the victory. Wounded in the spine, he was on his way to a dressing station when, hit a second time, he died. Bonfield-born Peter Gaudette (407075), a 22-year-old teamster from North Bay, appears to have died on 26 September 1916, the first night of the Battle of Thiepval Ridge. Gaudette's unit, the 15th Battalion, was part of the 1st Canadian Division. The army first classified Gaudette as "Missing in Action," but soon decided that he was "for official purposes ... presumed to have died."

Next, in early October, the Allies tried to capture what had been labelled "Regina Trench." (Trenches seem to have been assigned names arbitrarily, though often with the hope of gaining them as Canadian territory; Sudbury Trench was a small side extension nearby.) Regina Trench was in German hands but would soon be captured. Joseph Aubin (448870), a labourer from North Bay barely past his 20th birthday, was killed in action on 3 October when fighting there with the

22nd Battalion of the 2nd Canadian Division. The struggle for Regina Trench cost an estimated 2,688 casualties.[80] The second part of the attack alone had cost 1,364 Canadian casualties, in addition to another 1,324 before and after 8 October.

Some 20,000 of the 65,000 in the Canadian Corps became casualties during the Battles of the Somme, and most of the survivors were exhausted. By November the soldiers were coping with snow, sleet, and heavy rain. In charge of the Allied offensive, French General Joseph Joffre chose to fight in an area without "great geographical advantages" and despite British advice that it might be wise to await the arrival of more troops and ammunition.[81] The many who died included Arthur Hardman (178173), a jeweller from Cochrane with parents in Kapuskasing. He had been assigned to the 87th Battalion, and died on or about 17 September 1916 during a bombing raid. A mine exploded just as he reached German lines. Enos Grant (11484), a mill hand from New Liskeard, who had been in the 97th Algonquin Rifles militia before he enlisted, served with the 4th, and then was transferred to the 44th Battalion, suffered a similar fate on 19 September 1916. Another was Wesley Hager (472904), a farmer who came from the hamlet of McCool, just west of Thornloe (though he enlisted in Saskatoon on 3 January 1916 and thus served with the 46th Battalion). He met his fate near Courcelette on 11 November 1916.

The Battle of Vimy Ridge, part of a British initiative based in Arras, began on Easter Monday, 9 April 1917, and lasted a week. Vimy is probably the best remembered Canadian campaign of World War I. German forces occupied Vimy Ridge, a high position between Festubert and Givenchy and Lille and Lens in German-occupied France (fig. 3.5). British and French soldiers had tried and failed to dislodge the Germans from the ridge though they had captured some of the area around Vimy. But Canadian soldiers managed to take the ridge. A huge and frequently photographed monument now marks the spot, and such popular writers as Pierre Berton and Ted Barris have written gripping books about the Battle of Vimy. Berton and Barris depict the battle as a force for Canadian nationalism.[82] No longer were Canadians merely British subjects who lived outside the United Kingdom: "Canadians could grumble that Ypres, the Somme, and Passchendaele were bungled by the British," Pierre Berton writes. "But Vimy! That was Canada's, and nobody could take that victory away."[83] His indictment of futility of the battle in general and the use of poison gas by Canadians would be forgotten in what became the "myth" of Vimy Ridge.[84] Far more important was the fact that the four divisions of the Canadian Corps proved their mettle compared to any other troops.

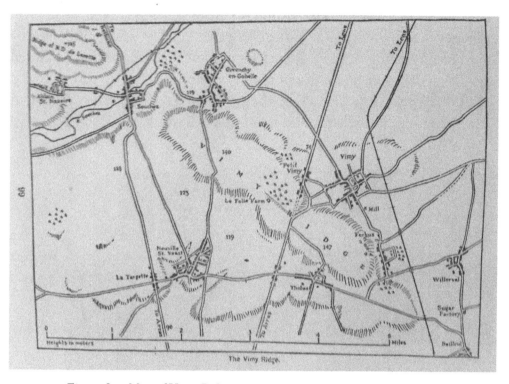

Figure 3.5. Map of Vimy Ridge area. The sugar factory at Courcelette is in the bottom right corner. (*Canada in the Great World War* [Toronto: United Publishers of Canada, 1920], 4:98.)

Yet historians question the larger military significance of Canadian soldiers' individual and group accomplishments at Vimy. J.L. Granatstein does not want "to belittle the Canadian achievement of Vimy Ridge."[85] However, in *The Greatest Victory* he argues that "Vimy did not change the course of the war" to any significant extent because the British High Command had no plans to exploit the gains. At a cost of 10,602 Canadian casualties, Canadians advanced 4,500 yards.[86] German forces simply retreated "a few miles eastward" to the western outskirts of Lens. As for the soldiers, their commanding officer Lieutenant-General Sir Julian Byng believed in a war of attrition. Granatstein reminds his readers that "a strong majority of the men in the Canadian Corps at Vimy were British-born recent immigrants to Canada."[87] The implication is that Vimy was a British victory as well as a Canadian one. Nonetheless, the combatants at Vimy included many Canadian-born soldiers, some from Northeastern Ontario, and hundreds lost their lives that week. Perhaps typical was a Scottish-born Cobalt miner, Arthur Adamson (57781). Next to his will in the service file is written, "Killed in Action 9.4.1914 [sic]" followed by "Taken from Living 8.9.17," suggesting that he died after being wounded (fig. 3.6). Adamson had enlisted on 8 September 1916 in Toronto with the 20th Battalion. In France he took a machine gun course. Wounded numerous times in the neck and hand (fig. 3.7), he finally died at Vimy.

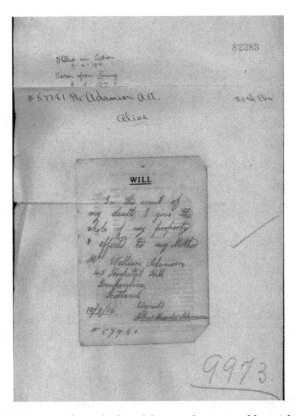

Figure 3.6. Excerpt from Arthur Adamson's service file, with his will and the notice of his death. (Courtesy of Library and Archives Canada)

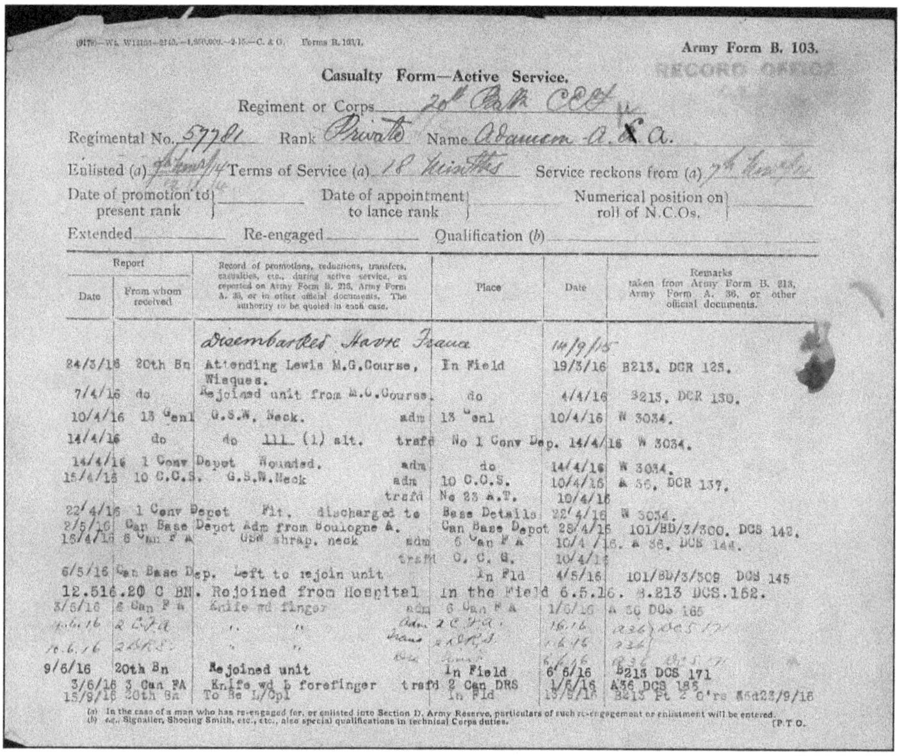

Army Form B. 103.

Casualty Form—Active Service.

Regiment or Corps 20th Batt CEF

Regimental No. 57781 Rank Private Name Adamson A. A.

Enlisted (a) 9th Nov/14 Terms of Service (a) 18 Months Service reckons from (a) 7th Nov/14

Date of promotion to present rank ______ Date of appointment to lance rank ______ Numerical position on roll of N.C.Os. ______

Extended ______ Re-engaged ______ Qualification (b) ______

Report: Date	Report: From whom received	Record of promotions, reductions, transfers, casualties, etc., during active service, as reported on Army Form B. 213, Army Form A. 36, or in other official documents. The authority to be quoted in each case.	Place	Date	Remarks taken from Army Form B. 213, Army Form A. 36, or other official documents.
		Disembarked Havre France		14/9/15	
24/3/16	20th Bn	Attending Lewis M.G. Course, Wieques.	In Field	19/3/16	B213. DCR 125.
7/4/16	do	Rejoined unit from M.G. Course.	do	4/4/16	B213. DCR 130.
10/4/16	13 Genl	G.S.W. Neck. adm	13 Genl	10/4/16	W 3034.
14/4/16	do	do 111 (1) slt. trafd	No 1 Conv Dep.	14/4/16	W 3034.
14/4/16	1 Conv Depot	Wounded. adm	do	14/4/16	W 3034.
15/4/16	10 C.C.S.	G.S.W. Neck adm	10 C.C.S.	10/4/16	A 36. DCR 137.
		trafd	No 23 A.T.	10/4/16	
22/4/16	1 Conv Depot	Fit. discharged to	Base Details	22/4/16	W 3034.
2/5/16	Can Base Depot	Adm from Boulogne A.	Can Base Depot	28/4/16	101/BD/3/300. DCS 142.
16/4/16	6 Can F A	GSW shrap. neck adm	6 Can F A	10/4/16	A 36. DCS 144.
		trafd	C. C. S.	10/4/16	
6/5/16	Can Base Dep.	Left to rejoin unit	In Fld	4/5/16	101/BD/3/309 DCS 145
12.5.16	20 C BN.	Rejoined from Hospital	In the Field	6.5.16.	B.213 DCS.162.
3/6/16	2 Can F A	Knife wd finger adm	6 Can F A	1/6/16	A 36 DCS 165
[illegible]	2 CFA	" " Adm	2 CFA	1.6.16	A36 DCS 17[illegible]
10.6.16	2 DRS	" " trans	2 DRS	[illegible]	A36
		[illegible]	[illegible]	6.6.16	A36 DCS 1[illegible]
9/6/16	20th Bn	Rejoined unit	In Field	6/6/16	B213 DCS 171
3/6/16	3 Can FA	Knife wd L forefinger trafd	2 Can DRS	1/6/16	A36 DCS 185
15/9/16	20th Bn	To Be L/Cpl	In Fld	15/9/16	B213 Pt 2 O'rs 5d23/9/16

(a) In the case of a man who has re-engaged for, or enlisted into Section D, Army Reserve, particulars of such re-engagement or enlistment will be entered.
(b) e.g., Signaller, Shoeing Smith, etc., etc., also special qualifications in technical Corps duties.

[P.T.O.

Figure 3.7. Casualty form detailing numerous wounds sustained by Arthur Adamson during the war, including GSW (gunshot wound) to his neck and a knife wound in his finger. (Courtesy of Library and Archives Canada)

Casualties at Vimy included Andrew Peltier (754723) of Sault Ste. Marie, serving with the 52nd (New Ontario) Battalion; Mathew Hancock (408730), a tinsmith from Steelton with the 37th Battalion (organized by Colonel Penhorwood of Sault Ste. Marie); Percy Goudin Beck (184203) of Gore Bay in the 102nd (North British Columbian) Battalion; Frank Nighswander (754694) from Manitowaning, who started with the 119th Algoma Battalion; field ambulance worker James Hume (455121) of North Bay; Reginald Adshead (1006145), also of North Bay, who started in the 228th (Northern Fusiliers), then shifted to the 159th (Algonquins) and worked in the 5th Canadian Railway Corps before Vimy; and James Hollenbeck (754440) from the Iron Bridge area, who fought with the 52nd Battalion. Typical of the casualties might be Harvey Marshall (486556), an 18-year-old farmer from Green Bay on Manitoulin Island, who "Died of Wounds" on

11 April 1917: "While on duty in the trenches near Vimy he was wounded in the abdomen by shrapnel from an enemy shell. He received First Aid and was taken to a dressing station and later evacuated to No. 30 Casualty Clearing Station where he died."[88]

Many at Vimy were wounded because the Canadians had to move up a well-defended ridge. Victor Mullen (208323) wrote home about a piece of metal like an eight-inch pipe embedded in his thigh. Though born in New York on 3 June 1888, this miner enlisted in Timmins on 10 April 1916. His next of kin was his brother Richard, who also lived in Timmins. His medical record states, "was wounded at Vimy Ridge, [with] a piece of detonator tube, 10.5 inches long, passing through from outside of left thigh, through perineum piercing the urethra." This happened on 9 April 1917. The lasting effects of the wound were also described: "Wounded about groin has since had persistent urethral discharge." The injury proved incurable, and he was discharged as "medically unfit for service" in Toronto on 28 October 1918.

More than a month after Vimy, an account in the *Sudbury Star* on 23 May 1917 listed many of the wounded and stated, "no doubt Sudburians have read many vivid descriptions of how the Canadians did the impossible, but which naturally contained no record of the part played by those of the 159th." The paper then quoted from a letter by M.J. Quinn (648533):

> Many of us were on the ridge and went over the parapet. Ed Clement was wounded and is in Blighty [England], also Claude Lockwood. George Allen was killed in action, also one of the Dole boys, while the other brother was wounded. The Friel boys are with me and come through safe. There were many others from various parts of the north, but who are not known in Sudbury … but the district may well feel very proud that it was represented on almost every part of the front by boys from Sudbury, Copper Cliff, etc. Yes, and some of our little fellows made the big Huns drop their rifles and call for mercy Kamerad. I'm afraid that some of the Germans will have to ask Higher up for mercy, for they got very little here below [did they decide not to take prisoners?]. I am sorry that big Andy Duncan, my old officer in the 159th was killed in action.

Quinn, born in Ireland in 1886, had worked as a machinist in Copper Cliff. He had been with 97th Algonquin Rifles militia, and enlisted on 25 February 1916 at Frood. He trained with the 119th Battalion and was fined for drunkenness and being absent without leave. At Vimy he served with the 52nd, and died on 24 August 1917 near Lens. The Claude Lockwood (648544) he mentions was born in England in 1896, was transferred from the 159th to the 73rd Battalion, and was hospitalized twice with VD before being wounded in the hand and spending most of 1917–18 in England. One of the Friel brothers named above, James (648329), "died of wounds" on 30 June 1917. Born in Ireland in 1887, he was a labourer who enlisted at Frood. The popular officer, Andrew Duncan, had been born in Ireland in 1890 and was working as a broker in Swastika before the war. He enlisted with the 159th at Haileybury and went to France with the 38th Battalion in December 1916. For "gallantry" at Vimy he received the Military Cross.

Several battalions identified with the North had by this time come into being, including the 52nd and 94th (both from Northern Ontario, though more commonly identified with Northwestern Ontario), the 119th Algoma, the 226th and 227th (both called Men of the North), and the 228th (Northern Fusiliers, sometimes identified with Toronto). All had their own identifying insignia, such as cap badges (fig 3.8). The 227th even had its own song:

> The Northern boys are all in a line,
>
> From woods, stream, lake and mine,
>
> We're out on a trip to cross the Rhine ...
>
> We're from the Soo, and Sudbury too,
>
> We hunt the moose and caribou
>
> From Manitoulin Island and St. Joe's ...
>
> For Men 'f the North are we.[89]

The charming self-identification was lost upon the military leadership.

Figure 3.8. Cap badge of the 159th Battalion.
(Courtesy of David Deloye).

However, few of these battalions remained together as fighting units; some, such as the 119th and 159th were disbanded, and troops dispersed among other battalions. Soldiers such as John Friel (648387), born in Ireland in 1887 and working as a labourer in Copper Cliff when he joined on 22 February 1916 with the 159th, would be transferred to the 119th, then placed in the 52nd. While with that unit Friel was wounded and gassed, so he ended in the 18th Reserve in England. His brother James (648329), mentioned above, had joined a few days earlier. He had been with the 97th Algonquin Rifles militia, enlisted with 159th, was transferred to the 119th, and then was placed in the 52nd. These transfers caused consternation at home. The *Porcupine Advance* on 31 January 1917 summed it up with the headline "Future Destination of 159th Not Officially Known." The paper asserted that the men were "anxiously awaiting their turn in the trenches." By 17 February it could write "it would appear that the 159th Battalion, recruited largely from this district, is not to go to the front as a unit, as many expected and hoped." About 150 men had been placed in an engineering corps, and the paper concluded, "Thus the fine battalion from the North Land meets the usual fate of the [northern] Canadian unit overseas."

Table 3.1. Battalions from Northeastern Ontario in World War I

Battalion Name	Area of Recruitment	Fate
119th Algoma (Overseas) Battalion, nicknamed "Algoma Roughnecks"	Sault and Manitoulin in late 1915	Operated as reserve regiment, with men transferring to replace losses in other battalions; disbanded early 1918
159th Algonquins Battalion	Sudbury and Haileybury in early 1916	Operated as reserve
227th Men of the North Battalion	Northeastern Ontario, mostly Algoma and Sudbury, after mid-1916	Men transferred into other units on arrival in England
228th Northern Fusiliers	Nipissing district	Operated as reserve, identified with Toronto, and later became the 6th Battalion Railway Construction Troop

If military historians agree that "the Battle of Vimy Ridge did not change the strategic picture of the war,"[90] and the larger Allied offensive failed, the battle for Hill 70 had similarly devastating results. The fighting between 15 and 25 August 1917 near Lens cost 9,198 Canadian casualties, 8,677 of them at Hill 70.[91] The officers' purpose in the fight for Hill 70 came down "to seize [it] … and let the Germans waste their men trying to take it back."[92] To test such inhumane calculations, many men, like Charles Holbrook (648425), a surveyor from North Bay with the 24th (Victoria Rifles) Battalion, died by sniper fire. Others were shot and/or shelled. Corporal Sidney Elms (141902), a piano and organ tuner from North Bay with the 76th Battalion, received fatal gunshot wounds to his neck, legs, and arms. A teamster born in Scotland and working in Copper Cliff, Allan Bruce (27864) enlisted in September 1914. Assigned to the 48th Highlanders as part of the 15th Battalion, he, too, died at Hill 70: "he was employed as a stretcher bearer, and while searching for wounded in a forward position was hit by a machine gun bullet. When being carried out of the line he was again hit by a fragment from an enemy shell and instantly killed."[93]

The next campaign, at Passchendaele, began late in July but intensified in late October and early November 1917. Also known as the Third Battle of Ypres, it has gained almost universal notoriety. So many lives lost, so much effort expended, for so few results. Passchendaele, a small Flemish village, provided the site for the final two of the eight battles of the Passchendaele campaign. The Allies had several goals, almost none of them achieved, as leaders on the western front were making their plans in reaction to events in the east and south of Europe. In March, Russia had had the first of two revolutions that year. The Czar abdicated, and the government, led by Alexander Kerensky, promised that Russians would continue to fight against the Central Powers (the German, Austro-Hungarian, and Ottoman empires). However, British authorities had doubts. Further, Romania, which had declared war on the Central Powers in 1916, faced defeat. The British calculated that an offensive in Belgium would keep the German Army busy during the eastern front's instability. Moreover, an attack in Belgium would engage the Central Powers to the point where Italian soldiers might attack Austro-Hungarian territory and discourage the Central Powers from launching a counter-offensive.

Another factor was Germany's return to unrestricted submarine warfare, announced early in 1917. As a result, in April, the US government abandoned neutrality and declared war on the Central Powers, but it would take some time for trained US soldiers to reach Europe and for the US navy to deal with the submarine threat. Sir John Jellicoe, commander of the British navy, did not want the German navy to have any bases in western Belgium (none of the eastern Belgian seacoast held by the Germans had useful ports).[94] Meanwhile, the offensive at Passchendaele was not going well. One historian maintains that before Field Marshall Haig called upon Canada for assistance, the United Kingdom, Australia, and New Zealand had suffered so many casualties at Passchendaele between July and October (an estimated 200,000) that their armies could not otherwise retain what they had taken at such cost. Under such circumstances, French soldiers might mutiny and force their country's withdrawal from the war.[95]

In his official history, Nicholson cites the tremendous effort of the United Kingdom and the Dominions (Canada, Australia, New Zealand, India, and South Africa) at Passchendaele. Before the conflict ended, 51 out of 61 of their divisions were engaged. Lieutenant General Arthur Currie, the commanding officer of the Canadian Corps, distrusted the British leadership and accurately projected 16,000 casualties. *Passchendaele*, the movie produced by and starring Paul Gross, vividly portrayed the mud and bloodshed and psychological trauma, as well as the dilemmas of recruiters, during those terrible months. But the reality exceeded literary and cinematic power (fig 3.9).

Figure 3.9. Passchendaele's battleground, with mud and duck boards.
(Courtesy of George Metcalf Archival Collection, CWM 19930013-480,
Canadian War Museum, Ottawa)

The whole effort allowed the Allies to advance just seven kilometres (4.5 miles). The German army retained control of Belgium's eastern ports and soon regained any territory it had lost. The only "benefit" Nicholson identifies involves the convoluted estimate that, although casualties on both sides were horrendous, the British could absorb the loss of 260,000 of their men better than the Germans could deal with the loss of 202,000.[96] The thousands killed included Samuel Robinson (648770), a labourer from New Liskeard of the 4th Canadian Mounted Rifles, and James George (754342), a woodsman from Blind River with the 124th Battalion. Albert Giverman (755067) from Thessalon, with the 227th, died when he was hit by a shell casing in the front-line trenches at Passchendaele. The casualties from Northeastern Ontario came from all over: farmer Pulford Bishop (1004188) from Hilton Head on St. Joseph Island, chauffeur Joseph Baker (255178) from Popular on Manitoulin Island, clerks Orland Morrow (649387) from Frood Mine and Russell McIntyre (1003078) from Sudbury, sailor William Rousseau (451298) from Killarney, and railwayman Arthur Duquette (1007104) from Mattawa.

Perhaps the most positive account of Passchendaele has been that of Daniel G. Dancocks, who notes that within two weeks of the start of the Passchendaele campaign, Canadian soldiers won nine Victoria Crosses, about half of the sixteen subsequently awarded during all of World War II.[97] Against all odds, Canadian soldiers managed to capture Passchendaele with casualties similar to those at Vimy.[98] The Canadian prime minister, Sir Robert Borden (1911–20), certainly did not share Dancocks's perspective. He told his British counterpart, David Lloyd George (1916–20), "If there is ever a repetition of Passchendaele, not a Canadian soldier will leave the shore of Canada so long as the Canadian people entrust the Government of my country to my hands."[99] Some of that amounted to bravado because he simultaneously organized increased recruitment and conscription (announced in April 1917 but introduced slowly, in the face of immense public opposition). Historian John Keegan finds the effort at Passchendaele "inexplicable." Almost 70,000 soldiers died and more than 170,000 were injured. Whether or not German casualties were worse, the Germans had another contingent that they could transfer from the collapsing Russian front. The British had no such reserves.[100]

Hard on the heels of the Passchendaele campaign came the Battle of Cambrai, renowned for being the first time tanks would be crucial, not peripheral, to the battle. The Russians were no longer fighting and the Italian front had collapsed, so the Allies faced a difficult situation. Tanks offered the possibility of smashing through the German line between Cambrai and St. Quentin. Commanders chose flat and treeless ground suitable to tank warfare. The plan involved 300 tanks. As the tanks rolled, the infantry captured Bourlon Wood. The Allies enjoyed the element of surprise: tanks could easily roll over barbed wire laid by the enemy, and thus advance bombardment of the target area would be unnecessary. The assault began on 20 November 1917.[101] News of an Allied "victory" reached England, where church bells rang in celebration. Unfortunately, the celebration proved premature. The Battle of Cambrai, despite the tanks, was a costly British defeat, though historians continue to debate its significance.[102] Canadian casualties again ran heavy for little result, though few came from Northeastern Ontario: John Friel (648387) of Copper Cliff, mentioned above, was gassed and wounded in his hand.

By autumn 1917, the Canadian government resorted to conscription to fill the huge gaps in the battalions resulting from three years' losses. That change in policy had important consequences. Everywhere, attacks on shirkers became commonplace. In Sudbury and elsewhere, many of British background increased their verbal attacks on alleged aliens and accused the local French population of not supporting the war; they even changed street names.[103] The police went out in pairs to collect draftees. In one case, searching for a French Canadian farmer in St. Charles (south of Sudbury), they mistakenly accosted his brother plowing a field and caused the horses to bolt. The man died in the melee.

Avoiding enlistment toward the end of war became as common as enthusiastically volunteering had been at the beginning. Under the conscription system, all men of service age (20–45) had to register (through the post office). They could appeal, based on personal circumstances such as being the sole supporter of a wife, mother, or children, or having an occupation vital to the war effort. By late 1917 most men, having heard about the killing fields of Europe, tried to avoid the draft (fig. 3.12). However, appeal boards tended to be biased in favour of filling the ranks. To shame eligible and fit men to become soldiers, public naming became commonplace. Those who appealed had their cases publicized in local newspapers.

Figure 3.10. As this article from the *Sudbury Star* (14 November 1917) demonstrates, by the third year of the war, the eagerness to defend the British Empire and fight Germany had waned, and appeals for exemption vastly outnumbered those willing to "do their bit." (Courtesy of Sudbury Star, a division of Postmedia Network Inc.)

A compilation of hundreds of exemption cases reviewed by tribunals held in Sudbury for most of the Northeast (from the Sault to North Bay and north) provides insight into the process.[104] The judges' findings appeared in the *Sudbury Star* starting in November 1917. A sample from 10 November reads:

> Holmes, John Williams, Walford Station, farmer. Appeal by himself. No case made out. Did not appear. Disallowed. Doust, Ami, woodsman, Massey Station. Exemption claimed by Spanish River [lumber] Co. Disallowed. He appealed. Has no dependents and work not of national importance. Did not appear. Disallowed. Thibeault, Wilfred, Mile 62 A.E.R. [Algoma East Railway], Espanola, lumberjack. Exemption claimed by himself. Disallowed. Appeals. Has no dependents, does not contribute to support of parents, his work not of national importance. Did not appear. Disallowed.

Even appeals made by men working at Copper Cliff as metal chemists and supported by the company were disallowed. Four of the exempted happened to be prisoners at the Burwash Industrial Farm. A number from Foleyette received temporary deferrals, including farmer Ernst Frault, teamster Alfred Lajoie, and woodsman Emile Mercier. A barber, Hector Audette from Foleyette, was given time to sell his business, while a woodsman, Alfred Diotte, would be exempted if he returned to farming. Some of the individuals received the right not to serve immediately, while most of those conscripted after mid-1918 probably lucked out in that by the time they finished training the war had ended.

The long lists of conscripts who pleaded to stay home illustrate the resistance to state decisions about which occupations served the national interest and which did not. Many farmers and employers received exemptions, while school principals, mechanical draftsmen, locomotive foremen, surgeons, blacksmiths, freight agents, and nearly all labourers had to serve. For example, medical student Clifford Smylie (3233548), born 22 October 1893, was required to present himself for service on 26 October 1917. He signed an attestation on 4 April 1918, giving his mother in New Liskeard as his next of kin. In England he worked in a tank battalion. After the war, he practiced medicine in Earlton and Monteith.[105] A sampling of the tribunal findings suggests that less than 10% received exemptions or temporary stays of conscription. Much resentment would have been fomented when the state sent police to corral men. One French Canadian, Emile Barbe, conscripted in November 1917, asserted to his family that "the [Roman Catholic] priests had sold them to the army," and believed that the church was paid for supplying names and locations.[106]

Despite the losses and the difficulty of filling the ranks, the war continued through a period of setbacks following Passchendaele, including changes on the political front. In November 1917, a second revolution took place in Russia, leaving the Communist Party in power. On 3 March 1918, that government concluded a peace agreement, the Treaty of Brest-Litovsk, with Imperial Germany. Peace with Russia allowed German authorities to reinforce the Western Front, where they launched an offensive that lasted until 6 August, two days before the

Battle of Amiens. Throughout March and April of 1918, Canadian forces stood guard near Lens, "a ruined coal-mining town,"[107] and Vimy Ridge, where they protected the most convenient source of coal (the principal source of energy) and an Allied communications centre. As spring turned into summer, the Allies—with the Canadians playing a major role—launched what turned out to be their final, successful offensive, a series of battles in northeastern France and Belgium. Canadian forces liberated one community after another.

The Battle of Amiens started on 8 August 1918. There were at least 54 casualties from Northeastern Ontario, many from Manitoulin and the Sault area. Historian J. L. Granatstein has devoted his book *The Greatest Victory: Canada's 100 Days*, to the period between Amiens and the Armistice of 11 November. He describes the period, with some exaggeration, as "unquestionably Canada's greatest contribution to the Allied victory" and "the most important Canadian role in battle ever, the only time that this nation's military contributions might truly be called decisive."[108] Amiens was followed by a brief stalemate that lasted until 20 August. However, even the lulls in fighting could result in casualties. Frederick Bryan Atkinson (755079) of Sault Ste. Marie had enlisted on 2 March 1916 with the 119th Algoma Battalion. While serving with the 52nd, he was wounded on 19 February 1918. He died on 13 August 1918, when struck "by a bomb from an enemy aircraft."[109]

On 22 August, Lieutenant General Currie described to his subordinates his plan for capturing the road between Arras and Cambrai, and by 26 August, the troops had advanced to a major German defensive position, the Hindenburg Line. Currie thought that the 1st Canadian Division had fought particularly well. Both sides suffered heavy casualties in the weeks that followed, when more fighting occurred near Bourlon Wood, but on 8–9 October the Canadians captured Cambrai, a distribution centre. In order to make that advance of 30 kilometres (23 miles) between 26 August and the capture of Cambrai, during the course of which they liberated 54 French communities, Canadians had to overcome what Nicholson terms "very strong resistance."[110] Canadian casualties numbered 1,544 officers and 29,262 men of the ranks; they captured 18,595 German prisoners-of-war, 371 guns, and almost 2,000 machine guns. During the battle over Cambrai (at Abancourt),

William Merrifield (8000) from Sault Ste. Marie and Sudbury took out two machine gun emplacements while wounded, earning the only Victoria Cross awarded to a Northeasterner. John William Drysdale Black (142072), a draughtsman from Sudbury, was probably involved in the same battles as Merrifield because both fought with the 4th Battalion. Black provided a strong contrast to Merrifield. Born on 23 May 1892, he enlisted on 14 August 1915 and spent much time in English hospitals, with appendicitis in 1916 and venereal disease (gonorrhea) in 1918. On 23 November 1918, the *Sudbury Star* published a letter, under the heading "Killed Ninety Huns," which Black had written to his parents. The text repeated the outlandish claim. His service record indicates that he received a badge for participation, but contains no hint of any heroic action.[111]

From France, the Canadians' war moved into occupied Belgium, to the city of Mons, which Canadian troops liberated hours before the Armistice. German forces had occupied Mons early in the war and benefited from its coal mines, which, unlike the ones in France, had not been sabotaged and were still producing coal. On 9 November, the Battle of Mons began, and Canadian soldiers entered Mons an hour or so before midnight, late on 10 November. Fighting continued overnight until dawn, by which point the last Germans had left Mons. Troops at the battlefront learned only at 9 a.m. on 11 November that an Armistice would take effect two hours later. The taking of Mons cost the lives of 9 officers and 107 others from the 3rd Division, as well as 22 officers and 343 others from the 2nd. At least 18 officers and 262 Canadian men of the ranks died, suffered injuries, or were captured during the last two days of the war. On 11 November itself, "there were one fatal and 15 non-fatal casualties."[112] Many from the units raised in the North, the 119th, 159th, 227th and 228th, suffered the same fate in the last push of the war though most were serving in other units, like labourer Wilbert Durrell (3230999) who had been drafted in Haileybury with the 228th in November 1917. He gave his mother in North Bay as next of kin, arrived in France in June 1918, took a Lewis (machine) gun course, was first wounded on 2 October, and then was "dangerously wounded" by a shotgun to his shoulder on 6 November. He died two days after the Armistice.

Many died after the fighting stopped. John Blanchet (3111233), a conscript born in North Bay in 1895, arrived in England on 16 September 1918. In November he complained of pains and chills, later combined with coughing and vomiting. By December his temperature reached 103°F, and despite (or because of) doses of cyanide of mercury, he died of meningitis on 5 February 1919. Some succumbed to the great influenza epidemic, including, on 6 February 1919, George Flannagan (648315), a paper maker from Sturgeon Falls who enlisted at North Bay after serving in the 97th Algonquin Rifles militia and the 159th Battalion. Like many, he had been placed in the 8th Reserve, then the Railway Construction Corps, before being transferred to the 4th Battalion. James Durrell (226981) enlisted in 1917 in Sudbury, though his father lived in North Bay. After being wounded in September 1918, he returned to duty in October but reported pain. He would die on 26 April 1920 before being demobilized. Randall Forder (2250351), who had also enlisted in Sudbury, died of myelitis on 1 October 1921, while the death of Claude Craig (408060) as late as 1927 would be attributed to "overseas" effects.

Some men returned from war very late because they were sent to intervene in the Russian Civil War. The British thought, wrongly, that intervention on the side of the so-called Whites who opposed the Bolsheviks might reopen the eastern front.[113] The Allied governments shared a fear of communism and convinced Canada to commit 4,000 soldiers to the mission. Some were sent to Murmansk, European Russia's principal Arctic port, and some to Vladivostok, Russia's principal port on the Pacific Ocean. As an insufficient number volunteered, the Borden government filled the gap with men conscripted under the legislation of 1917.

Among these was St. Charles farmer Emile Barbe (3038922), born in Ottawa on 1 February 1897 and conscripted on 3 November 1917. He signed his attestation papers on 12 September 1918 in Toronto. After a short leave with family in Warren, he rode the train west because he had been assigned to the eastern Russian conflict (fig. 3.11). He sailed for Vladivostok from Vancouver on 22 December 1918 (after the Armistice and after he received punishment involving his conduct), arriving on 22 January 1919. Unlike the Canadians at Murmansk, those at

Vladivostok experienced no fighting. By early 1919, the Russian Whites had basically lost the war and most politicians acknowledged that intervention would waste more lives. A shortage of shipping combined with ice conditions in Vladivostok's harbour delayed the Canadian soldiers' return. Barbe sailed back from Vladivostok on 19 May 1919 and demobilized at Toronto on 11 June 1919, giving his residence as Warren, Ontario. He would not have seen much of Siberia but gathered experiences on the way there and back. Those included being told the Canadians' job involved protecting the deposed Czar, suffering -50°F cold, and stealing two loaves of bread and a large tin of strawberry jam because of insufficient rations. In the meantime, his older brother George (3035667), conscripted on the same day in November 1917, signed his attestation on 18 April 1918, and then enjoyed his stay in a series of English hospitals with measles and then scarlet fever. The nurses thought him cute because of his curly hair.[114] He too only demobilized late, because of his illnesses, on 18 July 1919 in Montreal.

Though the fighting in Europe ended on 11 November, the troops still had to be demobilized.[115] Demobilization moved slowly until a peace treaty replaced the Armistice because the possibility existed that Germany might not accept an imposed peace. Furthermore, transport constraints existed, especially a lack of ships to move troops back to North America. Some men, such as Claude Craig from Sudbury, served in the occupied western area of Germany (the Rhineland), and returned only in mid-1919. In a few instances, drinking and fights over British women led to riots, though whether men from Northeastern Ontario were involved is not clear. Some of the men lived in concentration camps (here meaning simply camps where troops gathered before demobilization). One, at Witley, formerly a training camp in England, was named "Canadian Concentration Camp"!

Captain Donald Cameron, a Sudbury hotel manager before the war, became quartermaster at Witley. As a young Scot he had participated in the South African War. Later widowed, he left his son with a guardian to seek his fortune as a prospector in Canada. He claimed 13 years with the 97th Algonquin Rifles militia when he enlisted in 1915. Wounded in 1917, he received the Military Medal but was found unfit for regular duty. He was given a position in the supply system and was eventually posted to Witley. He would not be demobilized until September 1919, when he returned to Sudbury, where he held leading positions in the local militia and became a justice of the peace. His formal blazer with crest, symbolizing his service in the regional militia and veterans' organizations, remains on display in the Bunker Military Museum at Cobalt.

Figure 3.11. Emile Barbe. (Courtesy of Noreen Barbe, Sudbury)

Many have raised questions about the purpose of the war and the methods of fighting it. Many historians have suggested that the war left the world a worse place, with Hitler rather than the Kaiser in charge of Germany.[116] Few would say that the disintegration of the Habsburg Empire meant happier lives for those who lived in its successor states. The collapse of the Ottoman Empire also did not bring peace and stability to the Middle East. For decades, confrontation, ideological or otherwise, between Communists in Russia and people in the rest of the world fed ideological strife and stealthy wars. Regardless of these consequences, the young men who fought, died, were injured or captured, or continued to do battle originally believed that they acted responsibly, doing what political and military leaders expected of them, and mostly doing it well. Some went to war for adventure, some because their mates were doing it, some to avoid unemployment or from other, more difficult-to-discern motives. Those from Northeastern Ontario who fought in World War I sacrificed their health and even their lives. They made an important contribution by playing their part in this conflict, which shaped their country and the world in the opening decades of the 20th century.

Notes

Notes

Part 2: Experiences

The experiences of war in every region of Canada have been different. Francophone areas generally questioned conscription and often resisted participating in the major conflicts. Some people fought verbally (pacifists) and some physically (riots in Montreal; disappearance into the northern bush) to stay out of wars. The burdens and benefits of war were not shared equally since some regions suffered more casualties, and war profiteers and beneficiaries mostly resided in industrial and financial centres. Even overseas and on the front, officers (who came primarily from larger centres) lived in relative comfort, while common soldiers went hungry in World War I.

Part 2 relates Northeasterners' experiences of warfare, but it offers only a selection of the available stories. Those chosen highlight individuals and groups, special situations and many surprising and unknown events. This collection reveals the diversity of experience and the richness of military social history in Northeastern Ontario.

CHAPTER 4

Individual Encounters, 1914–19

T hough war is a group activity, many experiences are very personal. Some soldiers kept diaries, most wrote letters, and a few wrote memoirs to record their personal perspectives. This chapter explores individual wartime experiences.

A Sudbury Soldier's Diary

Rain and snow. Mud, hunger, fatigue, cold. Enemy bullets, poison gas, deaths of buddies, the risk of your own death or capture. These were daily realities for thousands of young Canadians who fought in World War I.

Many judgments on the war are based on information from the records of contemporary political and military leaders. However, in the twentieth century, with high rates of literacy and despite censorship, regular soldiers also left their views in letters and diaries. The war's outcome depended upon the grunts, those who *did* the actual fighting. For them, World War I meant months or years of living in the trenches of northeastern France and Belgium, aware that death or serious injury could strike at any moment. Interspersed were the horrendous battles—Ypres,

St. Julien, Festubert, Givenchy, St. Eloi, the Somme, Vimy, Passchendaele, Cambrai, Amiens, and Mons—that cost tens of thousands of deaths, often in exchange for minimal territorial gain. Training and retraining for the new type of warfare with machine guns, artillery barrages, and telegraph and radio communication took up as much time as the fighting.

Claude C. Craig (408060) of Sudbury, 23 years of age when he went overseas, left a wartime diary.[117] Raised in Ottawa of Irish Protestant background, Claude moved to Sudbury with his father, step-mother, and half-sister in late 1913. His father, Rufus James Craig, served as coal superintendent for the Canadian Pacific Railway (CPR). Claude worked at the CPR's telegraph office, at that time the most common means of rapid communication. He had been found medically fit on 14 April 1915. Like all other recruits, he pledged allegiance to the Crown, and he promised to obey all orders. He signed up at Niagara-on-the-Lake Camp on 12 June, declaring that he had been born in Ottawa on 4 November 1894 and naming his father in Sudbury his next of kin.[118] For occupation, he wrote "telegraphist." The attestation papers describe him as five feet six inches, of dark complexion, with grey eyes and black hair. His chest expanded to 34 inches and he had two marks on his left arm. Religious designation: Church of England.

Claude Craig dedicated his diary "to whoever will read it," and added as a preface:

I never wrote nothing before

I'll never write nothing no more.

There won't be no second edition

For, you see, the war it is o'er.

So please don't be hard on the writer.

I did the best that I could.

I can't get ideas into my head.

You never can into wood.

Despite his modesty, Craig provided a vivid description of his experiences, which 100 years later should cause readers to be grateful that they have lived in an era of relative peace.

Claude Craig joined the 97th Algonquin Rifles militia late in December 1914 but did not go overseas for another 12 months. His enlistment form states that he had also been with the militia in the 43rd Regiment (headquartered in Parry Sound) for two and a half years.[119] So anxious was he to go that he accepted a demotion from the rank of sergeant. His diary gives no hint of lack of faith in the cause, even as it vividly portrays the horrors of war. He does not give his motives for enlisting, whether patriotism, adventure, or advancement—the military did offer opportunities for someone in his trade. Signalling information proved crucial to the war, and he was attached to a signals unit. He trained in Canada, and then trained other signallers for nearly two years in England. In February 1917, he made it to the fighting front in France.

At the front he found mud. On 4 April 1917, he reported, "went into a couple of nasty shell holes full of mud and had to be pulled out of one." Four days later he described what he had to carry: "Battle order consists of the skeleton equipment with the haversack strapped to the back, rifle, ammunition, water, iron rations and all the grub that one can carry. Then there are bombs, flares, shovels, phones, flags, flappers and a host of other things." The difficulty of carrying supplies and personal gear through the endless mud became a recurring theme in front-line soldiers' war experience.

Craig fought in the Battle of Vimy Ridge (9–14 April 1917). For days in advance, the enemy bombarded them with shells, while somebody had to run back and forth—through the mud—with food and other supplies. Yet Craig could see some humour in it all: on 29 March, he wrote, "The officers ... were shelled out of their dugouts at 1 a.m. and the Brigadier had to stay in the muddy ditch ... in his night-clothes for 2 hours. I would have liked to have seen him." On 8 April, the day before the battle began, the Canadians headed toward what would be the battlefield: "We left about 9:30 p.m., and we were carrying an extra water-bottle, which, by the way, is a sure sign that one's battalion is going over the top [confronting the enemy] or are going into a 'dirty place.'" On 9 April, Easter Sunday, the soldiers reached their destination at 3 a.m.: "Looking around the dugout at the fellows sitting and lying around, one couldn't help wondering who was to come back and who wasn't."

The Canadians gained ground at Vimy Ridge, and on 14 April, Craig and his friend Herbert found themselves in a German dugout with seven dead enemy soldiers. Craig reported, "as we couldn't move them out we slept with them in the same place. It wasn't nice smelling, but it was much better than in the mud, which was very bad." He later reported that "we lost all track of the time … I don't remember much of it as I was too sick to care where we were going."

Craig's accounts of the major battles of 1917 and 1918 say much about the intensity of the fighting. About Passchendaele, where thousands died, mostly due to poor British planning, he noted on 6 November 1917 that his unit had "100 casualties in 20 minutes." The next year, on 26 August 1918, he described another battle near Lens: "The Fritzies [Germans] were sitting on top of a ridge and I guess they thought that we couldn't put them off. We did, in half an hour, killing about 70. I got one, wounding a hundred and taking about 150 prisoners."

Between the battles, Craig reported other difficulties caused by the inadequacy of the military's preparations. In a letter in September 1916, he asked his father to send his raincoat from Sudbury, as the rainy season was approaching. The coat eventually arrived. His diary reports that, on the night of 3–4 September 1918, Claude and his buddies marched for so long that they reached their destination too late for breakfast. The next night they slept crowded but warm, and then "slept and played cards all day." Not quite two weeks later, they marched more than six kilometres "for a bath … but we were turned back as there wasn't any water." Many Canadian soldiers had similar experiences as the army struggled to organize adequate food, shelter, and clothing in concert with troop movements.

The chaos of war could have far more serious results. Craig was on night reconnaissance in late September 1918 when he and a buddy became lost, ended close to the enemy trenches, and discovered that they had wandered three kilometres in no-man's land. In the artillery-scarred battlefield between the opposing armies, few landmarks survived. Even medical care for the wounded could be hard to find. On 1 October, a bullet went through Craig's wrist. He walked four kilometres to the closest first aid station and another two to reach a bus. While the army had ambulances and stretch-bearers for serious casualties, those capable of walking often fended for themselves. At Camiers, Craig wrote from the hospital: "I was very sorry that I ever was in this Hospt, at all. It was very cold, and the grub was very, very poor, and not enough of it at that."

Fortunately, Craig returned home after some time in western Germany in early 1919. Unlike some veterans, he came home to a job, working in telegraph offices of the CPR's Sudbury Division. The 1921 census registered Claude Craig as a "stenograph" at Byng Inlet near Parry Sound, and his obituary stated that he had held such posts at train stations all around the Sudbury area. By 1926 illness had curtailed his career, yet he married Virginia Leclair of Espanola on 18 January 1926 and lived long enough to sire a daughter. However, he too appears to have been a casualty of war. Early in April 1928, while still in his early thirties, and after spending some time in the Sudbury General Hospital, he suffered a stroke and died. The obituary attributed his death to "overseas service."[120] Sometimes it is forgotten that the war's consequences continued long after its official end, especially for the wounded or shell shocked.

At least two other soldiers from Sudbury/Copper Cliff left diaries. Clerk Alfred Baggs's (7933) diary can be compared to his service record.[121] After obtaining permission to marry an Englishwoman in November 1915 (he had proof of a pre-war engagement), he seemed to lose interest in returning to Canada, as after the war he demobilized to Britain, where he received a Meritorious Service Medal. During the war, he had also received 168 hours Field Punishment #2, which probably involved extra duties, for "cruelty to a horse." He wrote of endless mud, and admitted to food theft due to limited rations. His diary describes fighting at Ypres and Hill 70, a gas attack, suffering Belgian refugees, and officers "cheerfully" encouraging soldiers "eager" for their initial engagement. He suffered from shell shock and was hospitalized for an ingrown toenail, and in 1918 he served in the Canadian military police before settling in Britain.

Sudbury printer Frederick John Cressey (2527351), working behind the Allied lines from April 1918 to June 1919, also kept a diary in the form of a chronology.[122] He had been in the 97th Algonquin Rifles militia for a year before he enlisted on 21 September 1917 with the 58th Battalion in Hamilton. He was transferred to the 8th Reserve before going to the front with the 58th. On 19 August 1918, he received a gunshot wound in the thigh that put him in the hospital for nearly a month. After the war he participated in the interwar Sudbury militia, rising to the rank of captain and serving as a recruitment officer during World War II. The diary relates his bureaucratic tasks in 1918–19: organizing work parties to repair bridges or trenches, mustering men for parades, and updating the nominal role or list of men. The frequent mention of food and billets underscores the shortage of the former and the poor quality of the latter (fig. 4.1).

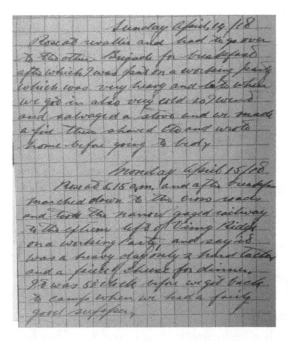

Figure 4.1. A page from Frederick John Cressey's World War I diary.
(Cressey Papers, 58A1 1.10, George Metcalf Archival Collection,
Canadian War Museum. Reproduced courtesy of the Canadian War Museum)

An Engelhart Soldier's Hardships

The letters home from Englehart soldier Harold Austin Phillips (648713) provide first-hand insight into a soldier's life.[123] Born in Leeds County in southeastern Ontario in 1900, Phillips moved with his family to Englehart in May 1910. Eager to serve, he lied about his age when he enlisted in the 159th Algonquin Battalion "B" Company at Haileybury on 25 January 1916, a mere three days after his 16th birthday. (The legal age was 18.) At the time he stood at five feet five inches and weighed 133 pounds. He gave "butcher" as his occupation. Phillips and his fellow recruits marched from the armory in Haileybury to the railway station as crowds cheered and the band played "The Girl I Left Behind Me." At that point, the fun appears to have ended.

After training at Camp Borden, Phillips willed his earthly possessions to his father, instructed the army to send $10 of his pay each month to his father, and set sail for England in 1916. His ship landed at Liverpool, and the 159th Battalion then travelled by train to Seaford, east of the resort town of Brighton on the English Channel. Phillips wrote to his father on 20 November 1916: "Well, this is some place. Mud to the eyes and lots of drill. The camp is right close to a town so I go down nearly every night. We had a good trip over but they used us like cattle. We were packed into the boat like sardines." Phillips considered himself fortunate to be living in a hut rather than a tent, but he shared that hut with 29 others. He signed the letter "Pte [Private] Harold A Phillips No. 648713, Signaling Section 159th B.N., C.E.F. [159th Battalion, Canadian Expeditionary Force]." The 159th Algonquins started as a special battalion recruited in Northeastern Ontario in late 1915, but overseas its soldiers were spread among other units.

In 1917, Phillips was transferred to the Railway Construction Corps, which sent him to France. After a spell there, his letters begin to sound bitter and disillusioned. From "Somewhere in France," he wrote to his father on 17 June 1917: "Don't ask me how long this confounded war is going to last, for you know more about it than we do … Yes, it is too bad they did not have conscription in Canada long ago. It would please the poor devils out here to see some of those momma's pets sent out here." Being in the railway corps, exposed to enemy artillery and sniper fire while laying track and bringing up supplies, may have influenced his deteriorating outlook. On the positive side, he thought the weather good, although in August he complained to his sister Gwendoline about "some very hot weather." Money did not pose a problem, he told his father. Soldiers received enough money "to keep us going in smokes." Mail service proved fast. By 17 June he had received the letter his father had written on 27 May, and his letter to sister Gwen dated 23 August acknowledged hers written 30 July.

From that point, Phillips's situation deteriorated. On 20 October 1917, he received 14 days of Field Punishment #1 and forfeited $15.40 in wages because he had hesitated to obey an order from a non-commissioned officer and sworn at him. Field Punishment #1, inherited from the British Army, had in 1881 replaced flogging as a punishment for minor offenses. The soldier who had misbehaved was tied to a stake, gun carriage, or other fixed object for at least two hours a day regardless of weather, for a maximum of 21 days. Humiliating in itself, Field Punishment #1 could be even worse if it took place within range of enemy gunfire, if the soldier had to face into the sun, or if he had lice.

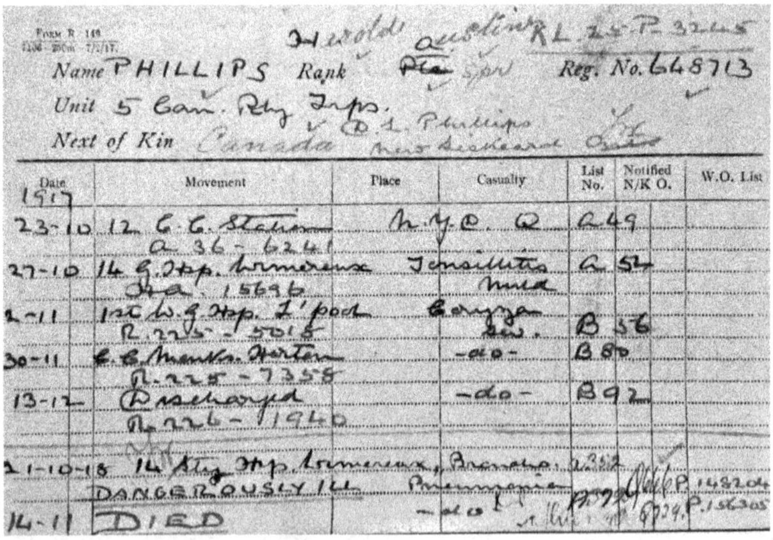

Figure 4.2. Harold Phillips's service record.
Note the tonsillitis that put him in the hospital on 27 October 1917.
(Harold Phillips [648713], Service file, RG 150, Accession 1992-93/166, Box 7796-8, *Personnel Records of the First World War*, Library and Archives Canada, www.bac-lac.gc.ca/eng/discover/military-heritage/first-world-war/personnel-records. Reproduced courtesy of Library and Archives Canada.)

Poor health may have been behind Phillips's insubordination. Three days after being sentenced, Phillips became a patient at No. 12 Casualty Clearing Station because of what appeared to be tonsillitis (fig. 4.2). His condition was so serious that he was sent by train to Antwerp and then back to England. After weeks in English hospitals for bronchitis and other ailments, he was deemed fit for duty in January 1918 and returned to France. The French winter may have been cold but dry (unlike England's), and Phillips appreciated the absence of steady rain—and other diversions. On 26 March 1918, from "Somewhere in France," he explained to his father that he had been unable to write "as I had my finger smashed playing ball." On 18 September, he told his sister Gwen that he had applied to the RAF, the British air force, but had been rejected. Instead, he had become a sapper (a soldier whose duties include tunnelling under opposing lines to blow them up).[124] Shortly thereafter, Phillips fell victim to bronchial pneumonia and influenza, and died at the No. 14 Station Hospital at Wimereux, France—near Calais on the Strait of Dover—on 14 November 1918, three days after the Armistice.

Whose Hero? William Merrifield and His Mysteries

Who can take credit for heroic soldiers? This question is raised by the case of William Merrifield (8000), a Victoria Cross winner (fig. 4.3), whose exploits have been connected to communities ranging from Hull and Ottawa, to Sudbury and Sault Ste. Marie, to Brentwood, England.

Figure 4.3. William Merrifield, on his way to receive the Victoria Cross, January 1919. (*Canada in the Great World War* [Toronto: United Publishers of Canada, 1921], 6: facing page 304.)

On 7 January 1919, the *Ottawa Journal*'s banner headline read "Victoria Cross for Gallant Deed." In slightly smaller print, the subtitle reported, "Hull Boy Attacked Two Enemy Machine Gun Emplacements Which Were

Holding Up Advance, Killing Both Crews." Then the paper quoted the official *London Gazette* announcement of Merrifield's award:

> … for the most conspicuous bravery and devotion to duty during the attack near Abacourt, on October 1, 1918, when his men were held up by an intense fire from two machine gun emplacements. He attacked them both single-handed. Dashing out of a shell hole he killed the occupants of the first post and although wounded continued the attack on the second post and with a bomb killed the occupants. He refused to be evacuated and led his platoon until again severely wounded.[125]

The Ottawa paper claimed him as a "Hull Boy," but wrongly identified him as a farmer. On 28 January, the *Journal* repeated the account when it reported on the ceremony where the king awarded Merrifield the Victoria Cross (VC), the highest British military honour. This time the paper provided an address on Aylmer Road and asserted "he is well known in Ottawa."

On 19 and 26 April 1919, the *Sudbury Star* also described Merrifield's accomplishments. The *Star* added that he had received the Military Medal for courageous action at Passchendaele. The article announced that he would be in Sudbury on 20 April and raised the issue of whether Merrifield was a Sudbury or Sault hero, since he had lived in both cities before the war. In an interview on 9 May 1919 in the *Sault Star*, Merrifield confirmed that he worked for both Inco and the Algoma Central Railway. He clearly had ties in both cities.

But Merrifield's story is more complicated.

Born 9 October 1890 in Brentwood, just northeast of London, England, Merrifield came to Canada as a youth. One report stated that he arrived at age 10 (in 1900),[126] and his granddaughter claimed 12 (1902),[127] yet he does not appear in the 1911 Census of Canada. When he enlisted in August 1914, signing his attestation at Valcartier, he gave as next of kin his father, William Merrifield, of Aylmer Road in Ottawa. The 1915 nominal roll of the 2nd Battalion again gives his father, at the Aylmer Road address, as next of kin, as does a February 1916 entry in his file when he was being treated for shell shock. In a postwar interview in the Sault, however, he claimed an uncle in Ottawa as his only relative in Canada, yet he seems not to have visited his father (or uncle) in Ottawa/Hull after his demobilization. Did the father die between 1916 and 1919? Merrifield seems to have no connection to Ottawa or Hull in his later years.

Many communities have laid claim to Merrifield, one of only two Northeastern Ontario bearers of the Victoria Cross. Brentwood has honoured him with a memorial stone. The *Sudbury Star*, as related above, claimed him for Northeastern Ontario, yet he started the war with the 51st Soo Rifles militia and was among the 127 volunteers listed on the front page of the *Sault Star* when they left on 20 August 1914 (fig. 1.6). He was transferred to the 2nd Battalion, but by 1915 appeared in the 4th (identified with central Ontario). Before returning to Sudbury after his Toronto demobilization in March 1919, he went to Brantford with comrades from the 4th Battalion, where "he was identified and greatly welcomed."[128] In the end, Merrifield returned to the North. His service file initially gave his intended address on demobilization as Box 1555, Sudbury, though that has been corrected to 308 Hudson Street, Sault

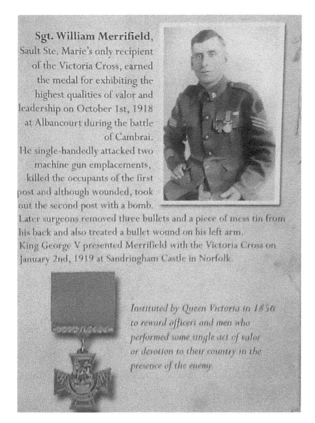

Figure 4.4. Tablet honouring William Merrifield, VC. (Courtesy of Sault Ste. Marie Museum)

Ste. Marie; it is not clear when the change was made. On 9 May 1919, the Sault gave him a tumultuous welcome, and in his interview with the *Sault Star*, he hinted that the warm reception influenced him to stay in the Sault, where he is honoured in the military room of the local museum (fig. 4.4). Since he survived the war, his name does not, of course, appear on the Sault Ste. Marie World War I monument commemorating its war dead. However, a plaque honouring his exploits sits in front of the monument, probably erected after his death in August 1943.

Despite his life in and evident preference for Northeastern Ontario, Merrifield's northern identity has been overlooked in a brochure handed out by the Canadian War Museum, *Canadian Recipients of the Victoria Cross*.[129] While the residence of most VC recipients is included in their short biographies, for William Merrifield the brochure notes only his birth in England and his death in Toronto. Between, it lists his battlefield achievements, but gives no hint of his Northeastern Ontario life and work. Nonetheless, Merrifield is listed in the 1919 and 1920 Sault city directories as a brakeman working at the steel plant and living on Gore Street. In 1921 he married Maude Bovington, with whom he would have four children. When the New Ontario soldiers' reunion took place in the Sault in August 1923 (see ch. 8), Merrifield participated in a demonstration of trench warfare, though he received no special acknowledgement, despite his VC. He died in 1943 after a massive stroke in 1937, and is buried in the Sault's West Korah cemetery, in an Imperial War Graves Commission plot.[130]

Perhaps the question of who can lay claim to Merrifield's heroism is wrong, since he acknowledged ties to more than one place and the motives for his actions are unknown. We know that he spent months in the hospital (in January 1915, November 1916, and February 1919) being treated for VD, and that he was not always a model soldier. Unlike his fellow soldier from the Sault, Edwin Durham, Merrifield offered few insights on his war experiences, except to say that he cherished gifts from his comrades more than his VC. He added that many soldiers deserved the medal, but their deeds had not been witnessed by officers. Humility—the sure sign of a hero regardless of what place claimed him—marked his outlook.

Being a POW: Onions and Theatre

Hundreds of Canadians became prisoners of war (POWs) at the second Battle of Ypres in April 1915. Wounded in the stomach, then in his buttock, Edwin Durham (7954) surrendered as the battle continued (fig. 4.5). In letters home and in his detailed memoirs, Durham recounted that a German officer took pity on him lying in a trench and asked in French if he was cold. In response to his "yes," the officer covered him with blankets. "I was carried to a field station,"[131] Durham later reported.

Figure 4.5. Edwin Durham. (Durham Papers, 992.13, Sault Ste. Marie Public Library Archives)

The next day he was bandaged, but remained at the field station because the hospital was full of worse cases. A day later his guard took him by train to Siegburg, across the Rhine River, where he was transferred to a horse-drawn ambulance. Since lying down made his wounds hurt, he sat with the driver, helping to manage the horses. At a military hospital for war wounded from all countries, which had been established at a monastery, doctors agreed that the bullet had left a jagged stomach wound that had to be cauterized. He pointed out his other wounds, and "A pretty little sister [nurse] ... got me one of those rubber donuts to lie on."[132] He reported, "they were very good to us and we were well fed there. We didn't know how well until we got to Cologne."[133] Over the next six weeks he met other captured Allied troops, noting that he got on well with the Hindus, but that the French disliked the Algerians. He met a "professional hobo" from Canada, known simply as China Booth, who loved board games but played a different form of checkers.

Once he was transferred to Cologne, Durham found "it was military and that was very different ... it was a starvation diet there."[134] For breakfast they received a slice of black bread, and *ersatz* coffee made from acorns. Their diet was monotonous. He described the soup:

they'd bring up about half a horse, it was quite well dressed [butchered], and boil that in a large cauldron. Then they'd take out the bones and meat, take all the meat off all the bones and put the meat through the grinder and back into the soup, the broth, and so many ladles of that would be put into the other cauldron with vegetables to make up the soup … Now in the case of potatoes they were peeled by a potato peeler that scratched the skins … it was like a larger grater, a revolving grater. So they were losing some starch there."[135]

He also described another meal frequently fed to POWs: "sometimes it would be fish soup and you could see the fish eyes in it."

Prisoners found it hard to survive without parcels from home. Durham explained how newly captured men were instructed by the experienced POWs to think of the names of friends and relatives, and to write to them all requesting parcels. Those who had been captive for a while would share their packages with newcomers, who were expected to share when they started to receive their own. Durham did not care for the homemade wine that the Poles and French concocted or had sent to them, and he concluded that "the German rations were impossible."[136] As Craig's diary also reveals, food meant much to soldiers because of their strenuous workload, and it was hard to keep supply lines open due to the constant bombardment. In hospitals the problem was compounded by the need to make sure fighting men were fed first. Rations for POWs were supposed to be the same as for the opponent's soldiers, but the Central Powers did not have sufficient supplies after the British blockaded Europe. Cultural differences about what was normal and nutritious food also played a role. Central Europeans appreciated black bread and it was, like fish eyes, highly nutritious but unpalatable to British and Canadian tastes.

Durham spoke about how the Germans treated them:

There weren't many bad ones. We were very fortunate in being in amongst the Saxons. And the average farmer [for whom POWs had to work], he had nothing against England. He just wanted to till his land and be left alone. And the strange thing about it, there was a certain understanding between prisoners and Germans who had been at the front, as opposed to a young German who had never been to the front.[137]

He related stories of helping grow cabbages and the use of dried fecal matter that POWs had to spread for fertilizer. They were sometimes allowed to keep the smaller cabbages. Relations with the guards were complicated:

> I hadn't been sorting onions for some time and I thought I'd get away with a couple onions but I didn't. He [the guard] took them off me and I was a little disappointed not so much in losing the onions as disappointed in him. Anyway I went back to my barrack and I was sitting down and in came the little devil and he had the onions that I swiped and a couple more for me.

The guard may have disliked the strict rules or simply sympathized with the hungry prisoners. Barriers prevented exchanges between POWs in different barracks, yet they could easily talk to each other over the wires separating the barracks, and those sorting onions would throw some to those on the other side.

Some of Durham's stories are droll. Once, when going drinking with a guard, Durham told the guard he had no money. The guard replied that it did not matter: "So I get up and on our way to the pub, little corner pub there, he gave me some money to pay for the beer. He couldn't be seen in the pub paying for my beer!" Durham became the camp electrician and fixed lights and bicycle lamps as a favour to the guards, so he may have received more liberties than others.

He also gave detailed descriptions of the clothing, a rough uniform with an armband, though they could wear other clothing if they had it, and they would dress up to go into town.

The POWs at the Stendal camp, where Durham spent three years, were a mix of French, British, Poles, Russians, and some "colonials." They organized endless variety, music, dance, and orchestra shows, as well as language and music lessons. The Durham Papers contain printed programs and photos. At one point, the British organized a very popular musical revue, *The Joy Boys*, in which Durham participated (figs. 4.6 and 4.7). The prisoners could go into town to print programs and used the local cinema for presentations. The French orchestra also provided mimeographed programs for their audiences.

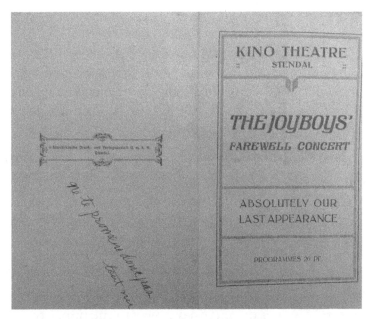

Figure 4.6. Theatre at Stendal POW camp.
(Durham Papers, 992.13, Sault Ste. Marie Public Library Archives)

Figure 4.7. Photo of the Joy Boys, Stendal POW camp.
(Durham Papers, 992.13, Sault Ste. Marie Public Library Archives)

This visual evidence provides a very different picture of captivity than that painted by some Canadian historians, who describe much rougher treatment.[138] Durham, a member of the Sault Legion for years and a respected veteran, does not speak of mistreatment, except for the food shortages shared with his captors. Though food was unfamiliar and in short supply, when examined after captivity most POWs were found to be in good physical condition. The photos of those repatriated and those still in the camps show quite healthy men, unlike the skeletons that came out of Japanese or German camps after World War II. This is not to deny that some POWs were mistreated. A comparative study has demonstrated that brutalization of POWs occurred among all the major powers.[139] The practice of using POWs for labour just behind the fighting lines was begun by the British, for example, and the Germans, in reprisal, did the same.[140]

A different POW experience comes from a Timmins soldier. A story in the *Porcupine Advance* from 29 May 1918 reported on a repatriated POW who referred to his captors as "German beasts." Percy Dunbar (28018) announced his joy at being free, and advised, "Never allow anyone who is tainted with one drop of German blood to speak to you or yours." However, he described no examples of mistreatment. His service file reveals that he was repatriated to the Netherlands in March 1918 after three years in POW camps at Cassel and Soltau. His medical examination did find "debility" from "exposure," but also found him fit again by December 1918. Another Northeastern Ontario POW was Major Robert Russell McKessock, a magistrate from Sudbury. He was shot in his right leg at Ypres on 23 April 1915, and wounded in the head on 24 April. He became a prisoner of war in a series of German camps (Bischopswerde, Crefeld, Schwarmstedt, Holzminden, and Freiburg Baden). Due to his declining health, he was part of a prisoner exchange and was interned in the Netherlands in 1917. He made a statement to a medical board in England in December 1917: "since 1916 he has been feeling below par and physically unable to stand sustained effort, due to conditions in prison camp in Germany." He was given three months without duties to recover from "debility": at enlistment, he had weighed 195 pounds; when interned in the Netherlands, 165; and at demobilization in 1919, 185. In sum, his experience was far less positive than Durham's.

Edwin Durham was born 31 August 1894, and he had enlisted with his older brother Elliott, born 8 December 1892, immediately at the war's outbreak. Both were found fit at Valcartier on 22 September 1914. They had been in the 51st Soo Rifles militia in Sault Ste. Marie. Edwin had trained as an engineer, while Elliott was a clerk with the rank of lieutenant. Elliott returned to England after his war service. He later became the Sheriff of Nottingham and in that role attained fame because he pardoned Robin Hood for his 13th-century thefts from the rich. Edwin served in the 2nd Battalion and would be repatriated in January 1919. When demobilized in May 1919, he had scars from his posterior wounds and a "slight weakness of the abdomen." He served in the local Sault militia in the 1920s, and after World War II gave presentations on his war experiences, cautioning that efforts should be made to maintain peace.

Special Cases: Deserters and Punishment

Some Northeastern soldiers' files leave big mysteries. Among the thousands examined for this book, the case of William James Connors (754150) offers just the bare bones of what might be a much larger story. On 28 January 1916, this locomotive fireman enlisted at Massey, giving his father in Lindsay, Ontario, as next of kin. Born 28 August 1892, Connors claimed to have been in the militia for three years, but did not specify where. His thin file indicates that he was recruited for the 119th Battalion. However, a note at the top of his service summary in the short and perhaps incomplete file reads "Original is not available." One of two terse entries records that on 7 April 1916 he was transferred to the 224th Canadian Forestry Battalion in Quebec. A much later entry from 30 July 1923 reads "Ill[egally] absent 20.4.16 SOS [Struck off Strength, or discharged] as a Deserter." Did he change his mind about going to war when assigned to a forestry job? Where did he go, and where is the original file? Why was the designation "deserter" entered only in 1923?

Joseph Deroches (1003335) is a similar case. A labourer from Blind River whose next of kin, his mother, lived in Gaspé Bay, Quebec, Joseph was born on 25 December 1891. He enlisted at Blind River on 30 May 1916 in the 227th Battalion, at a time of aggressive recruitment drives. Again, someone has noted at the top of the file that the original is unavailable. On 12 September 1916, Deroches left the Hamilton training camp without authorization, and by 12 October he was designated a deserter. A court of inquiry called on the case left no record of its findings. Where did he go, where is his original file, and did he simply hide out in Gaspé Bay?

Somewhat different is the case of Frank Dukoski (186556), who claimed to be born at Victoria Mines, Sudbury, but also claimed not to know the address of his next of kin, brother Sam. Though this labourer enlisted in Winnipeg on 10 November 1915 and claimed residence in Sudbury, he probably lied, because by January 1916 he was Away Without Leave. By February he was designated a deserter. Could he have been a so-called alien who pretended to enlist because he did not want to report every month to police? These are the kinds of cases that require literary imagination, since historical evidence is absent.

The case of Raywood Douglas Leffler (7993) is equally intriguing. On 24 February 1915, Edwin Durham wrote to his parents about men from the Sault who were to be recognized for heroism. He mentioned that "that fat baker," Leffler, might be the recipient of a Military Cross.[141] Though Leffler did not receive an award, his service file makes interesting reading. Working in a field ambulance unit, he would have had many dangerous experiences bringing wounded back from the front. However, he was hardly a model soldier.

Leffler was born in London, Ontario, on 19 April 1895, but had been a member of the Sault militia before the war. He gave as next of kin his mother at Sault Ste. Marie where he enlisted, though he officially signed his attestation at Valcartier on 22 September 1914. Leffler was big, at five feet ten inches; his chest expanded to nearly 40 inches. Like Durham and a hundred recruits from the Sault, he would be placed in the 2nd Battalion. In January 1915 he lost three days' pay because of "18 days hospital, VD." He arrived in France on 8 February 1915 after training in England. He soon sprained his foot and spent a few days in hospital at Versailles in June. On 13 August he was "fined 3 days pay" for "scandalous and insulting language to an NCO." Leffler's misbehaviour became worse: in September he was "sentenced to three months FP#1 [Field Punishment #1] from 7/9/15, viz 91 days," less one month for his good conduct under fire. He would die of multiple wounds to face, arms, and lungs on 31 December 1915. One can only imagine what this short summary of his misdemeanours and punishments meant in terms of emotional stress for the baker-soldier.

The daily experiences of soldiers from Northeastern Ontario may not have been greatly different from others serving in the mud of Flanders, going hungry and carrying the heavy burdens of warfare or undertaking heroic action. Yet their specific and very diverse cases have mostly remained untold over the decades since the war.

Notes

Notes

CHAPTER 5

Special Units and Identities

How many have claimed that a grandfather or uncle fought at Vimy or Ypres? It is just as likely that they might have served in the forestry or railway corps, cutting wood or laying railway ties.

In war, many situations arise requiring skilled men and special materials. Soldiers do more than fight: getting personnel, supplies, and munitions to the battlefields, maintaining them, and building defenses all require a variety of experts, often organized in special units. In World War I, at least three new units drew on the expertise of soldiers from Northeastern Ontario, because lumbering, railroad building, and tunnelling were skills northerners exercised daily. Two groups who had such skills were Indigenous men and Francophones, who were often placed in the forestry, rail construction, and tunnelling units. Officers, too, can be seen as a special group.

The Canadian Forestry Corps (CFC)

Canadians have been stereotypically identified as hewers of wood. The British certainly had that impression and thus turned to Canada when a shortage of wood became a crisis by late 1915. Two reasons explain the lack of wood: the sheer quantity of timber needed at the front; and the difficulty of importing it from North America because ocean transport was dangerous and political leaders had prioritized the shipping of troops, war materials, and food. In early 1916 the British made a special request to Canada for 1,500 forestry workers: 700 tree fellers, 450 sawyers, 250 carters, and 100 engineers, sent immediately in batches of 50.[142] Canada agreed to provide experienced woodsmen and managers to set up mills and cut timber in English, Scottish, and western French forests. Eventually 22,000 Canadians served in the timber operations of the Canadian Forestry Corps. They also cleared forested areas for over a hundred aerodromes.[143]

The importance of wood in 20th century warfare is often forgotten. In World War I, wooden timbers supported the wet walls of thousands of kilometres of trenches and dugouts. Wooden slats, known as duck boards or trench mats, lined the bottom of hundreds of miles of muddy trenches. Wood was needed for storage buildings, barracks, hospitals, airplane hangars, and even plane parts. Rifle butts, axe handles, stretchers, and coffins (when they were used) required wood. Ammunition boxes and barbed-wire stakes required wood. Railways required ties. Making tea or hot soup in the trenches required fuel and the local supplies quickly disappeared. If the film *Paths of Glory* overdramatizes the fighting scenes and senseless "going over the top," it does illustrate the use of wood, especially in trenches and dugouts.

Within six weeks of the British request, by April 1916, 1,600 men had been recruited and assembled at Quebec City. The first group took along a portable mill, and by 13 May it was operating. Northeastern Ontario newspapers repeatedly called for men to join the forestry battalion, or listed the names of those who had signed up. On 19 July 1916, for instance, the *Porcupine Advance* declared, "New Forestry Battalion Recruiting in the North: They will not be engaged in fighting but will be employed in cutting timber in forests of Britain and France for use at the front— Expect to go overseas in September—Are necessary to success" (fig. 5.1).

Figure 5.1. Recruiting office for forestry corps in Timmins.
(Courtesy of the Timmins Museum National Exhibition Centre)

As the shortage of men and wood continued, the recruitment drive intensified. On 4 April 1917, the *Porcupine Advance*'s front page read, "Business Men Assisting with the Forestry Draft." A week later, it headlined "Nine More Recruits for Forestry Draft" and listed the new recruits by name, emphasizing the high quality of their timber skills. Another story, reprinted from a YMCA pamphlet, expressed Britain's gratitude for the "good work." The Y had service huts that provided non-alcoholic refreshments and entertainment nearly everywhere that the Forestry Corps worked in Britain and France.[144] In France the Y made special efforts to direct the timber men away from brothels and toward concerts, cinemas, lectures, religious meetings, Bible classes, and athletic games.

Figure 5.2. A Canadian timber camp in Scotland. (C.W. Bird and J. B. Davies, *The Canadian Forestry Corps: Its Inception, Development and Achievements* [London: H.M. Stationary Office, 1919], 7.)

By 1918, 150 forestry companies of approximately 100 men each had been organized. Complete timber-cutting mills accompanied the men from Canada. Most came from New Brunswick, Northern Alberta, British Columbia, and northern Quebec and Ontario. A high proportion, including Indigenous recruits, came from Northeastern Ontario. The organizers divided Britain into six districts and France into three. The companies worked mainly with horses but also with small railways or trucks to extract the trees and then transport them to mills. There the trees were cut and dried before being reworked or shipped to the front. The British government later complimented the Canadians for their efficient actions and for the huge quantity of wood processed in two years (figs. 5.2 and 5.3).

Figure 5.3. Stacked lumber along a light railway. (C.W. Bird and J. B. Davies, *The Canadian Forestry Corps: It Inception, Development and Achievements* [London: H.M. Stationary Office, 1919], facing page 26.)

Lieutenant-Colonel Sydney Lewis Penhorwood, one of the deputy commanders of forestry operations in southern England, came from Sault Ste. Marie, where he had been one of the organizers of the Soo 51st Rifles militia unit in 1913 and then a recruiter for the 37th Battalion in 1915 (fig. 5.4).[145] In England, he became a personal friend of King George V, went to horse races and attended formal dinners with the royal family, and helped rebuild the monarch's fishing lodge in Windsor Great Park; the lodge would be renamed in honour of the Canadians' work there. In 1919 when the Prince of Wales came to Canada, he asked to see Penhorwood in Sudbury, and Penhorwood met King George VI and his wife, Queen Elizabeth, on their 1939 Canadian tour. In 1959, Penhorwood was one of the guides for Queen Elizabeth II.

Figure 5.4. Colonel Penhorwood of Sault Ste. Marie. (Courtesy of Sault Ste. Marie Public Library Archives)

Penhorwood's papers reveal that the forestry soldiers at Windsor Park had their own chicken coops and athletic competitions, engaging in "mop races," "mixed shoe races," "mounted pillow races," and "fatmen (over 200 lbs)" races, as well as baseball. One photo shows two men, one white and one black, in baseball outfits. Non-white recruits were generally assigned to forestry or construction, rather than fighting units, and here men of different races clearly worked and played together. However, despite the games, timber work had priority, as a 11 September 1917 letter from the general commanding the corps reveals. He instructed Penhorwood to tour forestry districts 3 and 4 because "production is on the wane at several of our camps and it is necessary to visit the operations personally in order to impress on the Officers Commanding the urgent need of speeding up, so that the maximum output can be achieved and maintained."[146]

Lieutenant-Colonel Charles Hugh Lepailleur Jones, who joined the Canadian Forestry Corps command at Sunningdale in June 1917, also came from Sault Ste. Marie, where he had been head of the 51st Soo Rifles militia. In October he was transferred to the forestry corps in France, eventually becoming deputy assistant director. In May 1918 he was "mentioned in dispatches," meaning that he was recognized for meritorious service, and was named an Officer of the Most Excellent Order of the British Empire the following month. On 8 September, he was transferred back to England, and he left military service on 31 October, just before the war's end.

If Northeastern Ontario provided capable officers to the Canadian Forestry Corps, the workers who cut the wood and prepared it for the front were also worthy of praise. They operated under all sorts of conditions, where food often consisted of porridge, camps were wet and cold, and work was dangerous. The urgent need for wood at the front kept production quotas high, but speed when working with heavy equipment could mean more danger from accidents. Thomas Chappise (1004119), for instance, "fell astride of a log" in April 1919 while serving in the 54D Forestry District with the CFC, receiving a crushed testicle—not a common war wound! This Indigenous trapper from Chapleau gave his brother at the Indian School there as his next of kin. Born on 24 December 1897, Chappise joined up on 2 January 1917, at the age of 18. His medical report noted "no previous illnesses, tobacco, alcohol in moderation ... well nourished ... no evidence of disease, venereal or otherwise." Another trapper from Chapleau, Robert McWatch (1003334), born on 27 May 1898, enlisted on 29 May 1916. Of course he had been found "fit" when recruited by the local police chief for the 227th forestry battalion. He trained at Camp Borden, where he lost pay for missing parade. McWatch reached England on 22 April 1917. At first he worked at timber camps in England, but as of September 1918 served at the front. When he left the service in February 1919, medical officers found that he had "congenital deafness in both ears." The military decided that he had had "Defective hearing all his life—no change in condition," and he received no extra pension.

Even a sailor from Manitoulin could work in forestry. Gordon Ames (2626969), born on 3 January 1897 at Manitowaning, enlisted on 8 December 1917, arrived in England on 31 December 1917, and was assigned to Sunningdale forestry base. Because of "scar right knee" (almost a code for a leg injury) he would be returned to Canada in February and discharged on 1 April 1918. An Indigenous labourer, Steven Ashawasaga (1004190), allegedly born on 2 December 1898 at Pickerel River, was described "complexion: Red (Indian)." Before enlisting, he had worked for the Silver Lake Lumber Co. for $2 a day. After recruitment into the 227th Battalion on 16 February 1917, he was found to be under age and "medically unfit," though he worked for a short time at Sunningdale. Further, his file lists "scar right knee" and "underdeveloped" on 28 August 1917. He was discharged at Toronto on 13 December 1917. His file acknowledges, "This boy states that he is 16 … no birth certificate is available. He is fit."

Even though the newspapers declared that the forestry battalions would not be fighting, many were still reluctant to join up. Emile Canie (648130 and 2251135) of Timmins worked (or mostly avoided working) in France, twice signing up for the forestry battalions. Originally recruited in 1916, specifically for the forestry draft, Emile had typhoid fever and could not go. The army thought he had deserted but later corrected his file. He reenlisted on 13 April 1917, and in July transferred to Sunningdale with the forestry division, before being sent to France on 30 July 1918. His life thereafter became a list of punishments. With the 60th forestry company, Canie was "sentenced to 28 days FP #2 [Field Punishment #2] 6.8.17 for 1) Drunkenness 2) A. W. L [AWOL]" for a day and a half. He lost 2 days' pay. On 1 October 1917 he received the same punishment for insubordination. On 24 November he received Field Punishment #1 for missing parade and being out of bounds without a pass, so lost 5 days' pay. On 14 January 1918 he was sentenced to 21 days' Field Punishment #2, and on 21 June and 1 August he was again punished for being AWOL, losing 3 or 4 days' pay for each transgression. His behaviour did not change despite being transferred among four forestry companies. He even spent a day in prison in Paris after the war ended. Partly because of his misdemeanours, he would not be demobilized until May 1919.

A quite different case is that of Kenneth Deacon (2498411), a clerk from Timmins who enlisted on 10 September 1917. Born on 29

September 1898, Deacon was a tall man at five feet ten inches, weighing only 116 pounds. His character and conduct were judged "very good," and he was found "fit to serve." After training he took up a clerical post with the 140th Canadian Forestry Company on 31 December 1917 in England. He was hospitalized in February with chest pain. The doctor noted that he was free of all communicable diseases, including VD and "vermin." The dentist saw bad teeth and poor hygiene. Less than a year after he enlisted, on 14 August, the review board decided that he should be discharged, deeming him "Over grown, poorly developed and badly nourished. Not able to march." Deacon's war amounted to four months in English hospitals.

Few accounts exist of the men's own views of their work. However, in a letter dated 15 April 1917, Malcolm Lang gives us a forester's view. At age 42, he was an older lieutenant, and he had been with the 97th Algonquin Rifles militia before enlisting from South Porcupine on 13 July 1916. After training with the 159th Algonquins at Camp Borden, Lang was transferred to the Forestry Corps in February 1917. He thought he would not get to the front for the "spring show," but was satisfied with his lot:

> I am near enough to hear the noise but not to take part in the big show but kept good and busy as you will understand when I tell you we arrived in the wood we are cutting on March 10th with nothing on the ground and erected our mill and had it running in 10 days, Captain Pete Ferguson of Haileybury is in Command of the company and he has two other subs besides myself.

Then he described his own work:

> I have charge of the wood operations; that is, the cutting and the hauling to the mill and so far they have never had to wait for logs. It is a fine beech forest ..., and we use up every bit of the timber and brush for material for roads, trenches and mine timber ... I am working about 300 men and about 45 of these are Canadian recruits and the balance are from the east of us [prisoners of war] where they are bagged and taken in the same as the Canadians did at Vimy Ridge last Monday. We are with an Imperial division and about 15 miles south of any Canadian division.

His letter, published in the *Porcupine Advance* on 23 May 1917, closed by reporting the good health of a few other soldiers from the area. Lang himself moved up to the rank of captain, then major, and as an officer received two weeks of leave in Britain every six months.

William Harcourt Milne of North Bay moved even further up the ranks. He started as a lieutenant in January 1917 when he reached England with the 159th Battalion, and was then transferred to the 8th Reserve. However, by March he was posted to the base depot of the forestry corps and in April promoted to captain. He must have been an efficient manager, for by September he headed the 6th district and the next month became a major. After managing timber operations in France for a few months, in February 1918 he was transferred back to the base depot in England, and then joined the command of the 55th forestry district in Scotland. That July he reached the rank of lieutenant-colonel—only 18 months after arriving in England as a lieutenant. Just before the war ended he was hospitalized in Edinburgh with influenza, but by December was back at work. After returning to Canada, he was made an Officer of the Most Excellent Order of the British Empire (OBE). During the last year of the war, at his last rank he received approximately $5,000 dollars a year—15 times the pay of a common soldier. Milne was among the founders of North Bay Legion Branch 43 in 1926 (when it changed from a veteran's league); the branch now bears his name. Being in the forestry corps did not prevent him from having a stellar military career.

Many more were recruited from the Northeast to serve in the Forestry Corps, including, in Timmins in mid-1916, G.A. Sykes, Earl Neil, Ronald A. Pecore, Andrew W. Wood, Joseph Laughton, Fred Leduc, John McDonald, T.C. Rush, J.A. Bird, and Ralph B. Martel, all appearing in just one of many lists of forestry recruits in local papers. Their experiences were probably not very different from those described above: some injured by the dangerous work, some too weak or ill to serve, and some recognized for excellent service, moving up in the ranks.

Railway Construction Troops

If wood was crucial to warfare, putting it to use required much manpower. Though horses and mules moved most military goods at the beginning of the war, as the war became a stalemate of trenches and artillery pounding dug-in positions, bigger and heavier shells and equipment had to be quickly moved to the front. Men too had to be shifted quickly between different points in the trenches. By mid-1915, small railways had become crucial.[147] Ties and rails needed to be brought forward, and the rails had to be moved as the army advanced and retreated. Special railway construction troops were developed.

Railway battalions were at first British-run and manned. But with the shortage of manpower by late 1915, just as on the forestry front, Britain asked Canada to lend an experienced hand. Canada had had thousands of men building regional and national lines before the war. Northeastern Ontario had many experienced labourers, signalmen, locomotive drivers, and system managers. The CPR recruited the first 500 men from its employees. When that proved insufficient, whole battalions were recruited with the special occupations in mind; other battalions were converted to construction and transport. Canada eventually supplied 13,000 men for this service.

Canadians brought their own railway construction equipment, including steam shovels, scrapers, concrete mixers, pile drivers, track-layers, and box cars. They built rail yards, sidings, and standard gauge track in England and France. Trucks bogged down in mud, and the Canadians soon convinced the British that a smaller gauge, lighter rail system would better move men and materials. Eventually, some units specialized in building light railways "to relieve traffic on the heavily travelled roads and to ensure rapid delivery of all kinds of supplies."[148] Trains ran night and day, and averaged 1,500 tons of ammunition, thousands of men, and tons of foodstuffs per run (fig. 5.5).

The 228th Northern Fusiliers Battalion was converted to railway construction. The men came from Nipissing district north to James Bay; 12 of the 31 officers came from Northern Ontario and at least a dozen recruits were Indigenous. The nominal roll listing the battalion's personnel in 1917 shows a higher proportion of Canadian-born enlistees than in the army as a whole (fig. 5.6). By 1918, the 228th was working primarily at light rail construction. These soldiers were paid the same as those in the trenches. Their job generally did not include fighting, but their situations could be dangerous. They usually had no weapons. They laboured behind the lines, but sometimes *just* behind them, where they were vulnerable

Figure 5.5. Troops moved by Canadian light railway. (*Canada in the Great World War* [Toronto: United Publishers of Canada, 1920], 5: facing page 320)

to gunfire and artillery. The enemy sought to destroy supply lines, so it rained shells on railways. However, most of the men of the railway troops were lucky. Few of them suffered major injuries, though some contracted illness, including VD, scarlet fever, and influenza.

Men came to the railway troops from a variety of backgrounds. Ernest Smith (1007161), for instance, was born on 28 May 1892 in South Shields, England, but was working as a bank clerk in Timmins when he enlisted with the 228th on 23 January 1917. He arrived in France on 2 April, and served in the 6th Canadian Railway Troop without incident. He was hospitalized with scarlet fever in March 1919 before being discharged in Toronto on 23 April 1919. Wilfrid Rochon (1007135) was a Canadian-born lumberman who enlisted with the 228th four days before Smith during the same Timmins recruitment drive. He handled ties with the 6th Railway Troop in France, but he is also listed as "bushman" and "sapper." He must have celebrated the end of the war, because his file lists

Regimental No.	Rank.	Name.	Former Corps.	Name of Next of Kin.	Address of Next of Kin.	Country of Birth.
	Lieut.-Colonel	Earchman, Archibald	34th Regt and S.A.	Earchman, Mrs. Grayce	Mill Brook, Ont.	Canada
	Major	Dillabough, James Vidal	C.O.T.C.	Dillabough, Mrs. Annie Louise	141 Eugenie St., Norwood, Man.	Canada
	Major	Eppes, David Douglas Rand	36th Regt. and S.A.	Eppes, Mrs. Louise Ann	77 Spruce Hill Rd., Toronto, Ont.	Canada
	Major	Ferguson, William Walter	97th Regt.	Ferguson, Mrs. Maude A.	North Bay, Ont.	Canada
	Major	Fraser, Daniel William	34th Regt.	Fraser, Mrs. Margaret Florence	103 Sunnyside Ave., Toronto, Ont.	Canada
	Major	Reed-Lewis, Ellis Watmough	34th Regt.	Reed-Lewis, William	Bexhill-on-Sea, Sussex, Eng.	U.S.A.
	Captain	Chadwick, William Albert	12th Regt.	Chadwick, Mrs. Dora Ellen	Birch Cliff, Ont.	England
	Captain	Frid, Herbert Percival	Can. Eng.	Frid, Mrs. Flora	c/o Dr. J. O. McGregor, Hamilton, Ont.	Canada
	Captain	Magindery, William John M	97th Regt.	Magindery, Mrs. Laura M.	New Liskeard, Ont.	Canada
	Captain	McMurchy, Archibald Henry	C.A.M.C.	McMurchy, Mrs. Annitta	North Bay, Ont.	Canada
	Captain	McNamara, George Andrew	34th Regt.	McNamara, Mrs. Sarah	Penetanguishene, Ont.	Canada
	Captain	McNamara, Howard Dennis	34th Regt.	McNamara, Mrs. Sarah	Penetanguishene, Ont.	Canada
	Captain	Piercy, Charles Murison	34th Regt.	Piercy, Mrs. Edith Margaret	Porcupine, Ont.	Canada
	Captain	Spears, William Johnston	36th Horse	Spears, William	Kinglassie, Fife, Scot.	Scotland
	Lieutenant	Beaudro, Rocque Francis	30th Regt.	Beaudro, Mrs. Mabel Louise	143 Edmonton St., Winnipeg, Man.	U.S.A.
	Lieutenant	Beith, Robert Elwood	31st Regt.	Beith, William	174 Howland Ave., Toronto, Ont.	Canada
	Lieutenant	Bourke, James	34th Regt.	Bourke, John	North Bay, Ont.	Canada
	Lieutenant	Christopherson, William Wallace	34th Regt.	Christopherson, Louis Aldous	North Bay, Ont.	Canada
	Lieutenant	Currie, Thomas Dickson	34th Regt.	Currie, Mrs. Euphemia	88 Auburn Ave., Toronto, Ont.	England
	Lieutenant	Davies, Ernest	97th Regt.	Davies, Mrs. Constance Margaret	P.O. Box 707, North Bay, Ont.	England
	Lieutenant	Duncan, William James A	34th Regt.	Duncan, Mrs. W. A.	94 Gloucester St., Toronto, Ont.	Canada
	Lieutenant	Gatacre, Geifry William	34th Regt.	Gatacre, Mrs. Zoë B.	North Bay, Ont.	England
	Lieutenant	Hett, Sibbald	34th Regt.	Sibbald, W. M.	Sutton West, Ont.	Canada
	Lieutenant	Kert, Lawrence	97th Regt.	Kert, H. T.	Englehart, Ont.	Canada
	Lieutenant	Macdonald, George Alfred	Can. Mil.	Macdonald, Mrs. G. A.	15 Peel St., Brantford, Ont.	Canada
	Lieutenant	Osborne, Colin Carter	10th Regt.	Osborne, J. P.	Beamsville, Ont.	Canada
	Lieutenant	Reed-Lewis, William John D	34th Regt.	Reed-Lewis, Mrs. Jessie McLeod V	Barrie, Ont.	U.S.A.
	Lieutenant	Smith, William Henry	31st Regt.	Smith, Mrs. Mary B.	1351, 3rd Ave. E., Owen Sound, Ont.	U.S.A.
	Lieutenant	Stallwood, Robert James	S.A.	Stallwood, Dr. John	Beamsville, Ont.	Canada
	Lieutenant	Weegar, Elwin Carl	34th Regt.	Weegar, Sylvanus	92 Worthington St. W., North Bay, Ont.	Canada
	Lieutenant	Young, Russell Booth	34th Regt.	Young, Mrs. Gertrude Irene	North Bay, Ont.	Canada
1006241	Sergeant	Abbott, James Robert	23rd Regt.	Abbott, Mrs. Nellie	19 Washington St. W., North Bay, Ont.	Scotland
1005344	Corporal	Ackert, Robert John	Nil	Ackert, Robert	Cobalt, Ont.	Canada
1007008	Private	Adams, William Walter	Nil	Adams, Mrs. Harriet Priscilla	98 Givens St., Toronto, Ont.	England
1006680	Private	Adams, William John	Nil	Adams, Mrs. Kathleen	Plymouth, Devon, Eng.	Ireland
1007010	Private	Alaks, Joseph	Nil	Alaks, Joseph	Palator Farm, Dakla, Kuos State, Russia	Russia
1006692	Private	Allan, Harold	Nil	Allan, Michael	Quyon, P.Q.	Canada
1006984	Sergeant	Allan, John Maxwell	Nil	Allan, Rev. Robert	Bartonville, Ont.	Scotland
1006580	Private	Allen, Gordon Charles	Nil	Allen, Arthur	Port Perry, Ont.	Canada
1006075	Private	Allibon, Joseph	Nil	Allibon, Mrs. Sarah	Earlton, Ont.	England
1006651	Private	Anderson, Allan James	Nil	Anderson, John James	Cobalt, Ont.	Canada
1006147	Private	Anderson, James Calder	Nil	Anderson, Mrs. Martha Thomson	North Bay, Ont.	Scotland
1006005	Private	Anderson, Leonard	Nil	Anderson, Mrs. Ethel	North Bay, Ont.	Canada
1006326	Private	Anson, Thomas	Nil	Anson, Mrs. Rose	Haileybury, Ont.	England
1006333	Private	Antler, Robert	Nil	Antler, Mrs. Carolina	Tomstown, Ont.	Canada
1006413	Private	Antram, William Henry	Nil	Antram, Mrs. Jeanette Amelia	Englehart, Ont.	England
1007178	Private	Anyan, George William	Territorials	Anyan, Mrs. Elizabeth	P.O. Box 434, Englehart, Ont.	England
1006840	Private	Anyan, Harold	Nil	Anyan, Mrs. H.	Englehart, Ont.	England
853065	Private	Arbour, Amos	Nil	Arbour, Narcisse	Victoria Harbor, Ont.	Canada

Figure 5.6. A page from the nominal roll of the 228th Northern Fusiliers Battalion. Next of kin is one clue to a soldier's origins. (Courtesy of Library and Archives Canada)

repeated treatment for syphilis during demobilization in England and after his arrival in Halifax on 25 March 1919. Lectance Joseph Olivier (3037705), a Sudbury Francophone who had been born in Sturgeon Falls on 14 June 1895, was drafted on 9 May 1918. As a locomotive foreman, he brought much-needed civilian experience to the 3rd Canadian Railway Battalion. He remained in England, transporting troops, and thus survived the war. In contrast, Bertie Nackogie (10069310), an Indigenous recruit from James Bay, never left Canada. He signed on with the 228th on 20 July 1916 at Moose Factory. He gave his aunt there as next of kin and his occupation as "guide and hunter." He was found fit at his medical inspection on 26 December 1916, but soon died of pneumonia at the base hospital in Toronto (fig. 5.7).[149]

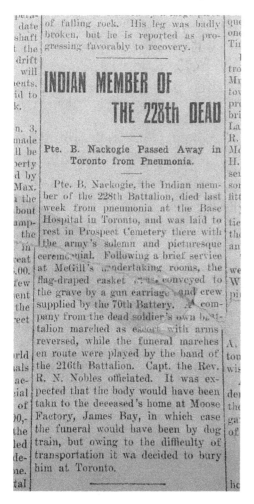

Figure 5.7. The *Porcupine Advance* notice of Bertie Nackogie's death on 3 January 1917. Because the railway did not reach James Bay until September 1931, winter travel to Moose Factory would have been by dogsled. (Courtesy of Timmins Museum National Exhibition Centre)

The railway workers were no freer of blemish than any other soldiers. Miner Norman Martin (649418), born in Muskoka on 6 January 1893, was living in Schumacher when he enlisted with the 159th Battalion in Timmins on 2 June 1916. He was transferred to the 4th Canadian Railway Troops, and they sailed on 31 October. After more training in England, the unit was sent to France on 24 February 1917. On 16 July, Martin was sentenced to 3 days of Field Punishment #2 for "Neglect of Duty." He was in and out of hospitals for various reasons, including VD, during his stay in France, but served until his discharge in Toronto on 3 April 1919. Joseph Laforest (1007132), born in St. Urbain, Quebec, was working as a labourer in Timmins when he enlisted with the 228th Northern Fusiliers on 10 January 1917. He named his brother Edgar of Montreal as his next of kin. Laforest's unit sailed on 16 February 1917, and on 3 April 1917 he joined the 6th Canadian Railway Troops in France, where he became a sapper. Twice he received Field Punishment #2: on 28 June 1917 for 5 days for "being absent from work without leave from 1 p.m. to 5 p.m."; and on 12 July for 10 days "for (1) neglecting to obey an order; (2) Insolence to an NCO." He survived the war and was discharged in Canada on 29 March 1919, his insubordination forgotten. George Charron (3231484) is more problematic. Born in Quebec, Charron lived in Blind

River, where he worked as a lumberman. He signed his attestation in Toronto on 5 January 1917, naming his father Mack as his next of kin, but he does not appear on the 1917 nominal roll and he received his last pay on 18 February 1918. On 14 March he was deemed "illegally absent," and the file indicates that he was "struck off as a deserter."

Among the older recruits, Edward George Hayward (1007126) was a 34-year-old Timmins miner, who also served as a sapper after he enlisted in 1916. He sailed with the 228th Battalion on 16 February 1917 and worked at railway construction in France, though he was in hospital with influenza from 28 June to 8 July 1918. When he enlisted, Hayward was married with three children in New Liskeard. He was discharged in Toronto on 21 March 1919 and would die at age 50 on 3 December 1932. James P. Lennen (1007133) was also older than most recruits, having been born in 1877. At five feet eleven inches he was also much taller. He signed up on 23 January 1917 in Timmins, where he had been a millwright. He was blind in his right eye yet he was still found fit to work construction. He was promoted to corporal in October 1918, just before the war ended.

Figure 5.8. The light railway moved wounded from the battlefield to clearing stations and hospitals. (*Canada in the Great World War* [Toronto: United Publishers of Canada, 1920], 5: facing page 26).

Some soldiers did move up in rank. Sgt. Joseph Lavoie (1012644) of Iroquois Falls enlisted in Ottawa on 30 September 1916 and served with the 230th Battalion (identified with Montreal). His next of kin was an uncle in Montreal, Lavoie's birthplace. Lavoie was promoted to corporal, then sergeant before he went to France on 24 February 2017. He served as an administrator until he was discharged on 13 February 1919 after severe influenza. Sidney Robert McCoy (1007148) was born in Ottawa on 6 August 1896, and his parents still lived there when he left his job as "stenographer and accountant" in Timmins to enlist with the 228th Battalion on 27 January 1917. McCoy went to France with the 6th Canadian Railway Troop on 3 April 1917, serving there and in Belgium. He must have done well because he was promoted to lance corporal on 20 March 1917 and sergeant on 26 August 1918. He demobilized in Toronto on 26 March 1919. The skills men brought to the war, whether organizational training such as McCoy and Lavoie would have had, or a railwayman's experience with the mud and muskeg, blackflies and mosquitos of Northern Ontario like Olivier, made these men valuable resources in England and France, where they kept men and materials moving to and from the front (fig. 5.8).

Going Underground to Fight: Tunnellers/Sappers

The term *soldiers* took on a different meaning for the tunnellers, or sappers, of the Canadian Tunnelling Companies. Like the foresters and railway builders, tunnellers shared the dangers of the front, but they also faced other hazards: suffocation, cave-ins, and underground explosions. More than two dozen soldiers in the tunnelling companies came from Northeastern Ontario.

In World War I, tunnelling companies came into being because of the stalemate of trench warfare. Charging the enemy's trenches across the no-man's-land between the battle lines had become increasingly costly, but if one could not advance on the surface, tunneling offered an alternative. The Germans were the first to use tunnelling (also called mining), reviving the old methods of siege warfare where they went under fortress walls because they could not get over them. By December 1914, the Germans were secretly digging tunnels to damage the Allies' defenses from below and make an above-ground attack possible. The tunnellers dug vertical shafts, and then excavated tunnels measuring about two metres high by three metres wide toward and under the opponent's trenches, parallel to the ground. Next, they placed explosives in strategic spots, often like the ends of the fingers of a hand at the leading end of the tunnel. At their beginning point well behind Allied lines, the tunnels could be many metres high and wide, supported by wooden frameworks; most tunnels ran hundreds of metres. When the miners detonated the explosives, horses, men, equipment, and artillery would collapse into the earth. Sometimes they were buried, but always, the collapse gave an opportunity for a surprise attack.

The British soon imitated the Germans, and the foes sometimes ran into each other's tunnels, fighting hand-to-hand in the dark. Sophisticated listening devices and ever-deeper tunnels and ever-larger caches of explosives were employed, until near Messines in 1917 the British, helped by Canadian tunnellers, set off a blast heard in London, some 260 kilometres away. It was the largest non-nuclear explosion ever created, and the resulting hole buried, by some estimates, ten thousand German troops. Tunnellers also excavated huge caverns behind their own trenches so as to secretly bring up men, ammunition, and artillery for massed attacks. Some of these tactics proved decisive in helping to win battles at the Somme, Arras, and Ypres. Under Vimy, the tunnel system was especially extensive (fig. 5.9).[150]

Figure 5.9. Tunnels under Vimy Ridge. ("World War I - Vimy sector tunnel.jpg," *Wikimedia Commons*, 28 September 2017, https://commons.wikimedia.org/w/index.php?title=File:World_War_I_-_Vimy_sector_tunnel.jpg&oldid=260150509. Reproduced under Creative Commons Attribution-Share Alike 3.0 license.)

To develop the tunnelling companies, the British called upon Canadian expertise, partly because of manpower shortages. Between late 1915 and the middle of 1916, three companies were assembled. Most men from the Northeast served in #1 Company.

They often worked with British units, and their activities lacked the attention given to the above-ground battles or air engagements. However, the service files reveal that this was very dangerous work. Tunnels could collapse because of wet soil, and the Germans could tunnel underneath and explode the tunnel. The tunnellers' own explosives could detonate and bury them. In long tunnels, suffocation was also a possibility, and air quality was likely always a concern.

Miners and mining engineers from Cobalt and Timmins signed up in the late 1915 recruiting drive. Regimental numbers 501006 to 501019 were assigned to men from the Northeast, suggesting that they enlisted at about the same time. Between 15 October and the first week of November, at least a dozen men signed attestation forms in Haileybury (which was, like Timmins and Sudbury, a recruiting centre). A number signed on 30 October. They reached England in December, and disembarked in Le Havre on 16 February 1916. The #1 Canadian Tunnelling Company trained at Rouen and Sainte-Marie-Cappelle, and then set up its headquarters at Armentières from 7 March to 10 May, when it moved to the front at St. Eloi. For more than a year, the men dug tunnels beneath the front near Ypres. Then, in April and May 1918, the company operated at Arras and Vimy. Where precisely the men from Northeastern Ontario worked is not clear in the unit's war diary.[151]

The tunnellers shared some traits. Most were older than the regular recruits. One was in his mid-forties, and a number in their thirties. These were experienced old-timers. They tended to be bigger, reflecting the fact that mining required size and strength. However, they suffered more illnesses, perhaps from working underground in damp, dark, confined spaces (though about the same percentage had "self-inflicted wounds," the military term for venereal disease). Some soldiers' medical histories speak of lung and respiratory problems. Patrick McAndrew (501173), a miner from Timmins, attributed his TB to working in France. The heart problems suffered by Joseph Michael McGuire (501336), a clerk born in Collingwood, Ontario, on 21 June 1897, might also have resulted from the physical toll of tunnelling. McGuire enlisted with the 1st Tunnelling Company at Pembroke, despite the fact that he declared his "present address" as Haileybury (where his mother also lived). In France he did well, and in 1916 he was promoted to corporal and then sergeant. However, in April and May 1918, he was hospitalized at Étaples with syphilis. He lost 10 pounds that year, and suffered heart problems and shortness of breath to such an extent that he was declared medically unfit. Few of the disabilities were recognized as permanent. Many of the men were British-born and some had mined coal in Britain (or Nova Scotia, which is often credited with supplying tunnellers), but some also had very different peacetime occupations, such as cook and clerk.

Tunnellers were exposed to many of the dangers facing those fighting in the trenches. For instance, Scottish-born sapper William Connell (501008), a miner when he signed his attestation form in Haileybury on 30 October 1915, died as a prisoner of war at Hameln, Germany, on 4 February 1917. He probably died of wounds that preceded his capture in July 1916. English-born William Jackson (501018) never recovered from a gas attack at Ypres during October 1917. He survived the war but died before he could sign his demobilization papers and move home to Cobalt. Sapper Stanley McDonald (501015), who had moved from Cape Breton to work as a miner in Cobalt, was shot in his right wrist during the campaign of the last hundred days. Back in England on 2 January 1919, doctors diagnosed him as a victim of myalgia (pain in the muscles) and deemed him "Medically Unfit." Sergeant Malcolm McQuarrie (501062), another Nova Scotian transplant, was a miner in Timmins when he enlisted in 1915. He took shrapnel in the knee. Sapper Hugh Millar (501111), a Scottish-born miner from Cobalt, died of his wounds on 7 August 1918, one day before the Battle of Amiens. Another miner from Cobalt, English immigrant 2nd Corporal Harry Pixton (501014), died near Ypres on 2 January 1917: "While sleeping in a small dugout ... he was instantly killed by an enemy shell that made a direct hit."[152] Yet another Cobalt miner from England sapper Arthur Walker (501012), suffered permanent eyesight and hearing loss that same day. A medical report written on 19 December 1918, more than a month after the Armistice, explained his condition as the result of a "shrapnel explosion in which he was blown up in air. He had several wounds from shrapnel fragments in legs ... Was in bed about one month. In hospital six months doing light duty."

Lieutenant William Fordyce Gowans (501330) was more fortunate than Pixton or Walker. Born in Dundee, Scotland, on 1 November 1880, Gowans had fought in the South African War, and then moved with his wife to Haileybury, where he worked as a mine superintendent. Like others in the 1st Tunnelling Unit of Canadian Engineers, Gowans arrived in France on 16 February 1916, and because of his performance in the field, on 19 May 1917 the French president awarded him the Médaille Militaire. After the war, Gowans and his wife settled in Timmins. William Mainville (501172) also returned safely from the war. Born in 1894 at Bonfield, he stood 5 feet 11 inches and was one of the miners who enlisted at Cochrane on 19 November 1915. Where he worked specifically is not clear, though he arrived in France on 16 February 1916 and survived the war. Such cases indicate that the experience of hard rock mining in Northeastern Ontario provided special skilled labour for the underground Hades in Belgium and France.

The "Indian Draft"; or, Indigenous Experiences

As this chapter has illustrated, many Indigenous men were recruited for the Canadian Forestry Corps and Railway Construction Troops. As minorities within the general population and within the military, their war experiences were different because of language and prevailing attitudes.[153] Their service files often feature the phrase "Indian draft" or "Canadian (Indian)," suggesting that the military thought of them as a distinct group within these services.

A note in the collection of the Anglican Diocese of Moosonee archival fonds lists former students of Bishop Horden Hall, the residential school in Moose Factory, who enlisted in the 228th Battalion and the Forestry Corps in World War I (fig. 5.10).[154] The service files of these men reveal a great deal about Indigenous participation in the war. When the war began, Indigenous people were discouraged from enlisting.[155] However, by early 1916, the losses at the front from battle and disease led to a change in government policy: Indigenous volunteers were now acceptable. A desperate recruitment drive sought ever more men to fill the ranks. Those encouraged, or pushed, to join included Cree from communities on James Bay.

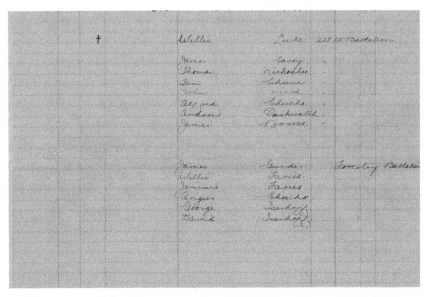

Figure 5.10. List of former residential school students who served in the Canadian Forestry Corps and the Railway Construction Troops. (Anglican Diocese of Moosonee fonds, Laurentian University Archives)

Many of these men served through to the end of the war. Coming first on the Anglican Diocese list, William Luke (1006962), born 1 June 1898 at Wasnwanaby [Waswanipi, Quebec], on the James Bay coast, enlisted on 24 July 1916 at Camp Borden. Relatively tall at five feet eight and half inches, he gave "teamster" as his occupation. He died on 29 October 1917 while serving in a railway troop as part of a construction battalion in France, which often meant working in unprotected areas. He had attended residential school in Moose Factory until 1906, and gave as his next of kin his father in Metagami, but he willed his possessions to an uncle in Elk Lake. His family may have been one of the "Indians at Elk Lake" who received support from the Patriotic Fund (see pages 132-133). James Carey (1006926), a blacksmith's helper from Moose Factory, also enlisted in mid-1916. He contracted tonsillitis in April 1918, and then pneumonia in July while serving with the railway troop. He was demobilized in Toronto in May 1919.

Many others also came from Moose Factory. Sam Chena (1006928), a hunter and guide, enlisted there on 25 July 1916 in the 228th Battalion. For a contact address he gave "teacher at Indian Residential School

Moose Factory." Once in England he was transferred to the 6th Railway Construction Troop. He survived the war unscathed. Alfred Cheechoo (1006996), a tall hunter and guide from Moose Factory, enlisted with the 228th on 4 October 1916 (signing with an X). He was placed in a railway construction troop. He would die of influenza in France on 12 January 1919, awaiting demobilization. A Hudson's Bay Company (HBC) boatman at Moose Factory, John Mark (1006963) survived the war. Born on 18 October 1895, he enlisted on 26 July 1916, leaving parents, a wife, and child at Elk Lake. He was listed with a construction battalion, but his designation included "sapper." James Kooses (1006992), another Moose Factory guide and hunter, was born on 5 February 1897, and went to Bishop Horden Hall residential school in 1906. He enlisted on 4 October 1916. Early in 1918 he was gassed and spent a month in hospital. When demobilized he had, according to the reviewing doctors, "no disability." The fact that so many enlisted in July 1916 (Luke, Chena, Mark) suggests a recruitment drive focused on the Indigenous community as casualties increased in mid-1916.

The next summer reveals a similar pattern. Angus Cheechoo (2498464), a Moose Factory hunter born on 4 June 1897, volunteered for the forestry corps in 1917. His file refers to an "Indian Draft Forestry Depot" under the "Railway Construction and Forestry Depot" and identifies Cheechoo as "Canadian (Indian)," suggesting that the army saw Indigenous men as a distinct unit. Cheechoo received a very positive bill of health on 4 August 1917 when he signed his attestation forms in Toronto. He worked at forestry in southern England from late 1917 to early 1919, and was discharged on 18 June. The Faries brothers from Fort Albany, William Richard (2497975) and James Walter (2497959), were born on 17 July 1895 and 25 August 1896 respectively. Both were students at the residential school, William from age 11 in 1906, and James starting a year later. They enlisted in Toronto, on 9 and 17 July 1917, and worked in Scotland harvesting timber. James Walter suffered a "severely crushed toe" on 7 January 1919 when a logging rail car ran over it. William's medical record reads "joined on enlistment: Indian draft," and James Walter's reads, "Transfd to Indian Dft 17.7.17." The racial identity of all three men is underscored in their files, and all three signed up in Toronto, suggesting a pattern.

Among the most interesting are the last on the Moosonee Diocese list. Brothers David (2497989) and John George Iserhoff (2497990) signed up on the same day, 11 July 1917, at Toronto. On both files is typed "Indian Draft" and "Canadian (Indian)." An unmarried HBC clerk, David came from Martens Falls, Albany River on James Bay, where he had been born on 16 February 1899. He left to attend residential school with his older brother in 1908. He was just old enough to serve in 1917. John Iserhoff was married and worked as a "servant" (a worker in the fur trade) with the HBC. They worked in forestry at Nairn and Sterling in Scotland until 1919. David was hospitalized for nine days in July 1918 with influenza, and spent another 44 days in hospital with "severe" measles in early 1919. He was not demobilized until June. John also had influenza in 1918, and in January 1919 he contracted "a very bad case" of measles, with pneumonia and eye complications. It "cleared up" in time for him to be discharged in April.

The high number of men who, like the Faries and Iserhoffs, enlisted within two weeks in July 1917 raises questions: did they volunteer, were they dragooned, or was "Indian draft" simply the military's term for a batch of recruits it identified by race (fig. 5.11)? Their regimental numbers are very close together. If we explore the files of soldiers with regimental numbers in the same range, going backward or forward from those on the Moosonee Diocese list, an intriguing pattern emerges. Take the case of Isaac Goodwin (2497991), one number after George Iserhoff. Goodwin's file, too, is stamped "Indian draft," as is that of Solomon Sutherland (2497988), a Cree from Attawapiskat whose number comes just before the Iserhoffs. Goodwin, born on 10 August 1895, marked his X on his attestation form on 3 July 1917. He was assigned to the forestry depot in Scotland. He had bronchitis but, more importantly, he was re-examined in early 1919 after he refused food for days, exhibiting what his file calls excitability, poor memory, and childish judgment. Though he had been found fit when he enlisted, now he was diagnosed with "imbecility," and institutionalized in Canada. Yet when he was finally discharged on 28 February 1920, the bureaucrats found "no pensionable disability."

Figure 5.11. James Bay Indigenous recruits at enlistment. (*Canada in the Great World War* [Toronto: United Publishers of Canada, 1919], 3: facing page 316.)

ON ARRIVAL AT CAMP BORDEN

ONE WEEK LATER
JAMES BAY INDIANS

Many recruits came from Attawapiskat. Sutherland, born there in April 1897, worked as a sailor. He made his mark on 7 July 1917. Like many of the other Indigenous recruits, he was a big man at six feet one inch. George Kiaki (2497987), a hunter, also made a mark instead of signing his name on 9 July 1917. He was just old enough to serve, having been born in June 1899 and baptized Roman Catholic. His attestation is also labelled "Indian draft," and includes the entry "Transfd to Indian Dft 9.7.17." He was assigned to railway construction and to the forestry company of military district 2 (which encompassed much of Northeastern Ontario), and worked in timber in Scotland. Though normal math makes his age at enlistment as 18, the bureaucrat wrote 20, and his attestation papers identify him as a five foot nine inch Roman Catholic. A later medical entry changed his age back to 18, and he also lost two inches in height, suggesting that the enlistment process was more interested in making its quota than in factual accuracy. Kiaki was hospitalized on 12 February to 4 March 1918 for a "circumcision." He was also hospitalized 21 January 1919 with a sprained ankle and influenza, and then suffered a "severe attack" of measles. He demobilized in April 1919.

Injuries and illnesses plagued Indigenous forestry workers. Men found "fit" at enlistment seemed to have difficulties dealing with different food and exposure to pathogens. Like Kaiki, Jacob Edward (2497986), another Roman Catholic hunter from Attawapiskat, made his mark instead of signing his name on 10 July 1917 in Toronto. Born in February 1899, he was found fit to serve. Yet at the forestry headquarters at Sunningdale, on 17 November 1917, this five foot six and a half inch soldier was diagnosed with a "debility": "present condition: small, underdeveloped physically and mentally. Cannot speak or understand English and will not work. Chronic cough." Despite this, his discharge paper reads "character and conduct: Very good." Equally inconsistent evaluations came out of the Toronto General Hospital. A report dated 11 March 1918 stated, "This man was in my ward for a month. Admitted with bronchitis which ran a normal course. Then had middle ear disease. Drum was punctured and he was kept here till cleaned up. I always considered him bright and intelligent. He is able to read and write his own language." However, C.K. Clarke, chief of the Psychiatric Clinic of the Toronto General Hospital, wrote on 29 April to Capt. T.J. Duff, Medical Officer of the Ravina Barracks: "This man is an imbecile and has the mental age of between six and seven years. He should be discharged from the army as unfit for service." A 2 May entry in his file observes, "Does not speak English. Apparently complains of pain-MT-wound." Edward's discharge board found him "1. Mentally deficient. 2. Otitis Media." Only the latter was considered a post-enlistment condition; that is, the pain and buzzing in his right ear was caused by his war work. The medical board found the injury or disability permanent, but thought he could resume his previous occupation. Whether he received a pension is unclear.

Another "Indian draft" recruit, Nona Chakasuam (2497985), a labourer from Attawapiskat, signed up at Toronto on 3 July 1917, and arrived in England on 15 September 1917. He died in Sterling, Scotland, at the Royal Infirmary on 7 July 1918 of pneumonia. Similarly, "Indian draft" labourer Robert Linklater (2497984) came from Attawapiskat, though he was born at Moose Factory in November 1898 and signed up on 9 July 1917 at Toronto. His service file only recounts that he worked in forestry in Scotland and had boils and measles. Like many other recruits, his discharge occurred late in April 1919. A bit older, John Jakazom (2497983), born in February 1891 in Attawapiskat, also signed (with an X) on 9 July 1917 at Toronto. His file, too, reads

"Indian draft" and "Canadian Indian" at the top of the enlistment form. His wife was left behind in Attawapiskat, where he had been working as a labourer. Like others, he served in railway construction and forestry in Scotland, had pneumonia July 1918, and returned to Canada in April 1919. In answer to the question of whether his father was alive he said, perhaps with sarcasm, "Yes. (No address known in bush)." Many of the Attawapiskat recruits identified themselves as hunters, often giving their mothers as next of kin: Michel Nepin (2497982) and Thomas Noah (2497981) both signed up on 9 July 1917; Joseph Okimow (249780), made his mark on 10 July 1917. Another "Indian draft" hunter who signed with his mark at Toronto was Albert Metat (2497979) from Port Albany, who enlisted on 4 July 1917. Born June 1897, he too gave his mother as next of kin. Notably big-chested at 40 inches, he worked in forestry in Scotland, suffering an injury to his right hand, and a severe case of measles that put him in hospital for a month. He was discharged in April 1919.

The number of men who came from Attawapiskat, Moose Factory, or Fort Albany, as "Indian draft" recruits for the Forestry Corps, raises the question: what did "Indian draft" mean before conscription became law? Did these men volunteer because during wartime the demand for fur and guides declined? Many would have faced unemployment, and military service offered both the lure of excitement and regular pay. Many knew each other and had even gone to school together, so some may have signed up because their friends were going. Given the number who enlisted at the same time, one suspects that they were pressured to enlist, as the label "Indian draft" suggests. It cannot be coincidence that so many men from James Bay suddenly enlisted within two weeks in Toronto. The log of the Anglican Diocese of Moosonee records groups of "recruits" leaving Moosonee by canoe for the railway in Cochrane, accompanied in August 1916 by Reverend William Haythornthwaite, and later by others.[156] Were they influenced by residential school authorities? The third and sixth on the Diocese of Moosonee's partial list, Nickoshee and Pushwatch, attended residential school after 1909, but seem to have no service record; nor does James Gunder, on the Forestry Corps list, although he too attended Bishop Horden Hall after 1907. Were their names misspelled, or did they simply agree because they were pressured, and then change their minds? So many questions, so few precise answers.

Somewhat different is the case of the Michael Cada (1003459), an Indigenous soldier from Morrisville, Manitoulin Island, born on 24 December 1883. Though he was older than most recruits and married with children, he enlisted on 15 June 1916. The Indian agent at Gore Bay (F.W. Baxter) found him fit, though he developed teeth problems after he arrived in England in April 1917. Cada served with the 8th Reserve, and then was transferred to the 54th Battalion (identified with Kootenay, BC). He was killed instantly on 30 September 1918 when struck in the head by artillery shrapnel. His children became wards of the Department of Indian Affairs because his "widow was granted pension but died before gratuity was issued." In the recruitment drives of 1916 and 1917, did Indian agents also pressure Indigenous men to enlist? Also enlisting in mid-June, in the 227th Battalion at Little Current, was an Anishinabe farmer from West Bay (now M'Chigeeng), Louis Jacob Norton (1003458), born on 25 November 1883. Found "fit" at enlistment, he died quite suddenly of pneumonia at Camp Borden on 28 August two months later. What happened to his 21-year-old wife is not known. Again, more questions without answers.

One early postwar report, "The Canadian Indians and the Great World War," reviews the enlistment patterns across the country:

> About fifty Ojibwas from Manitoulin Island and the northern shore of Lake Huron enlisted. One of their number, Francis Misinishkotewe [755136], was awarded the Russian Medal; another Frank J. Sinclair [754872] received the Military Medal ... the band located at Sturgeon Falls, which sent thirty-five from a total adult male population of one hundred and three; the bands in the Chapleau district, which sent forty from a total adult male population of one hundred and one.[157]

Misinishkotewe was killed in action at Vimy with the 73rd Battalion. Sinclair, a fisherman from Manitowaning, had joined the 119th Algoma Battalion on 19 February 1916. Serving in the 52nd Battalion, he survived the war.

In addition to the men who served and suffered, Indigenous communities also supported the war financially. The Patriotic Fund was established at the beginning of the war to help families whose breadwinners were absent. The fund received contributions from all over Northeastern Ontario (see chapter 6). Indigenous communities' contributions are listed in *Canada in the Great World War*: Cockburn Island, $200; Sheguiandah, $500; Manitoulin Island, $500; West Bay Band, $500; South Bay Band, $200; Dokis, $1000; Nipissing, $500; Sheshegwaning Band, Manitoulin Island, $500; Sucker Creek, $171; Wikwemikong Indians, $201.70; and Garden River (to the Algoma War Chest Fund), $200.[158]

After the war, Indigenous soldiers, who seem to have been deliberately recruited, and who worked and fought for the war effort, returned to a country where their lives were subject to persecution and governmental control. Even their military pensions were controlled by the Indian agent. Community memorials sometimes do not list their names (see chapter 8). In the century since the war, their sacrifices have often gone unremarked. It is worth noting, however, that in the immediate aftermath of the war, their contributions were acknowledged in reports such as those cited above—though this did not change the conditions of their lives in Canada.

Francophone Experiences

If Indigenous soldiers found it hard to adjust to conditions overseas, Francophones also faced challenges and experienced a different trajectory than their military counterparts. Far fewer French names appear among the enthusiastic early recruits of August and September 1914 than among the population in general. In Sault Ste. Marie, among the 127 enlistees for which the local newspaper supplied names, only three Francophones appear to have accompanied William Merrifield, Edwin Durham, and the other Sault volunteers to war on 20 August 2014.

The reasons are many. Members of the Canadian elite, primarily of British background, asserted that they were fighting for their motherland. For French Canadians, loyalty to Britain meant little. On the eve of the war, Ontario had imposed English as the sole language of instruction in the school system, and the "Prussians" of Ontario seemed a more immediate threat than those of Germany. Francophones also tended to live in rural areas, and farmers had less mobility than others and were less inclined to volunteer. The militias who organized the first volunteers were also not welcoming, with English-speaking officers who gave orders only in English. However, the idea that Francophones did not participate is simply wrong, although most objected to conscription.

As the experience of Arthur Baillargeon (1006658) shows, speaking French in the Canadian Expeditionary Force, which was at that time largely Anglophone, posed ongoing problems. Baillargeon, a lumber scaler (measurer) born in Montreal on 21 August 1893, enlisted in North Bay on 13 June 1916. His battalion, the 228th Northern Fusiliers, sailed on 16 February 1917. Placed in a railway construction group, he survived the war with few ill effects save VD, and demobilized in Toronto on 8 April 1919. However, his file is a mess of crossed out and corrected versions of his name. The military even mixed up his file with a Montreal soldier of a similar name, who had deserted in 1915. Not until nearly the end of the war, in May 1918, did the military officially recognize the spelling he provided.

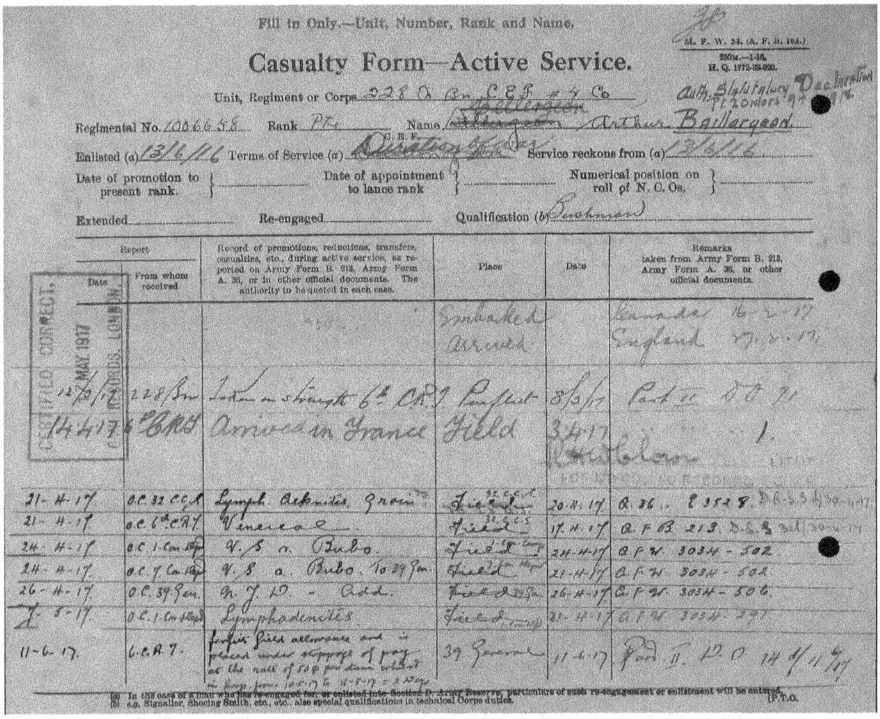
Fill in Only.—Unit, Number, Rank and Name.

M. F. W. 54. (A. F. B. 103.)

250M.—1-16.
H. Q. 1772-39-920.

Casualty Form—Active Service.

Unit, Regiment or Corps 228 O. Bn. C.E.F. #4 Co

Auth. Statutory Declaration Pt. 2 Orders

Regimental No. 1006658 Rank Pte Name Arthur Baillargeon

Enlisted (a) 13/6/16 Terms of Service (a) C.E.F. Duration of War Service reckons from (a) 13/6/16

Date of promotion to present rank. Date of appointment to lance rank Numerical position on roll of N. C. Os.

Extended Re-engaged Qualification (b) Bushman

Report: Date	Report: From whom received	Record of promotions, reductions, transfers, casualties, etc., during active service, as reported on Army Form B. 213, Army Form A. 36, or in other official documents. The authority to be quoted in each case.	Place	Date	Remarks taken from Army Form B. 213, Army Form A. 36, or other official documents.
			Embarked		Canada 16-2-17
			Arrived		England 27-2-17
12/3/17	228 Bn	Taken on strength 6th C.R.T.	Purfleet	8/3/17	Part II D.O. 71
14-4-17	6th C.R.T.	Arrived in France	Field	3-4-17	1.
21-4-17	O.C. 32 C.C.S.	Lymph. Adenitis, Groin	Field 32 C.C.S.	20-4-17	A. 36
21-4-17	O.C. 6th C.R.T.	Venereal	Field 32 C.C.S.	17-4-17	A. F. B. 213
24-4-17	O.C. 1 Con. Depot	V. S. a. Bubo.	Field	24-4-17	A. F. W. 3034 - 502
24-4-17	O.C. 7 Con. Depot	V. S. a. Bubo. To 39 Gen.	Field	21-4-17	A. F. W. 3034 - 502
26-4-17	O.C. 39 Gen.	N. Y. D. - Add.	Field 39 Gen.	26-4-17	A. F. W. 3034 - 506
1-5-17	O.C. 1 Con. Depot	Lymphadenitis	Field	21-4-17	A. F. W. 3034 - 297
11-6-17	6 C.R.T.	forfeits field allowance and is placed under stoppage of pay at the rate of 50¢ per diem whilst in Hosp. from 10-5-17 to 11-5-17 = 2 Days	39 General	11-6-17	Part II. D.O. 14

CERTIFIED CORRECT. MAY 1917 RECORDS, LONDON.

(a) In the case of a man who has re-engaged for, or enlisted into Section D, Army Reserve, particulars of such re-engagement or enlistment will be entered.
(b) e.g. Signaller, Shoeing Smith, etc., etc., also special qualifications in technical Corps duties.

P.T.O.

Figure 5.12. Service file of Arthur Baillargeon (1006658).
(Courtesy of Library and Archives Canada)

The problems created by the language gap were not just about spelling. A clerk or doctor's lack of understanding could have serious health ramifications. David Bernard (1006382) signed up at North Bay with the 228th Northern Fusiliers Battalion on 17 May 1916. One part of his file mistakenly makes him 63 when in fact he was 43 in 1916. He would be discharged after a few months at Camp Borden as "Too old—not able to carry on duties," despite his "good" conduct. Allen Bertrand's (1003800) heart condition should also have been caught at his enlistment. Bertrand was born at Papineauville, Quebec, on 3 December 1885, and cited his mother "Philimine [Philomene]" Bertrand of "Blizzard [Blezard] Valley" as next of kin when he signed his attestation in Sudbury on 4 July 1916. He joined the 227th Men of the North Battalion and reached England the following year. After his arrival, he was diagnosed with a pre-existing heart condition: "For past five or six years has had some shortage of breath on exertion … Hair turning grey and looks age stated [40]." He was discharged on 9 March 1918 and returned to Canada as medically unfit. How a person in his condition would have been originally found "fit" raises questions about the pressure recruiters were under in mid-1916 to deliver men to the front and possibly their willingness to ignore communication gaps.

Some Northeasterners chose to enlist in Quebec where they would be more likely to wind up in Francophone units. Arthur Ethier (3155013) was an unmarried labourer born in Warren on 24 June 1888. When he enlisted he signed his attestation form in Montreal, on 18 December 1917. He joined the 2nd Depot Battalion of the 2nd Quebec Regiment. After a medical inspection at Montreal on 6 February 1918, he sailed overseas. He was hospitalized with gonorrhea in mid-June 1918, and discharged at Witley from a "French Canadian Battalion" on 8 April 1919.

Most Francophone service files describe the recruit's conduct as "good" when discharged. However, a reluctance to serve is sometimes evident, particularly among those who enlisted after the fall of 1917, when conscription was instituted. Joseph Leclair (3231275), who had been born in Corbeil on 5 May 1894, signed his attestation form in North Bay on 5 November 1917. Drafted for service in "Canada only" on 22 January 1918, he trained with the 1st Central Ontario Battalion.

His pay was deducted for being AWOL, and then he was struck off the military list when he was found to be "illegally absent 23 August 1918." Despite frequent illnesses and this poor record as a soldier, however, he obtained a position as a guard at the Kapuskasing internment camp, where he assisted the director until October 1919.

Francophones could be as unlucky as any other soldier. Alphonse Lozier (1003334), born on 10 July 1892, worked as a lumberman. He signed his attestation form with a mark when he enlisted 17 June 1916 with the 227th Battalion at Chapleau as part of the forestry draft. Overseas he served instead in the 102nd, an infantry battalion. In September 1917, he picked up what was thought to be a dud bomb and it exploded. He sustained leg injuries and lost all hearing in his left ear. He was transferred to a forestry unit, but in January 1918 he was found medically unfit and returned to Canada. Francophones also suffered from disease as often as other soldiers—including the "self-inflicted wound," VD. Edward Joseph Bonhomme (318975), born in Bracebridge on 28 April 1898, cited his mother, a resident of Sudbury, as next of kin when he signed up on 10 May 1916. This printer contacted venereal disease during training in England. He spent 2 December 1916 to 22 January 1917 in the Shorncliffe Military Hospital with gonorrhea. He died of influenza in the same hospital in November 1918.

Like Anglophones from the Northeast, Francophone soldiers were also often transferred to battalions associated with other areas of the country. Telesphore Ducharme (648266), born at Moor Lake on 1 April 1895, enlisted at Frood on 26 January 1916. He gave his mother, Josephine Gagné of Sudbury, as next of kin and his trade as "labourer." Transferred from the 97th Algonquin Rifles militia to the 119th Algoma Battalion on 1 June, he sailed with his unit on 8 August 1916. Then he was transferred to the 73rd Battalion (Royal Highlanders), associated with Montreal (which, as a Francophone, he may have preferred). He was shot in the right eye in January 1917 but after a week returned to his unit. Two months later, on 1 March, he was missing in action. According to the *Circumstances of Death Registers*, he had "Previously [been] reported missing, [and was] now for official purposes presumed to have died."[159] No burial place is known. Harry Joseph Leclair (345122) served in a unit associated with southern Ontario. He was born in Trenton, and declared himself a commercial traveler based in Haileybury, a Roman Catholic, and single when he enlisted in Ottawa on 2 January 1918 with the 74th Battery of the Canadian Royal Artillery. After serving in France, he returned to Canada on 3 July 1919 and was discharged 9 days later. Albert Theodule Matte (3033836), a salesman from Sturgeon Falls, signed his attestation form in North Bay on 18 October 1917. He would be drafted on 20 February 1918 and placed in the Central Ontario reserve battalion. He arrived in France on 13 August 1918. Arthur Seguin (3231095) also served in France, with the 20th Battalion (Central Ontario). When he registered as a draftee in Toronto on 19 November 1917, he gave his current address as Haileybury and his mother, of Foleyet, as next of kin. He was called up on 18 January 1918 and served until he was demobilized in Toronto on 21 May 1919.

Perhaps because the railway and forest industry were major employers in rural Ontaro, Francophones were often assigned to forestry or construction battalions. Alfred Prevost (2497621), a boiler maker born on 30 March 1899, was drafted in Coniston (near Sudbury) on 5 July 1918. He served with the Railway Construction Troops behind the lines. Felix Lacombe (754508), a woodsman living in Blind River, enlisted there on 27 January 1916. His unit, the 119th Algoma Battalion, sailed for England on 8 August 1916. During training he received the right to wear "one good conduct badge." When the 119th was disbanded, Lacombe was transferred to the Canadian Forestry Corps, and after March 1918 worked at his trade in Inverness, Scotland. Unharmed, he returned via Southampton and Halifax in July 1919. His skill and experience may have meant more for his military career than being Francophone.

Officers and Men of the Ranks

Canada's social norms mirrored those of Britain: a deferential society looked up to superiors and respected authority. Militia officers mainly came from the propertied classes. When the war started, the officers of the 97th Algonquin Rifles militia included an engineer, a broker, a police magistrate, a contractor, a merchant, a school teacher, and an assistant surveyor, all more educated and better paid than the average person. They expected deference in their professional lives and carried that attitude into the military. Just as there was a social division between managers and labour in a factory or mine (reinforced by education, race, and assumptions about abilities), so there was a class line between officers and enlisted men. Most were of British background. Similar to the Algonquin militia's leaders, the officers of the 119th Algoma Battalion (fig. 5.13) included a surveyor (Austin Fellowes), a salesman (John McLurg), a manager (Charles Jones), and a bank manager (John Way).

Figure 5.13. Officers of 119th Algoma Battalion toward the beginning of the war. (Courtesy of Phil Miller, Sault Ste. Marie)

Military systems are inherently authoritarian and hierarchical; in theory, this allows organization, discipline, and responsibility, but in practice it also maintains social hierarchies. In such a system, knowing how to give orders is as crucial as taking them. The relations between soldiers and their superiors often make the difference between success and failure. Trust in those above and concern for those below are crucial, and in World War I, those relations were repeatedly tested by a war of attrition, where going over the top into machine gun fire was frequently the equivalent of suicide.

Reinforcing the social differences were the pay scales. Military pay depended on rank. Privates in the Canadian army received $1 per day as pay. In the field (i.e., serving at the front), they received an extra ten cents' field allowance. The scale of pay for officers dropped dramatically as one went down through the ranks. Majors received $4 per day plus $1 for field duty; captains $3 plus 75 cents; lieutenants and nursing sisters both received $2 plus 60 cents; sergeants received $1.35 plus 15 cents; and corporals $1.10 plus 10 cents. Nursing sisters held officers' ranks and received the same level of pay. Jessie Clarke, a nursing sister from Manitoulin Island, had a monthly income of about $110, from which she could afford to assign $50 to her relatives. She was also given a two-week leave from her work several times. To put her income into context, before the war an industrial worker's monthly income was around $30.

Such pay levels allowed officers to have a different quality of life. For example, as a recruiting officer in Chapleau, Lieutenant William Augustus Lyness received $2 per day (whether that would have been in addition to his salary as chief of police is unknown). He had eight years' militia service. After he went overseas in September 1917 and was promoted to captain, he was earning at least $80 per month, from which he assigned between $30 and $60 to his wife Alice. She moved to England for part of his time overseas, giving an address in North Holloway, London. Since he worked in the forestry corps, Lyness may not have received the full field allowance, though he served with that corps in France part of the time. Illustrating another privilege of officers, he obtained three 14-day leaves to the United Kingdom in March 1917, September 1918, and March 1919, presumably to visit his wife. POW Robert Russell McKessock, a captain when he enlisted and a lawyer before the war, earned a similar rate of pay. Promoted to major, he was captured and interned in the neutral Netherlands early in 1918. On a major's pay, he could afford to bring his wife there while he waited for the war to end.

Living conditions for officers during training and even on the front were reasonably comfortable. Senior officers had a batman or batboy, or a servant who polished shoes and brass, made the bed, cleaned and pressed uniforms, and served meals. Usually such servants came from the lower ranks; most were volunteers. In battle, they sometimes conveyed orders, dug trench holes, and acted as bodyguards for their superiors. Officers who became POWs lived comfortably with separate rooms, did not have to work, and could receive many parcels. This reflected part of the international code of warfare as well as a traditional military code of honour. If seriously wounded, officer POWs were more likely to be interned in neutral countries, especially Switzerland or the Netherlands and, like McKessock, could be joined by their wives. John Ernest McLurg, a sales manager born on 12 April 1875, was an officer with the 51st Soo Rifles militia when the war started. He became a lieutenant in the 2nd Battalion on 1 September 1914. After training at Valcartier, his unit sailed to England on 3 October 1914 and went to France the following February. McLurg was shot in the head and taken prisoner on 24 April 1915 at Ypres. He spent time in Lazarett Siegburg (Siegburg hospital), and Gefangenlager Heidelberg (Heidelberg POW camp), then Soltau. Suffering from his head wound and hip pain (which he attributed to sitting on a wet church floor when first captured), he was interned in Switzerland on 12 August 1916. He lived at Murren until he was repatriated on 22 December 1917. He was struck off the active list on 20 April 1918 as "medically unfit." Until then his wife in Sault Ste. Marie received $30 monthly support from his pay (of about $70 per month).

Despite their privilege, officers were often in the thick of things. Lieutenant Andrew Warwick Duncan came from the Presbyterian community of Antrim, Ireland, where he had been born on 6 May 1890. He became a broker in Swastika, and was a member of the 97th Algonquin Rifles militia. He cited his father, still a resident of Antrim, as next of kin when he signed his attestation form in Haileybury on New Year's Day 1916 receiving a commission in the 159th Battalion. The battalion left Canada on 31 October. On 9 December 1916, Duncan went to France with the 38th Battalion, and he fought and died at Vimy on 9 April 1917. Eight days later, on 17 April 1917, Duncan received the Military Cross. Another member of the 97th Algonquin Rifles, Lieutenant John William New, suffered a similar fate. Born on 30 December 1884 in Richwood, Ontario (west of Hamilton), New was a Baptist living in North Bay when he enlisted on 24 March 1916. He declared his father, a resident of Widdifield (near North Bay), as next of kin. He went to England with the

159th on 31 October 1916, and was transferred to the 38th. He was killed in action in France on 31 March 1917.[160]

Not everyone died on the battlefield, but the cost of war might be no less grievous. Lieutenant Jacob Raymond Myers was a Presbyterian, born in Morewood, Ontario, on 15 May 1890. Married to Eva Gladys Myers, he lived in South Porcupine, where he worked as a school teacher in New Liskeard when he enlisted in Haileybury on 17 June 1916. When he joined the 159th Battalion, he was a member of the 97th Algonquin Rifles militia. Myers's unit sailed for England on 31 October. After training he went to France with the 4th Canadian Mounted Rifles. On 26 October 1917, he was shot in the back of the head while serving on the front line. The wound proved so serious that he was sent to England, then back to Canada as "unfit" for further military service: because of pain in his eyes and elsewhere, he could not read; he also suffered from frequent dizziness and depression. Myers probably had post-traumatic stress disorder (PTSD). A 17 May 1918 summary of his "Subjective Symptoms" is telling:

> Insomnia, requires average of one hour to get to sleep each night. He wakens frequently, dreams very seldom, gets to sleep quite readily when he wakens during the night and feels tired in the a.m. JUMPY, sudden noises, unperceived, cause him to start. Is unable to go to Church as he breaks out into perspiration. If he goes to a theatre he is very fidgety. Vision impaired for close work.

Under "Objective Symptoms," the report states, "General health excellent. Does not appear nervous. No outstanding features of nervous disturbance … We find no disease in his eyes nor any sign of his eyes having been injured in service … We have given him at his request a prescription of a glass for reading." After the war, a report on his condition recognized "marked shell shock," noting, "Wound remain clptic [sic] for some time." The report concluded that, as he still complained about the symptoms, he was "Slightly incapacitated for civil life"; it recommended "a gratuity of $100." A 1921 document refers to Mrs. Gladys Myers of South Porcupine as a widow. Myers had died on 17 October 1920, probably because of the mental and physical toll of the war. He is buried at Mount Pleasant Cemetery in Haileybury.

A small matter made a special case of Captain Hugh Allan McDougall. Born in Glengarry on 18 October 1877, McDougall was working as a merchant in South Porcupine, where he lived with his wife Jean, when he enlisted. A Presbyterian, he had served five years with the 97th Algonquin Rifles militia before signing his attestation form at Camp Borden on 22 September 1916. He sailed with the 159th Battalion on 31 October 1916, and arrived in France from England with the 38th Battalion on 1 December 1916. At Vimy, on 25 April 1917, he suffered a shoulder wound plus a gunshot wound to his penis. A medical board wrote on 23 May 1917: "This officer was wounded at above place on above date … The Board finds the sustained GSW end of penis. The wound is now healed, there is tenderness in the area of the scar. He has some difficulty directing the stream while urinating." The army granted him three weeks' leave, and McDougall spent time in hospitals in Calais and London. After 23 May 1917, with a short interruption for VD treatment (he must have tested the healed member), he worked in the various divisions of the forestry corps in France, survived, and was demobilized on 9 June 1919.

More fortunate was Lieutenant Malcolm Lang, born in Eagle, Ontario, on 25 February 1874, a Presbyterian. Lang was working as a contractor in South Porcupine when he signed up in Haileybury on 15 April 1916. Like the others, he was a member of the 97th Algonquin Rifles militia. He declared his wife Lillian in Sturgeon Falls as next of kin. His unit sailed on 31 October. He served in England and France with the 159th Battalion, the 8th Reserve Battalion, and the Canadian Forestry Corps (the 27th, 69th, and 11th companies). Like other officers he demobilized long after the war, in his case on 14 October 1919.

Among those serving in the 119th Algoma Battalion one officer could always be seen: Austin Newcombe Fellowes (754288), known as "Tiny," measured six feet six inches tall. A civil engineer, he joined the 119th Algoma at Thessalon on 6 February 1916. He started as a sergeant but was promoted to lieutenant when he was transferred to the Canadian Railway Troop in England. During his time there he received permission to marry, a privilege granted more freely to officers. He was one of the rare men promoted to officer out of the ranks (fig. 5.14).

A bunch of us the morning *Tiny Fellows*
in centre got married.
Our padre on left.
"Tiny" is the big fellow in the centre.
"Me" on right next Bob Robinson

Figure 5.14. Officers of 119th Battalion celebrating Austin Newcombe Fellowes's (754288) wedding. (Courtesy of Phil Miller, Sault Ste. Marie)

As the stories of these officers show, many of them served in the militia before the war. Lieutenant-Colonel Charles Jones, head of the 51st Soo Rifles militia and later deputy assistant director of the forestry corps in France, is a typical example. A manager born in Montreal on 1 May 1876, he lived with his wife, Elizabeth, and four children at 17 Summit Avenue, Sault Ste. Marie. He served as a recruiting officer for the 227th Men of the North Battalion, and the song written about that unit was dedicated to him, perhaps reflecting his popularity (fig. 5.15). Jones signed his attestation papers in Sault Ste. Marie on 4 March 1916 and was found fit on 3 August. He held the rank of lieutenant-colonel, but in England, in April 1917, like so many other Northeasterners, he was transferred to the 8th Reserve. After serving four months at the headquarters of the Canadian Forestry Corps at Sunningdale, and most of 1918 with the forestry corps in France, he returned to civilian life, where he built a career working for the CPR and in the power generation and paper industries. His wife had received $60 of his pay of $270 per month while he was serving in the war.

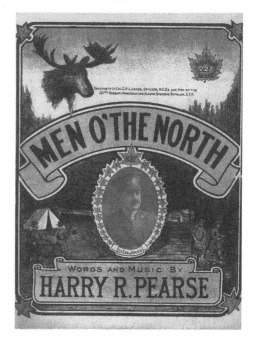

Figure 5.15. Cover of *Men of the North* songsheet. Note the dedication above the title. (Courtesy of Phil Miller, Sault Ste. Marie)

As Jones's history shows, officers as well as men were moved between battalions. Lieutenant John Hatherly Way's story follows the same pattern. His funeral notice reviewed his military career from the time of being made an officer of the 51st Soo Rifles militia in 1915 to his death in late August 1918 near Arras, France. He helped to recruit for the 119th Algoma Battalion, and then accompanied it to Niagara for training. More intensive training took place at Camp Witley in England during the summer of 1916. However, because officers received regular leave, he could also play tourist in England by, for instance, going to St. Alban's with fellow officers (fig. 5.16). Way was assigned to the 58th Battalion, where he served until Amiens. He is remembered on the Sault war monument and a plaque at Sault College (fig. 5.17).

Figure 5.16. Lieutenant John Hatherly Way with fellow officers Nursing Sister Hilda Bashford and Ken Dawson at St. Alban's. (Courtesy of Phil Miller, Sault Ste. Marie)

Many officers did not serve at the front, for both men and materials had to be managed at home and behind the lines. Major David Marr Brodie was born in Scotland on 4 February 1870, and emigrated to become a police magistrate in Sudbury. His designated heir was his wife, Agnes Stewart Brodie. A Presbyterian, he belonged to the 97th Algonquin Rifles militia when he signed his attestation form in Sudbury on 20 December 1915. He remained in the army through the war, but having served only in Canada and England, he was ineligible for veterans' benefits, since "as [a] soldier he did not serve in [the] actual theatre of war." Brodie was "struck off the strength … by reason of being surplus to requirements" on 27 August 1919. Some officers did not go abroad at all, but were involved in basic training at camps in Borden, Hamilton, Niagara, or Toronto. There, officers from the militia and later from regular battalions taught drill, shooting, and machine gun unit coordination, trying to create soldiers fit for the daunting tasks that awaited them in France and Belgium (fig. 5.18).

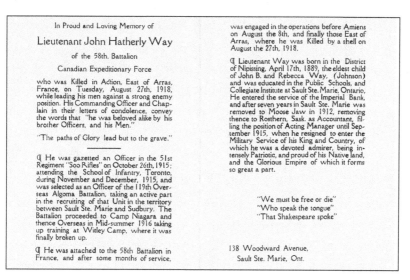

In Proud and Loving Memory of

Lieutenant John Hatherly Way

of the 58th. Battalion

Canadian Expeditionary Force

who was Killed in Action, East of Arras, France, on Tuesday, August 27th, 1918, while leading his men against a strong enemy position. His Commanding Officer and Chaplain in their letters of condolence, convey the words that "he was beloved alike by his brother Officers, and his Men."

"The paths of Glory lead but to the grave."

⁌ He was gazetted an Officer in the 51st Regiment "Soo Rifles" on October 26th, 1915; attending the School of Infantry, Toronto, during November and December, 1915, and was selected as an Officer of the 119th Overseas Algoma Battalion, taking an active part in the recruiting of that Unit in the territory between Sault Ste. Marie and Sudbury. The Battalion proceeded to Camp Niagara and thence Overseas in Mid-summer 1916 taking up training at Witley Camp, where it was finally broken up.

⁌ He was attached to the 58th Battalion in France, and after some months of service,

was engaged in the operations before Amiens on August the 8th, and finally those East of Arras, where he was Killed by a shell on August the 27th, 1918.

⁌ Lieutenant Way was born in the District of Nipissing, April 17th, 1889, the eldest child of John B. and Rebecca Way, (Johnson) and was educated in the Public Schools, and Collegiate Institute at Sault Ste. Marie, Ontario. He entered the service of the Imperial Bank, and after seven years in Sault Ste. Marie was removed to Moose Jaw in 1912, removing thence to Rosthern, Sask. as Accountant, filling the position of Acting Manager until September 1915, when he resigned to enter the Military Service of his King and Country, of which he was a devoted admirer, being intensely Patriotic, and proud of his Native land, and the Glorious Empire of which it forms so great a part.

"We must be free or die"
"Who speak the tongue"
"That Shakespeare spoke"

138 Woodward Avenue,
Sault Ste. Marie, Ont.

Figure 5.17. Lieutenant John Hatherly Way, memorial notice. (Courtesy of Phil Miller, Sault Ste. Marie)

Figure 5.18. Officers of the 227th (Men of the North) Battalion at the Hamilton training camp, April 1917. (Courtesy of Phil Miller).

Under the conditions of war and military hierarchies, relations between officers and men varied greatly, depending upon personalities and situations. At the beginning of the war, ordinary soldiers' letters home often made positive comments about officers they knew from prewar militia service, and officers commented equally positively on the men from the home region.[161] Hints of admiration for officers can also be found in the final letter from Way's commanding officer (fig. 5.17), and in the dedication of "The Men of the North" to Lieutenant-Colonel Jones (fig. 5.15). However, these informal relationships are visible only in private letters and diaries—and contrary evidence, such as Craig's glee at the general's spending a night in the mud (see chapter 4), is equally common. The service files suggest that by the middle of the war more men were being punished for not following orders and for swearing at non-commissioned officers. The conditions of trench warfare, the seemingly endless conflict, limited food, and transfers into different units away from familiar faces led to tension, but the hierarchies and privileges of rank may also have contributed to the social divide between officers and men.

Rank was not the only division within Canadian troops. Two depositions in a court martial tell part of the story of a conflict between New Liskeard soldier Graham Winters Hennessy, who had been promoted from the ranks, and a Toronto soldier. Hennessy enlisted with the 228th Battalion and was transferred to the forestry corps. Shipped to southern France in September 1917, he spent the next two months in hospitals being treated for syphilis. Then he returned to his forestry duties with the 60th company, and, in January 1918, came into conflict with Thompson.

A deposition by Andrew St. Denis (2251121) of Cobalt tells the story. Hennessy had put on a private's uniform and organized four of the men in his unit to help him "get" Martin Luther Thompson (2250102), who had been in a fight with Hennessy's batman that afternoon. St. Denis admitted that they had been drinking rum before they assaulted Thompson. A deposition by the batman, David Lalonde (2251120), confirmed St. Denis's account but maintained that rum was not involved. They lured Thompson out of a pub, and then Hennessy and his soldiers, including St. Denis and Lalonde, assaulted him. A bloody melee ensued.

Thompson was a Jamaican-Canadian immigrant from Toronto. The others were from Cobalt, New Liskeard, and Timmins. Was this a case of normal brawling among soldiers (northerners against a southerner), or was the attack racially motivated? Hennessy's actions were certainly premeditated and deceptive. Further, as an officer, he led his men into poor behaviour. He was found guilty of "scandalous conduct unbecoming of an officer and gentleman" in May 1918, and dishonourably discharged. Since Hennessy's accomplices received minor punishments for disorderly conduct, were they deemed to have merely been misled? The underlying causes of this incident, and the earlier fight between Thompson and Lalonde, remain a mystery. This is the only documented case of a Northeastern Ontario officer who was cashiered.

A Separate Service

The work of the foresters, railwaymen, tunnellers, and officers who served in World War I was crucial to the Allies' survival and successes, but these men also, in many ways, had a different experience from that of the ordinary soldier on the front. They shared much in common—shrapnel and bullets had no respect for rank—but the groups of men whose stories are told here also saw the war from a different perspective shaped not only by their work, but also, for the Indigenous and Francophone soldiers, by who they were. These men brought key skills in forestry, railway work, and mining to their service, marking one of the key contributions made by Northeastern Ontario in World War I. Who would have thought that so many would be cutting wood, laying track, or tunneling? These soldiers and officers shared the dangers posed by their professions, as well as the hazards of trenches, artillery, and disease. Few left records to tell us about their lives, perhaps because they were too busy surviving.

Notes

Notes

CHAPTER 6

Life When Not Being Shot At

War has always been about more than fighting. Daily life continues around the conflict, and since man cannot live by bread alone, time on leave helped satisfy other needs and desires. This chapter explores the lives of Northeastern Ontario soldiers off the battlefield, experiences that included travel, sex, marriage, and even hockey. This chapter also turns to the home front, the sacrifices made there, and the support that sustained families. Northeastern Ontario was not just a home front, however—the war experiences of enemy prisoners of war and so-called enemy aliens were shaped by camps established in the region.

War as Tourism

In all wars, some people join up for the adventure of travel in foreign lands. Many World War I soldiers' letters speak of "gay Paree" (Paris), others the sights of London. Many would explore England while on leave or recuperating from wounds. Since more than half of Canadian service personnel in World War I had been born in Great Britain, many were also going "home" to see relatives. To their Canadian homes they sent postcards of Folkstone, Dover Cliffs, and Stonehenge, the latter being close to one of the main training camps at Shornecliffe.

Letters to relatives and friends in Northeastern Ontario sometimes describe the sights only briefly, since details about drinking, visits to prostitutes, and overstaying leave would not have reassured families. The Young Men's Christian Association (YMCA) organized "comfort stations" and huts for the men as soon as the war started, providing places of quiet (sometimes to sleep off hangovers) as well as non-alcoholic drinks, and paper and envelopes for letters home. Refuges were established at the training camps and in Belgium, France, and occupied Germany. The YMCA tried hard to moderate soldiers' behaviour while on leave.

Some soldiers visited castles and historic sites, and as invalids they enjoyed the scenery of Wales or other rural areas where they recuperated. In France, the "Mademoiselles of Armentières" (a risqué refrain from a favourite soldiers' song) were worth a song and a dollar or two, but troops and nurses also saw Boulogne and Le Havre, and hoped to tour Berlin in victory. In reality, only Britain and a small part of Belgium and France were safe for tourism in the first years of the war. Some Canadians did go to Germany as POWs, and some occupied western Germany after the war. Soldiers who did not have relatives in Britain could take tours offered by the YMCA, or visit London, where the Y maintained a set of rooms known as the Beaver Hut (fig. 6.1). Arthur Studer (3110798) of Timmins wrote about his visit from Witley training camp on 22 September 1918: "Well, I was in the famous city called London. I had often heard of it but from my own experience, it is some barg [burg]. I visited the Houses of Parliament, clearly as big as Mr. [Charles] Pierce's store. I was in our Canadian YMCA called the Beaver Hut … It's a real home for Canadian troops."[162] His letter gave news of chums from home, mentioning prospector Paddy McCoy (3039379) and Sgt. McGregor, the former Schumacher constable.

If they were on longer leave, or working in Scotland with the forestry corps, soldiers could take the YMCA's "Red Triangle Tour No. 2 to Glasgow and West Highlands 'Scotch Lakes and Mountains.'" The brochure read, "A fairyland of scenery, for grandeur, impressiveness and quaintness, few places can equal it."[163] John McLean, on leave at the Borden training camp in England, wrote to his mother in Echo Bay on 17 October 1916 about his plans: "I am going to try and go on pass to Edinburgh Scotland with Jim Swan the end of this week for 4 or 5 days. It will be a rest from around the camp."[164]

For those fighting and working in France, the YMCA rented a special hotel in Paris with 330 rooms and 30 baths, but it also had to compete with brothels. The Y would not supply condoms unless the soldier had already contacted venereal disease, and it kept statistics on how many girls had been dissuaded from offering their bodies to the men.[165] The Y even had "huts" near the front which offered respite but hardly qualified as tourism (fig. 6.2).

A Self-Inflicted Wound: Venereal Disease[166]

Sick men are of no use to the military. Sick soldiers cannot fight. Sexually transmitted disease can undermine physical strength and mental focus. In World War I, syphilis

Figure 6.1. Poster advertising the YMCA's London refuge for Canada's soldiers. (Courtesy of Toronto Public Library)

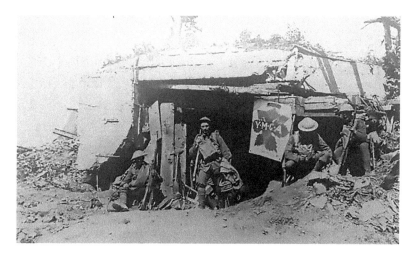

Figure 6.2. A YMCA hut in a converted German bunker. (Charles W. Bishop, *The Canadian Y.M.C.A in the Great War* [Toronto: National Council, 1924], 332.)

and gonorrhea caused problems both for the soldiers who suffered and the organization they served. Painful penis discharges, open sores, and fatigue required medical treatment and hospitalization. Without antibiotics, the treatments of the day (arsenic or mercury) were sometimes as painful and dangerous as the illness.

The high rate of VD among Canadian troops affected human resources and planning. The military saw VD as a "self-inflicted wound," so pay was deducted each time a soldier was hospitalized for syphilis or gonorrhea. By 1916, increasing losses on the battlefield meant that all fighting men were needed. Diseased soldiers upset generals' calculations. At the worst point, "28.7 percent of the [Canadian] men were reported to be infected; by the end of the war, some 15.8 percent of overseas enlisted men had contacted some form of venereal disease … almost six times the figure of that experienced by British troops."[167] In Canadians' defence, historian Tim Cook points out that British soldiers on leave could go home to wives and girlfriends, and that Canadians received more pay (and could thus afford the brothels). Further, the 16% figure was about the same as that for prewar Canadian adults. Given the high number of cases, however, the demobilization of thousands at the war's end could have created a serious public health issue.

In 1918, the military decided to inspect the troops during demo-bilization, in particular those who had been treated for VD. John Munroe (754638), a farmer from Bruce Mines, was one of the many soldiers who received treatment in this attempt to prevent the spread of disease. Munroe's military career started in January 1916 with the 119th Algoma Battalion and continued overseas in August 1916. He was transferred to the 52nd Battalion, and sent to France. He had hardly arrived when he was hospitalized for VD in early 1918. He was again hospitalized early in 1919 for VD and impetigo. His discharge from a Toronto hospital on 30 September took place after it had been agreed that he would continue further treatment as an outpatient for 183 days. His file reads, "He has been warned of the danger of transmitting infection. He has been informed that he may receive free treatment from the DSCR [Department of Soldiers' Civil Reestablishment]." The DSCR had been created in May 1918 to help resettle soldiers by providing vocational training, especially for the injured and disabled; it also helped to avoid public health problems such as the spread of VD. In October 1919, Munroe was discharged as "medically unfit."

Another well-documented case is George Wesley Fay (754500) from Tekummah on Manitoulin Island. This unmarried farmer, who had enlisted with the 119th Algoma Battalion at Providence Bay on 16 March, arrived in England on 19 August 1916. On 31 May 1917, after a second round of training, he was to ship to France with the 124th Battalion, but that day he was "Confined to Barracks" for five days due to "Disorderly Conduct" on morning parade. He reached France on 14 June 1917 with the 4th Canadian Engineering Battalion. On 10 March 1918, he received 14 days' leave in Paris. Within weeks, on 11 April, he was hospitalized with "V.D.G. [venereal disease gonorrhea]." Fay's case reveals the problems such repeat offenders created in an army desperate to fill positions on the front. He was transferred to the reserve pool of the 124th and was repeatedly hospitalized with VD. On 26 April 1918, he lost his field allowance and half his pay. An entry in his file on 20 July recorded "Forfeits F.A. and 50 cents per day while in Hosp from 13.4.18 to 13.7.18 (92 days)." These were normal punishments for not being able to fight. The loss of capable soldiers and the waste of medical and administrative resources is evident. A later entry in Fay's file reads "24/8/18 Forfeits F.A. and 50 cents per diem while in hosp, 18-7-18 to 15-8-18 (29 days)." Ironically, when he was discharged, his VD was found to have been "cured."

For many soldiers, VD was only one of the war's many adventures, though it still took time out of their lives and money out of their pockets. Immigrant John Gaalson (754360) enlisted on 10 March 1916 in Webbwood with the 119th Algoma Battalion. He reported that he had been born on 13 November 1896 at Arensburg, Finland, and gave his father (Mick Gaalson) there as next of kin. This Roman Catholic "lumber jack" measured an above-average height of five feet nine inches. After training, shipping overseas, retraining, and transferring to the 52nd Battalion, he was hospitalized with "parotiditis" (probably parotitis, an inflammation of the thyroid gland), in October 1916. At that time he made out a will to "Miss Gladys Hall 83 Blackfriars Road London, Eng." Then a diagnosis of rubella, later "ascertained [to be] V.D.G.," put him in the hospital on 5 January 1917 for two weeks. He fought at Vimy, and then at Passchendaele, where on 29 October he was admitted to hospital with severe head wounds. He would not be discharged from the Canadian hospital at Eastbourne, England, until 27 December 1917. In March 1918 he was again hospitalized for VD, this time in Kent, for five weeks. He was readmitted in June and not released until mid-August. On 17 December, the war over, he was posted to a "casualty company" and granted a "sub[sistence] allowance of 80¢ per diem from 17-12-1918 to 3-1-19 Home coming furlough," because his pay had been forfeited so often. On discharge he had a scalp scar about the size of a dime and his regimental number tattooed on his arm.

Gaalson's adventures were not over: two years later, he was serving with an American howitzer company in Camp Jackson, South Carolina, though on 15 November 1921 he changed his address to New York. He returned to Canada in 1929 to Widdifield (now part of North Bay) and bought a farm near Mattawa. He died on 2 August 1979. In fact, his real name was Johannes Ounpu and his relatives lived in Estonia.[168] Why he reinvented himself so many times remains a mystery.

The war service of many other soldiers besides Munroe, Fay, and Gaalson was interrupted by time spent recovering from VD. Numerous cases are sprinkled among the themes discussed in this book. Suffice it to note that what the YMCA termed "temptations" and the military called a "self-inflicted wound" had significant consequences. The problem would remain in World War II, when, according to a 1941 study of "medical non-effectiveness in the Canadian army," VD rates were at 30%, the highest cause of soldiers' inability to serve effectively.[169] The degree to which intervention and regulations limited this debilitating disease, often spread in conjunction with war, remains an open question.

War Brides

War brides, women whom Canadian men met overseas and married, changed the demography of Northeastern Ontario by decreasing the opportunities for Canadian women to find husbands at a time when battlefield deaths had already reduced the number of eligible men. The number of overseas marriages must have been particularly shocking to women from Chapleau: of 21 war brides on a list compiled from the *Sudbury Star*, six married men from Chapleau.[170] Perhaps small farming, lumbering, and mining communities needed women to balance the number of young men in those occupations. Unfortunately, as is common in that era, the names of the women often go unrecorded. A historical scrapbook for the town of Massey, for example, reports that "War Brides of Massey Servicemen were welcomed with a public reception and shower dance for each new arrival in the W[omen's] I[nstitute] hall." It then lists ten *men's* names. In larger mining centres such as Sudbury or Timmins, where men normally outnumbered women, the impact would have been much less. The total number of war brides in the Northeast is unknown, but in places like the Sault the newspapers prominently reported some marriages.

Some of these romances took place over a period of time. Scottish-born John Dingwall (178202), nicknamed "Scottie," a railway clerk in Copper Cliff, arrived in England a bachelor on 4 May 1916. Dingwall spent most of his war years in England, where he met Edith, a resident of London. His service records do not give the date of their marriage, but the ceremony took place before the end of the war. Sudbury steamfitter Captain Frank Rothery (11428), an Englishman born in Leeds, met his future wife Ethel when he returned to Leeds as a soldier visiting his parents. Frank and Ethel married in the summer of 1919. Lieutenant Wilfred Joseph Hough, a sub-contractor with the CPR in Coniston, met his bride when he was training in Yorkshire, having been seconded to the Royal Air Force on 24 July 1918. In the spring of 1920, the marriage of Hough and Gwendolyn Prosser took place at St. Joseph's Roman Catholic Church in North Bay, where the couple would live.[171] Sudbury fireman Sydney Thomas Dennis (648239) also met his bride in England. He served in England and France, and although single when he was discharged in Toronto on 2 April 1919, he returned to England late in the summer of 1920 and married Nellie Edwards of Northampton.

Some men moved more quickly when it came to love. Private James Land (166970), for instance, enlisted in Sudbury on 14 October 1915 with the Second Canadian Pioneer Battalion. Land arrived at Le

Havre, France, on 8 March 1916. On leave in England, he suffered such a severe case of influenza that he had to go to the King George Hospital in Rexhill, near London. There he met nurse Elizabeth Taylor, the daughter of John Taylor of Lancashire. They fell in love, and on 13 October 1917, Land received permission to marry. Sapper George Thomas Paul of Sudbury (166623) arrived in England on 14 December 1915, embarked for France on 2 March 1916, returned to England seriously wounded on 1 October 1918, and found an English bride. He returned home in 1919 with his wife and baby daughter, names unknown.

Not all hastily arranged marriages proved successful. Ottawa-born Lance Corporal Joseph Arthur Lauzon (550053), whose mother and heir lived in Sudbury, reached England on 2 December 1915. On 4 September 1917, he arranged a monthly payment of $25 for Mrs. Joseph Lauzon, a resident of London, England. He later married another Englishwoman. The prolonged periods of enforced celibacy in the trenches might have encouraged love at first sight and quick liaisons. With one exception (Alex Fraser, who served in France and married his French teacher), all the women on record came from England.[172]

More is known about the marriage of Lily Higgs and James Stewart McBain (754569). McBain, born on 13 July 1898 in Echo Bay, lived on the family farm until he enlisted with the 119th Algoma Battalion on 13 January 1916. After training at Camp Borden, he shipped aboard the SS *Matagama* and arrived in England on 19 August, finding that his farming experience had prepared him well for his military duties—caring for the mules.[173] McBain remained in England with the 4th Battalion until April 1918 (fig. 6.3). In London, according to their granddaughter, he met Lily Kate Higgs, born on 27 December 1899, a resident of Guildford, Surrey (fig. 6.4), and they fell in love. McBain spent the rest of the war in France, and returned to Canada for demobilization in June 1919. He joined the fire department in Sault Ste. Marie, and within a few months earned enough to pay for Lily's trans-Atlantic crossing, though she found leaving her English family hard. In 1927, McBain became an officer with the Ontario Provincial Police (OPP). Throughout his career, which lasted until 1963, he served in several communities in Northeastern Ontario. He held the position of district inspector in Sudbury when he retired.[174]

Figure 6.3. James McBain. (Courtesy of Bonnie Lachapelle, Sudbury.)
Figure 6.4. Lily McBain. (Courtesy of Bonnie Lachapelle, Sudbury.)

Since many men from Northeastern Ontario served in the Canadian Forestry Corps, and indeed were specifically recruited for it, it is worth noting that the official history of that unit during World War I claimed that Imperial ties had been fostered by their service: "That so many of the men will take back with them to Canada wives from Bonnie Scotland and other parts of Britain will only serve to make these bonds the closer."[175]

Hockey: By Whom? For Whom?

Was the best national hockey team in 1916–17 actually from a Nipissing-area battalion? The history of this winning team, comprised of soldiers, is one of the untold stories of Northeastern Ontario's war.[176] The 228th Northern Fusiliers Battalion was mainly recruited at North Bay from Nipissing District, starting in March 1916, but despite its name, it was recruiting not only soldiers but also hockey players for a team that played in the National Hockey Association. Organized primarily as a recruiting stunt, the team was made up of new "soldiers" with superb hockey records. Most had played with at least one professional team. Some enlisted because they intended to go overseas, but others joined with a tacit agreement that they would only play hockey. The 228th Northern Fusiliers joined the league as the sixth team for the 1916–17 season. Wearing khaki jerseys, the players became very popular and were soon the league's highest scoring team. Even when playing an all-star team drawn from the other teams of the league, they won 10 to 0. At New Year's, they were in first place and seen as contenders for the Stanley Cup. However, in February 1917, the *Porcupine Advance* reported that the 228th, which it considered its own, had been called overseas. The reduced league slowly disintegrated.

Some players were released, but others went overseas. Most transferred to the 6th Battalion, the Canadian Railway Troops. They laid track and moved supplies and equipment to the front. Some felt they had been misused by the league and their officers. The *Porcupine Advance* headline on 12 November 1917 reported that the league's highest scorer, "[Eddie] Oatman [1007011] Says 228th Used Him Badly." He had enlisted with the understanding that he would go overseas as well as being paid for playing hockey. Eventually he received some of his promised earnings; however, his service file stated "not likely to become an efficient soldier."

Oddly, the team became known as the "Toronto 228th Northern Fusiliers" (fig. 6.5) even though the players came from more northern areas. Oatman, for example, was from Parry Sound. An accountant, he had played for various southern Ontario teams before helping the Montreal Bulldogs win the Stanley Cup in 1912. Lieutenant James Duncan, an officer because of his militia service, came from Sault Ste. Marie. He enlisted on 12 May 1916. When he went overseas, he too served with the 6th Canadian Railway Troop. However, on 1 August 1917 he transferred to the Royal Flying Corps, where he became an ace credited with 11 victories. In one sortie he brought down three enemy aircraft after lengthy fights. On 26 July 1918, he received the Military Cross for gallantry.

Figure 6.5. Northern Fusiliers hockey team. FRONT ROW: Amos Arbour (played on the 1916 Stanley Cup–winning Montreal Canadiens), Captain Leon Reade (team manager), Lieutenant-Colonel Archibald Earchmann (battalion commanding officer), Howard Lockhart (goaltender). BACK ROW: Frank Carroll (coach/trainer), Gorden Keats, Archie Briden, Captain James Arthur Duncan, Captain Howard McNamara (captain, 1916 Stanley Cup–winning Montreal Canadiens), Captain Rocque Beaudro (scored the winning goal for the 1907 Stanley Cup–winning Kenora Thistles), Percy LeSueur (transferred to Toronto's 48th Highlanders and did not play hockey that season), George Prodgers (played on the 1912 and 1916 Stanley Cup–winning teams). (Photo courtesy of Captain Douglas Newman, Heritage Officer RCAF 22 Wing, North Bay.)

Another team member, Corporal Amos Arbour (853665), a butcher from Victoria Harbour, was born in Waubaushene, Ontario. He signed up on 3 July 1916 with the 177th Battalion (the Simcoe Foresters) at Barrie, but his record also says he joined the 228th and later transferred to the 6th (railway construction). On the front in France, he would be reprimanded for disobeying an order, but did not lose his rank as corporal. Leon Reade, a contractor with a wife in North Bay, enlisted on 29 April 1916 as a captain in the 228th. Howard Lockhart (648538) enlisted at Toronto on 5 November 1916, just in time for the hockey season. This machinist came from North Bay, though his mother lived in Cochrane. In 1918, he stumbled into a shell hole while playing football, developed knee problems, and was discharged as medically unfit. At demobilization, he received 153 days of outpatient treatment.

Percy LeSueur (799856) may have been the only player from Toronto, though he was born in Quebec City. His service file notes that he was "To be employed as an instructor in bayonet fighting and physical training at Divisional Headquarters." George Prodgers (1006620) came from North Bay, where he had been a mechanic. He put his skills to use in the 6th Canadian Railway Troop in France, was wounded in the back, but survived. Gordon Meeking (1006972) was a clerk (travelling salesman) and pro hockey player from Barrie. He would be discharged in February 1917 because he was "Not likely to become an efficient soldier" and was considered medically unfit because of attacks of epididymitis, or scrotal pain.

Most of the players, like the battalion, thus came from Northeastern Ontario, but Toronto took credit for the team and its recruiting efforts. Again we have to ask: Why was the team identified with Toronto, despite the 228th being a Northeastern battalion? It may have happened because the soldiers of the battalion were "adopted" by Toronto before going overseas. A *Toronto World* headline on 9 February 1917 read "Men from North in Need of Sox," and continued "Soldiers from Northern Ontario Should Receive Donations without Delay." A second headline patronizingly added, "Have Few Friends: Bushmen and Indians Leave to Do Their Bit Shortly." The article explained that "The 228th Battalion, from Northern Ontario, which was recruited in North Bay last April and went to Camp Borden in July some 900 strong, and has been quartered in Givens Street School since November, expects to leave the city for an eastern point within a few days." The report noted that 71% were Canadian-born and about 200 were "French Canadian and Roman Catholics." The paper claimed (wrongly) that since no ladies' auxiliary had been organized for the huge recruitment area, an "urgent need of socks and other comforts" existed, with some men even suffering frostbite:

> Drawn from the wide area there are hunters, trappers and guides, lumbermen, miners, prospectors, railway men and Hudson Bay Company employees. There are 43 Cree Indians from Moose Factory ... who walked 250 miles to Cochrane, the nearest station. Many of them are married and their families are now at Elk Lake and Bear Island. One squaw with her papoose on her back made the journey of 250 miles on foot to Cochrane. None of these Indians understood English before joining the battalion, and are among the best disciplined men in the ranks.

Church ladies and charity groups were asked to donate socks and money. The appeal assumed Toronto's generosity toward "her adopted battalion." The 228th Northern Fusiliers did have some ties to Toronto.

Animals at War: Beasts of Burden, Mascots, Pets, and a Dog's Tale of War

Eight million horses and mules died during the war. Only a few achieved the fame of the protagonist of *War Horse*. They suffered, hauling heavy loads through mud, and many were hit by bullets or shrapnel.[177] Some men with farming experience worked with these beasts of burden. Reuben C. Pettifer (57905), who came from Hanbury near Temiskaming Shores and enlisted on 12 November 1914, wrote home while with the 20th Battalion in England: "This is Sunday evening and I have just come off duty. I am on the transport, and we have got 20 more horses today, and four of us have had to picquet them. We have 68 horses here now."[178] A few officers rode horses for recreation: Captain Thomas Magladery of New Liskeard, quartermaster of the 37th Battalion, went for a ride every second day to clear his head from office drudgery.[179] More should be known about the relationships between soldiers and the animals that accompanied them to war—not only working animals, but the battalion mascots, the pets, and a dog who was a recruiter.

Figure 6.6. 159th Battalion with a bear cub mascot.

163

When the photograph of D Company (Haileybury) of the 159th Battalion was taken at Niagara training camp in 1916, in the centre front of the picture, held by a chain, sat a bear cub (fig. 6.6). Another photo showed a gangly moose, and possibly the same bear cub. For soldiers going into the unknown, there was doubtless comfort in the symbol of a beast representing home and its landscapes. Mascots provided companionship and entertainment. The 159th Battalion was not the only unit to bring a mascot to England. Another black bear taken from White River by Winnipeg troops and transported to London supposedly inspired the author of *Winnie-the-Pooh*.[180] Sadder is the moose whose story was told as an anecdote of war on 1 September 1932 by the *Porcupine Advance*:

> George Guppy, who was [nicknamed] O[fficer] C[ommanding] Mascots, used to lead the moose out aft for a breath of fresh air and it was pitiful to watch the huge, dazed animal propped up with his four legs braced at all angles against the rolling and pitching of the old *Empress of Britain*. With the bear it was another story. He quickly became the pet of the ship and was game to wrestle with all comers ... When England was reached there was some difficulty about getting the moose landed, because it was a hoofed animal ... But it was wartime, the regulations were judiciously loosened, and the two mascots were wangled down to Seaford in Sussex. There the moose promptly sickened and died ... On Sundays English visitors from the nearby towns thronged in and the bear did his stuff with gusto ... The troops, sensing the feeling of the crowd, spread the impression that bear wrestling was one of the major Canadian sports and every normal Canuck had his tussle with a bear every day before breakfast.[181]

When the battalion was disbanded and the men transferred, the bear posed a problem. It was hardly a domestic pet. Guppy received orders to take the bear to the London Zoo and simply leave it. However, British railways did not allow 400-pound bears on trains, even in third class ... except by bribery. Once in London, no cabbie would accept a bear, until Guppy hid the bear behind some crates, made a deal for a cab, then rushed the bear in despite the cabbie's protests. After a struggle, the bear ended in the cab: "Arrived at the zoo the boys led their captive within, tied him to the railing of the bear cage and loped off. He was still there two years later and quite a favourite." This bear may have provided the inspiration for Winnie-the-Pooh! Milne never specified which bear provided his inspiration.

Figure 6.7. Durham as a POW, with friend and a basket of kittens. (Photo album, 70, TED fonds, Sault Ste. Marie Library Archives. Courtesy of Sault Ste. Marie Public Library Archives)

Pets, like mascots, provide comfort. In POW camps, they also created a sense of normality. Edwin Durham (see ch. 4) noted in his memoirs that a cat played an important part "in my life and quite a few of the boys too" (fig. 6.7).[182] He told about a "quite wild mother cat" who was adopted by the POWs. Soon five black kittens appeared: "The biggest one the boys called 'M'Dralley the terrible Turk'" and the soldiers played hide and seek with him and the others using cardboard boxes: "One night I was walking down the compound and M'Dralley hit me about the middle of the back and went up on my shoulder and purred." Durham put the kitten on the ground. It meowed up at him, to show him a mouse it had brought for him. The kittens joined the men in bed and loved to have the covers lifted for them. The Germans raised rabbits to feed their guard dogs, and when a baby rabbit was caught on the barbed wire fence, Durham fed it to the kittens. What happened to the kittens after the POWs' departure, Durham does not say.

While wild-animals-turned-mascots and POW pets seem to have led relatively uncertain lives, a very different fate awaited Bobbie Burns, the dog that accompanied Lieutenant Jack Munroe (1769) to war. Born in Cape Breton in 1873, Munroe was already a well-known northern character as the founder of the silver town of Elk Lake (in the District of Temiskaming). He was an imposing figure standing just one-quarter inch shy of six feet, with a chest of 44 inches. He had served for three years in the US army, and he was famous for defeating the world boxing champion in one match, and fighting him to a draw in another 100-round fight. When the war broke out, he enlisted immediately on 22 August 1914 with the Princess Patricia's Canadian Light Infantry, naming his mother as next-of-kin but leaving his possessions to a mystery woman in Cape Breton. Munroe later became even more famous as an injured soldier who told his wartime story from his dog's perspective.[183] Where the prospector from Porcupine learned to write so well is not known, but he had impressive speaking and organizing abilities.

At Armentières in France, on 3 June 1915, Monroe suffered severe gunshot wounds to his right arm, shoulder, and chest, nearly paralyzing his arm. According to his service file, he went through a series of hospitals until the end of December 1916, when he returned to Canada. A medical report from 1 August 1916 summarizes his case:

> Patient was wounded by rifle bullet June 3rd 1915 which entered 1 inch below middle third of Right Clavicle, and emerged in back through Scpula near inner margin. He spat blood for an hour or two after he was wounded. The subclavian artery was injured and formed an aneurysm. There was also complete paralysis of shoulder and upper limb. Operation for ligature of subclavian and cure of aneurysm. Suture of brachial nerve trunks was performed December 8th 1915. Voluntary power is returning in muscles of upper arm, also pulse at wrist.

In Toronto he spent months in hospitals until discharged from the service in July 1917. Munroe became a well-known recruiter in the Timmins area in late 1917, attracting new volunteers for the war effort, including the forestry corps. At the same time, he composed his imaginative book. His preface is signed at Cobalt (fig. 6.8).

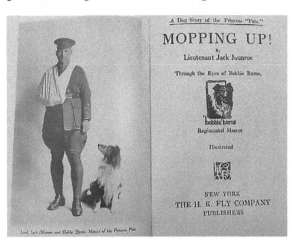

Figure 6.8. The title page from Jack Munroe's book *Mopping Up!*, which tells the story of his war experiences from the point of view of Bobbie Burns, a collie who accompanied him to war. (Jack Munroe, *Mopping Up!* [New York: H.K. Fly, 1918]).

Mopping Up! starts with the story of Monroe's first encounter with Bobbie Burns, a collie, in 1905 in Mexico City. He gives the panting and parched puppy some water, and from that day on they share a close bond. Later, when Munroe travels to Northern Ontario, Bobbie misses the train at North Bay, yet in ten days makes his way two hundred miles through the bush to Porcupine to rejoin his master. Bobbie becomes the narrator of Monroe's war story, since, as the author says, "I do not much care for a man's opinion of a dog. I am more interested in a dog's opinion of the man."[184]

At this point, the book changes narrators, and Bobbie himself picks up the tale of Munroe's war experiences. *Mopping Up!* provided solid recruiting fare for the military, portraying war as an exciting adventure with difficulties that are challenging but surmountable. Though also an anti-German wartime tract with numerous references to the dastardly "Huns," the book reveals many issues soldiers faced on the front. By using the dog's ability to overhear and understand conversations that Munroe could not have heard, the book allows the dog to relate the strategy of the officers as well as the travails of the common soldier.

Bobbie first hears of the war when camping with his master, whom he calls Pendy (short for Pendragon) during a prospecting trip at Nighthawk Lake near Timmins. When the men discover that the war has begun, they vow to give the Germans some of their own medicine. This makes the dog think that war might not be nice, since he has not liked medicine in the past. Pendy prepares to leave for the war, however, and Bobbie fears he will be left behind. In the end, he convinces Pendy to take him. The cheering crowds encountered en route suggest that war might be fun after all. They travel through North Bay to Ottawa, where Bobbie soon becomes the mascot of the Princess Pats and receives endless attention: "If this was war, why, I had as soon be at war always. But I could not understand the sympathy and good fellowship in it."[185] Even high-ranking officers dote on Bobbie, and he enjoys demonstrating his clever tricks, such as bringing his comb and returning it to its place.

When his master appears in khaki, Bobbie begins to show his bias, since he thinks it "the finest I had ever seen him wear."[186] Their journey to Valcartier begins with cheering crowds and bagpipes (which Bobbie detests). At the pier, the commanding officer refuses to allow Bobbie to come along, but Pendy and his buddies hatch a plan. Bobbie is smuggled aboard in a gunny sack: "My feelings at such undignified treatment may be imagined. A collie of the most royal blood of the Scottish Highlands crumpled in catch-as-you can fashion into a potato bag."[187] Hidden under a bunk, he begins to rethink his opinion of war. Later, on parade at Valcartier, he experiences his first troop inspection. When he is ambushed from behind by a big mongrel, Bobbie takes his cowardly attacker (who represents Germany) by the throat. The soldiers claim Bobbie's triumph as the first victory of the Princess Pats, exclaiming, "did you see Fritzie get the run?" Bobbie observes, "Now I knew. It had been war when I had been at the throat of the mongrel who had so wickedly assaulted me when I had not harmed him."[188] But, he sagely adds, "We had seen no war yet, we were just preparing. Somewhere some big mongrels of men must have attacked littler dogs of nations, and we were going to fight for the little dogs!"[189] The analogy equating the mongrel's ambush with the war's origins is false, but it made for effective war propaganda in the effort to attract volunteers. Bobbie and Pendy made a formidable team, and their adventures showed why more men were needed in the valiant but bloody struggle.[190]

On his return to Timmins, Munroe was hailed as a hero. On 29 January 1917, the *Porcupine Advance* announced, "Jack Munroe Home from the Front: Former Boxer and Mayor of Elk Lake Returning to the Porcupine." It listed the battles in which he had participated and the operations performed to restore his arm, the results of which he described in boxing terms as a "draw." The paper noted the further adventures of Bobbie Burns, who had returned to France, been gassed, but recovered and had come back to Canada with Munroe. What happened to Bobbie after the war remains a mystery.

Women as Active Participants

As in all wars, women as well as men played important roles. Women replaced men in some work situations, but mostly they performed their traditional supporting role at home—one that has often been underestimated.[191]

Women's main supporting role overseas was nursing, either at the front, or more often, in rear areas. About 2,500 Canadian women worked in hospitals in France and England to care for the wounded. Jessie Clarke of Evansville, Manitoulin Island, born 4 January 1886, worked for three months with the British Expeditionary Force, served in the US Women's Hospital (a charity organization), and then enlisted in the Canadian Army Medical Corps in February 1916. She served, with the rank of officer, in a number of hospitals in England and France. She sometimes fell ill herself, but worked until she was demobilized in June 1919.

The work of a nursing sister could be draining. Muriel Fell, also from Manitoulin Island, was born at Gore Bay on 26 September 1890 and enlisted on 18 December 1916. She served in at least seven different hospitals in England and was hospitalized three weeks with anemia before being demobilized in May 1919. Similarly, Evelyn McClelland of North Bay became so exhausted by her work that she had to be relieved from duties and caught influenza. Born on 21 April 1891, she enlisted on 3 February 1916 as a nursing sister, arriving in France during June 1917. By January 1918, she would be found unfit for duty at the front, though by August she was again ready to serve. She was instead discharged because of "strain of service." Her file stated that she "Had been at No.2 Gen. [Hospital] nearly eight mo[nth]s without leave and never off Duty ... Thin and debilitated." Handling wounded cases without a break must have been more than physically exhausting. At least three more nursing sisters (Irene Winifred Lamarche, Marion Georgina Soutar, and Eunice Weegar) and one doctor (Archibald H. McMurchy) came from North Bay. Lamarche had an affair with an officer, and the scandal forced her to return to Canada. Some Canadian nurses of British background can be hard to trace. Like Annie Saunders of Cobalt, many simply returned to the United Kingdom and joined the British nursing staff for the war's duration, rather than serving as Canadians.

On the home front, women worked hard to provide soldiers with "comforts," which could range from collecting money (for the Patriotic Fund, the Red Cross, or Belgian relief) to purchasing cigarettes, or knitting socks and organizing parcels with special treats. The *Sudbury Star* of 12 January 1915 describes the men's thanks for one shipment:

"The staff of the branch of the Bell Telephone Co received a collective acknowledgement from Copper Cliff boys now in France for Christmas boxes containing dainties and gifts which the girls thoughtfully forwarded." On 19 May 1917, the *Star* told of a Christmas parcel that had followed a Copper Cliff enlistee, James Duncan, all the way to Saloniki, Turkey, and then to Malta where he was recovering from his wounds. He gratefully acknowledged the women's work. Copper Cliff women even organized a formal Christmas Box Association.

Copper Cliff was not unique. A report summarizing the women's work appeared in the *Porcupine Advance* on 31 July 1918: "One of the officials of the Porcupine Consolidated Patriotic Club has prepared a summary of the amount of work done ... The Timmins Red Cross in the six months ending June 30th, 1918, made a record 700 pairs of socks, 202 suits of pyjamas, 2314 towels, 292 sheets, 407 pillows, 255 personal property bags, 648 handkerchiefs, 213 washcloths, 86 bed socks and 4 quilts." Similar lists from two other women's support organizations were also printed. The women of every town and village of the Northeast did the same. One letter from the front, printed in the *Sudbury Star* on 27 January 1915, read "thanks for your not forgetting"—especially since the soldiers detested European tobacco.

Women were expected not only to let their men go to war, but also to push men to enlist (fig. 6.9). By 1916 many official organizations and newspapers spoke against slackers and urged women to encourage enlistment. The Canadian government issued posters with few subtleties as to what was expected.

By the middle of the war, food shortages became a serious problem in Britain. Canadian women were encouraged to not waste food, plan "meatless days," and plant gardens to supplement their supplies, so more food could be sent overseas. In June 1917, the *Porcupine Advance* proclaimed, "Help Win the War by Eating Fish" and urged housewives to switch from meat and grains. Another article, on 10 June 1917, claimed, "Women Uniting for Food Conservation." The article told of a Timmins group that was educating housewives on the patriotic necessity of not wasting food. Young women from urban areas were encouraged to become Farmettes to help grow and harvest food. Since more than half the population was rural, farm women had to manage their farms while the men were gone, but also had gardens to tend, food to conserve, and children to mind. Yet many found time to volunteer for knitting bees with Women's Institutes.[192] Women's wartime contributions helped them achieve the right to vote after the war (Indigenous women and so-called enemy aliens were of course still excluded).

An important role, which mostly fell to women, was to write letters to the men on the front. While few of the letters survived because of the conditions there (they were useful for rolling cigarettes, among other things), soldiers in their own letters, constantly mentioned having received mail from home,

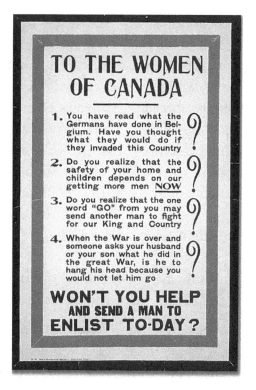

Figure 6.9. War poster appealing to women to persuade their men to enlist. (War Poster Collection, C 233-2-4-0-263, Archives of Ontario)

revealing how much word from home boosted morale. If mothers and wives needed a sign of life from their men, the men also needed signs that home life continued to sustain hope for a return to normal. Women were the main agents in this important activity though this emotional aspect of the war is difficult to document in depth.

Sharing the Burden of War; or Redistributing the Patriotic Fund

Nearly every community, especially in English-speaking Canada, made financial and material efforts to support World War I. Some collected for the Red Cross, some for displaced Belgians, some to buy machine guns. The largest organization to help families of enlisted men was the Canadian Patriotic Fund, modelled on similar organizations formed during the South African War. Over $48 million were collected between September 1914 and April 1919.

The postwar summary report in *The Canadian Patriotic Fund* (1919) notes that in August 1914 about 10,000 reservists or militiamen living in Canada were called to arms. The pre-war recession meant that many families were left with few resources: "Their wives and children were perforce left to live as best they could. Many of the men had been unemployed and had no reserve fund when the call came."[193] Other jobs had simply disappeared when war was declared and projects (like railways) cancelled. On 6 August the government announced it would recruit a contingent of 25,000 soldiers and within a few days more than that had enlisted. Who would care for their dependents? Privates in the Canadian army received $1 per day; in the field (when sent to the front), they received an extra ten cents' field allowance. Since the soldiers kept some money for themselves (for incidentals, tobacco, food), most assigned about $15 to $20 a month to their relatives as a separation allowance.

Many families could not survive on the allowance, and some cities and regions instituted a supplement, but often even that wasn't enough. "Patriotic" associations formed across the country to collect donations to support servicemen's families. The Patriotic Fund was the most important (fig. 6.10). It became a huge organization headed by national leaders with an Ottawa office and staff in place by late September 1914. Most cities and towns eventually had a Patriotic Fund branch. Two considerations were primary in providing support: the family's dependence on a soldier for income, and family need. The economic impact of enlistment became clear: the committees that reviewed families' needs tended to be parsimonious,[194] and the numbers who were eligible despite the stringent criteria reveal that for many, conditions must have been dire. Still, the fact that much of the Patriotic Fund remained unused in 1919 hints at the harshness of reviews of family situations. One study examined three Canadian cities and concluded that the fund primarily served to maintain social stability.[195]

Figure 6.10. War poster asking for donations to the Patriotic Fund.
There is an implicit promise that the family will be supported while the husband is at war.
(War Poster Collection, C233-2-5-0-268, Archives of Ontario)

The people of Northeastern Ontario donated to the fund through their districts. Cities and towns provided central collecting points. Circulars sent to workplaces suggested that each person might donate the equivalent of one day's pay, 75% going to the Patriotic Fund, 15% to the Red Cross, and 10% to other programs such as Belgian relief. In Algoma, for example, contributions were collected from 22 places, and relief committees were organized at Sault Ste. Marie and Blind River. By March 1919, $177,606.03 had been subscribed and $84,190.95 dispersed, of which $52,000 came from municipal grants. Some 312 individuals and families of the district received support. The surplus went to the central fund. Urban and industrial centres generally gave more than they received, while smaller towns and rural areas often had more needs than they could meet; for instance, in Temiskaming, Elk Lake donated $553 but the fund provided $7,178 to support 26 families, "including 16 families of James

Bay Indians who had enlisted" (see table 6.1).[196] As the previous chapter notes, Indigenous communities contributed generously to the Patriotic Fund.

Table 6.1. Northeastern Ontario Patriotic Fund contributions and disbursements by district/community between 1914 and 1919

District	Community	Funds subscribed ($)	Funds disbursed ($)	Families supported (#)
Algoma	Blind River	2,520	5,778	12
	Sault Ste. Marie (Algoma)	177,606	84,191	nd
Manitoulin	East	4,078	5,894	nd
	West	1,200	240	1
	Manitowaning	10,819	9,720	nd
Nipissing	Latchford	264	2976	nd
	Mattawa	6,575	14,800	50
	North Bay	≈95,000	101,320	450
Sudbury	Chapleau	6700	11,255	nd
	Copper Cliff	81,924	32,044	92
	Sudbury	125,540	58,113	181
Temiskaming	Charlton	216	6,550	nd
	Elk Lake	553	7,178	26
	Engelhart	1,400	15,231	nd
	Haileybury	54,702	21,601	nd
	Matheson	484	7,707	nd
	New Liskeard	5,812	28,961	58
	Porquis Junction	3,286	2,479	7
	Timmins/Porcupine	34,125	15,450	nd

nd = no data

Note: Table based on data in Philip H. Morris, The Canadian Patriotic Fund: *A Record of Its Activities from 1914 to 1919* (n.p., 1919).

The same patterns pertained throughout the Northeast: larger, richer places with industrial income could raise more funds than smaller, rural communities. However, after the war they faced a different situation. In Sudbury, where economic conditions worsened as the demand for metals fell when the war ended, the large donations to the Patriotic Fund were no longer available for relief. On 21 December 1918, the city council ordered that the "balance of the War Bounty Fund and Home Guard Fund be used for Soldiers' wives and families before Christmas."[197] However, postwar support was limited. Though veterans called each other "comrades," especially in the veterans associations (as they still do in the Royal Canadian Legion), the experience of war did not change the social structure of the country. If the Patriotic Funds were instituted so that families would not starve while the men were away, they made no provisions for rewarding soldiers well or creating equality. Once soldiers returned, they, not the government, were responsible for supporting their families. Sharing the burdens of war had limits.

Internment in Canada: Sault Ste. Marie and Kapuskasing

If being a POW in Germany was an ordeal, so was internment in so-called enemy-alien camps in Canada. Enemy aliens, immigrants from Central Power countries who had not yet been naturalized as citizens, were placed in internment camps along with enemy POWs. Indeed, one of the "services" northern Canada has provided has been to hold people in isolated camps.[198] The internment of Ukrainians during World War I has become fairly well known since the Canadian government's 2002 acknowledgement of the camps and creation of a fund to help educate Canadians about them. Of the 9,579 so-called enemy aliens interned, about 5,000 came from Galicia in the Austro-Hungarian Empire.[199] Most were ethnic Ukrainians, but about 2,000 were ethnic Germans and Austrians who had not been naturalized (some naturalized citizens were imprisoned as well). Toward the end of the war, leftists and objectors to conscription were also interned in the camps. In addition, more than 80,000 so-called aliens and enemy aliens (the terms were employed interchangeably by the press and public) were forced to register and report monthly to police, some until 1920. These were all immigrants who had been encouraged to migrate to Canada, and often enticed with offers of land and job opportunities.

In Sault Ste. Marie, the militia's armory served as an internment depot where those deemed a threat were processed before they were shipped to labour camps such as Kapuskasing. Some of the interned stayed in the Sault and worked for local industry (at the steel mill, pulp and paper mill, or canal locks). They were housed in rough barracks on Whitefish Island in the St. Marys River; their wages went to a government account though they could access some for incidentals. The internees received 25 cents per day (at the time, labourers received around $1 a day), thereby allowing the state to make a profit from prisoners.

The granddaughter of one internee, Cathy Beaudette, has found that at least 54 Sault Ste. Marie men were interned.[200] Her research has shown that the public knew of the internments. While morally unjustified, the actions met a low legal standard under the War Measures Act, which gave the government the right to curtail civil liberties. Local newspapers carried stories about the dangers posed by aliens, the process of incarceration, and the internment camp in Kapuskasing. Soldiers from the 51st Soo Rifles militia rounded up local aliens. On 13 July 1915, the *Sault Star* led with the headline "36 Austrians to Leave for Alien Camp Tomorrow," reporting, "interned alien prisoners, who have been taken in charge within the last few weeks, will leave under guard for the concentration camp at Kapuskasing, to which several other detachments of prisoners have been sent from the Sault in the past." The paper reported on the increasing number of prisoners at Kapuskasing, noting that money could be made: "Splendid Opening for Sault Merchants for the Sending of Supplies." As was often the case, patriotism and business went hand in hand. On 4 August the paper reported on the continued settlement of the Clay Belt despite the war and repeated that "there are now over 1,200 aliens interned there, and these with the soldiers of the guard makes quite a town, one which provides good business for those that are supplying it." By 1916, the war's demand for labour meant internments almost ceased, though the *Sault Star* and other newspapers kept propagating the dangers of alien threats to the war effort. The Sault was not alone in the hunt for enemy aliens. The *Porcupine Advance* reported on 12 December 1917 that about

400 aliens had been registered within the month, but the police chief intended to find and arrest some 30 who had not reported.

The "concentration camp" at Kapuskasing was a large complex hewn out of the northern Ontario wilderness (fig. 6.11). Located on the west side of the Kapuskasing River where the Ontario government intended to place an experimental farm to test the area for agriculture, the camp's isolation, controlled access, and the cold provided an ideal site. It was close to the CN rail line (MacPherson stop), 90 kilometres east of Hearst and over a hundred kilometres west of Cochrane. When the first prisoners arrived in January 1915, they found bush and cold. They had to build their own prison.[201] By early March, over 400 prisoners worked at cutting logs. The camp director described the work:

> 1. Clearing and stumping 1,000 [actually 1,200] acres of new land. 2. Erection of large barn on Experimental Farm. 3. Erections of bunk-houses, store-houses, fencing, etc. for troops and prisoners. 4. Making of roads in connection with station and farm. 5. Installing drains at station and farm. 6. Laying water pipes through station and farm.[202]

Figure 6.11. Kapuskasing Internment Camp. Prisoners lived under canvas until enough bunkhouses could be built. (Courtesy of Ron Morel Memorial Museum, Kapuskasing)

A thousand acres equals only one and a half square miles, but the clearing had to be done by hand, a challenge when taking out tree stumps or building roads while dealing with blackflies and mosquitos or snow and

-40 degrees. The wood was sold, so the government profited doubly from internment. A report published in 1919 described the housing:

> The prevailing type of accommodation in the remoter districts ... was modelled on the Canadian lumber camp. First a bunk-house, or series of bunk-houses, was erected, of log or frame construction, the bunks lining the walls, the heating supplied by stoves, and the whole made "healthy, clean, and decent," as demanded by the regulations. Around these were grouped the subsidiary buildings, with a liberal supply of open space to permit freedom of movement—all surrounded by barbed wire under the guard night and day of sentries whose boxes formed the final outposts of the establishment. Such, in the fourth year of the war, was the camp at Kapuskasing."[203]

Though men like Mike Bundziock of Cobalt, who had been beaten while being arrested, appealed their internment, nearly all appeals were denied.[204] Many simply could not understand why they had been arrested since they professed their loyalty to Canada.

Escape attempts usually resulted in capture, as happened with two escapees from Kapuskasing on 8 June 1918. They tried to go upriver, but were overtaken by a search party in four days. Though a few died while trying to escape, many were injured in accidents felling and moving trees. Many more became ill and some died, especially from tuberculosis, pneumonia, and influenza. Dozens suffered from severe mental and emotional instability, and had to be sent to mental hospitals or prisons.

All possessions and money were taken from the prisoners. Over $30,000 would never be returned, and confiscated property remained with the government.[205] At its height in 1916, this camp, Canada's largest during World War I, held about 1,500 prisoners under 256 guards. Following the Geneva Convention, Swiss, Swedish, or US (until it entered the war in 1917) neutral country representatives inspected the camp occasionally. In the first year, the guards were members of the 12th Regiment York Rangers of the Toronto militia led by Colonel F.F. Clarke (fig. 6.12).

Figure 6.12. Colonel F.F. Clarke and the guards from the 12th Regiment York Rangers
at the Kapuskasing Internment Camp.
(Courtesy of the family and Fairlawn United Church)

The militia members who had enlisted found themselves stationed in what they called "Canada Siberia." As well as overseeing their charges, they spent spare time hunting and fishing. They were gradually replaced by wounded soldiers and men thought fit more for guard than service at the front. This left a motley group of reservists and returned soldiers, some wounded, some shell shocked, in charge of reluctant internees. When a Swiss inspection pointed to the brutality of some guards, General William Dillon Otter admitted, "The various complaints made to you by prisoners as to the rough conduct of the guards I fear is not altogether without reason … and, I am sorry to say, by no means an uncommon occurrence at other Stations [camps]."[206]

Much has been written about the imprisonment of Ukrainian Canadians during World War I. and the indiscriminate and arbitrary fashion in which people who had been invited to come to Canada and to labour on its farms and in its industries and mines were treated. They had committed no crimes and had no chance to defend themselves. About a fifth of the prisoners were of German background. The discipline handed out to prisoners with German names is revealing: S. Konrad was assigned two days on bread and water for refusing to obey a guard order, W. Knittler received 168 hours of solitary confinement for insubordination, E. Hoyer received 72 hours of solitary confinement for using foul language in front of a guard.[207] It is past time to acknowledge the historical problem. German immigrants, too, had been enticed to Canada by officials, shipping agents, and publicity about "free land" in "Canada Das Land der Zukunft [Canada Land of the Future]."[208]

The incarceration of enemy aliens took place in a complex legal and labour situation during wartime. The public clamoured for incarceration in part because foreigners' loyalty was suspect and they supposedly took jobs from local miners, meaning mostly individuals who had been there longer or those of British background.[209] Imprisoning and isolating aliens in the hinterland was seen as the right solution, until in late 1916 a labour shortage meant that the government hired internees out to industry. Some were pardoned, but all were released only on promises of good behaviour and accepting the work—and this again placed so-called foreigners in competition with those who had not enlisted. The rules of war complicated the situation since some internees were officer POWs, who did not need to work, causing resentment among the rest. Enlisted POWs did have to work. Despite the tensions in the camp, much was accomplished that first year at Kapuskasing: "Between 1 May and 20 July 1915, 8,818 logs were cut, during the period 20 July to 1 September, 4,810 logs were cut, and between 1 September and 13 November, 6,911 logs were cut," resulting in over a million board feet of lumber (fig. 6.13).[210] Further, the prisoners roughed in 35 miles of roads and cleared acres of bush. Over 115 buildings existed by 1916. Sub-camps in tents were established once the lumber in the immediate vicinity had been exhausted (fig. 6.14).

Work conditions caused tensions at Kapuskasing. As in the Sault, internees were paid 25 cents a day. Many men resisted by working slowly. At least once they went on strike because of the treatment by the guards, the conditions of work (inappropriate clothing and lack of nutritious food), and the push for production.[211] The guards brutally suppressed the strike: "The casualties included one prisoner killed, nine critically wounded, and four others requiring medical attention."[212] Some prisoners simply could not stand the isolation, hard labour, or brutality and took their own lives. However, in keeping with wartime censorship, the local newspaper, the *Porcupine Advance,* on 11 April

Figure 6.13. View of the Kapuskasing Internment Camp, with the sawmill on the left.
The river is the Kapuskasing River.
(Courtesy of the family and Fairlawn United Church)

Figure 6.14. Five Mile Outpost, Kapuskasing Internment Camp. Although the main camp
had bunkhouses, at the sub-camps, prisoners lived in tents, even in winter.
(Guard Souvenir Album, Robert Atkinson collection, Laurentian University Archives)

1917 gave the camp a glowing report card and noted that a thousand more internees were coming from Kingston to Kapuskasing.

By late 1916, other Canadian camps were being closed as internees were assigned to work in industry. Kapuskasing received their leftover prisoners. Some refused to work and were imprisoned anew. Moving from one trying situation to another, one group of 39 who refused industrial work received sentences of hard labour at the Burwash Industrial (Prison) Farm in the bush just south of Sudbury (like the Sault Armory, another holding place).[213] Mostly, these men were innocent of any crime. Among the sad cases of those assigned to an industrial plant, George Werenka wrote to the minister of justice about the refusal of the Canadian Copper Company of Sudbury to grant him sick leave and threatening him instead with arrest. He pointed to others who had been jailed for six months because of refusal to work.

As late as December 1918, some 2,200 prisoners remained interned, of which 1,007 were at Kapuskasing. About 1,700 were ethnic Germans, including 800 merchant marines captured in the West Indies. In providing these statistics, Otter claimed 516 individuals were "hostile to authority and British rule, 134 agitators, 54 insane and 5 incurable with tuberculosis."[214] The camp closed in mid-1920. Kapuskasing's internment camp remains a dark chapter in Canada's history and the precise character of the issues has only begun to emerge.

Notes

Notes

CHAPTER 7

Away from Home, Wounded and Dying

Family Connections and Canada

During the war, the *New Liskeard Leader* printed letters written home by local soldiers. These letters are now available, along with many others, in the Canadian Letters and Image Project (CLIP). They repeat a litany of complaints, assertions, and descriptions typical of soldiers' letters from the front to almost everywhere in the British Empire. However, some also contain material unique to Northeastern Ontario.[215] Soldiers retained the world view and attachments formed in their prewar lives, even if some military history is written as though soldiers were either heroic individuals or all shared the same national characteristics.

The letters give a glimpse into the lives of World War I soldiers and their need to share their experiences. From Belgium, Captain Robert S. Robinson wrote to his wife in New Liskeard on 21 May 1915 about the destruction amid which daily life proceeded: "I could not have imagined that anything, even an earthquake could cause such devastation. Notwithstanding, a number of the business places are carrying on as usual, and a big trade is done with the soldiers billeted in the town." He noted heavy losses, especially in the cyclist company that carried messages under his command: "The work is very exposed and I fear our casualties will be higher than any other arm of the Division." The CLIP collection also contains a series of letters by John McLean (754576) from Echo Bay, who had enlisted while working in Sault Ste. Marie. He noted frequent thefts, and wrote to his mother on 21 December 1916 about the fate of her Christmas cake: "I got a box last night … and could tell that there had been a cake in it …" He commented ten days later on a normal pattern of service, as the men rotated into the trenches for three or four days, then out to recuperate, the respite allowing them to socialize behind the lines.

Letters in the *New Liskeard Leader* describe the soldiers' enthusiasm early in the war, then the mud, the lack of information about what was happening elsewhere, and especially all the deaths. At first the soldiers wrote with bravado about how easily they would beat "the Huns" (insulting slang for Germans, referring to Attila the Hun, who had terrified the Romans). Similar statements were made throughout the British Empire early in the war.[216] However, the Northeasterners' letters reveal a distinctly regional perspective. Alex Cadman (57035), a prospector born in Scotland who had been in the 97th Algonquin Rifles militia, wrote his mother in Haileybury on 30 October 1915: "As for mud it has Liskeard, Haileybury and Cobalt beaten hollow." Other letters try to share the excitement of the experience, as when Alf Johnson sarcastically wrote on 5 October 1915 to a friend in New Liskeard:

It's a great life. As long as it doesn't rain, you can enjoy yourself. But what a queer war, yourself and the enemy both hidden away along miles of sand bags, barbed wire and dugouts. Of course the artillery are the biggest trouble in the day time, and the rifle fire is kept up at night, by the use of flares, which looks just like a fireworks display, but the only thing is you keep ducking your head when the bullet whistles over. In each Company's line of trenches is a telegraph and telephone station, and we get scraps of news about what is going on in the line.

When Captain Robinson wrote to his wife on 31 May 1915 about the death of family friend Lieutenant A.N. Morgan, he lamented, "he will be missed in his social and business relationship in New Liskeard and vicinity." He noted that Morgan had had photographs of his wife and the Robinsons on him when he died.

Letters like this show how men tried to maintain ties with friends and family, partly because at first men who enlisted together served together. While still in training, Billy Thomas (47961) of New Liskeard wrote to his parents on 24 June 1915: "It is only two months since my pal, Fat [Angus McLean (47910)] and I joined ... We worked hard to get on in the drill, and we were as far advanced as some who have been on the job for five months." He described their desire to serve together: "When they picked out the draft [for those who would go overseas], Fat and I were pretty down-hearted, as all the other Liskeard boys were in it, and we were transferred to C Co., but we were only with them half a day when Sergt. Hicks was after us for the draft. We sure jumped at it." The desire to get to the fighting was at first common, but they wanted to do it with their buddies from home.

Letters from France and England show that soldiers kept track of each other, as if they had become a broader, new family overseas. Captain Robinson wrote to a friend on 1 August 1915 that he "met [Angus, known as "Fat"] McLean, [Billy] Thomas and [Sam] Bilow [633284]," all with the 48th Highlanders, 15th Battalion. In a similar vein, Billy Thomas reported to his mother on 26 July 1915 that he had seen Bill (W.S.) Smith and Tommy Weaver and that "Fat [McLean] is fine." Wilbert Beswitherick wrote on 24 October,

> We just came out of the trenches last night. I saw the boys from the north there, Billy Thomas, Angus McLean, S. Bilow. We met in the trenches yesterday. They were all looking fine and hearty. I am going to try and see Enos Grant some day this week. I heard Capt. Robinson was here and shall try to hunt him up. I also saw Tommy Faught [41648] who used to work at the [train] station.

Similarly, Angus McLean wrote on 8 October 1915, "Bill [Thomas] and I were over to see Claude Kennedy [36140] yesterday. Tommy Faught went with us. I haven't seen Capt. Robinson for six weeks." Bill Thomas wrote on 17 September 1915: "Angus [McLean] and I looked up Claude Kennedy, with Tommy Faught as our guide. Claude is looking fine. We also had a chat with Capt. Robinson. He was surprised to see us. He looks fine. Angus was talking to Herb Durand [63263] last night. We have not run across Enos Grant yet." The circle of acquaintances repeats the same names as though members of an extended family of northerners were having weekly get-togethers behind the front lines.

Like the group from New Liskeard, soldiers from Echo Bay also kept track of one another. John McLean's letters confirm the camaraderie and concern that resulted from having men who knew each other in the same unit. Before his death on 2 February 1917, McLean often wrote his mother about the young men she must have known (fig. 7.1). He asserted, in a letter written 16 November 1916, "All the lads are fine and we are still together and wont Be Broken up any more now. we dont know where the fellows we left in England are." On 22 November, he confirmed, "all the [Echo] Bay Boys are fine and are together now in one platoon." A month later, on 31 December 1916, he penned, "Ernie was not in the trenches at all this time I think he is working on a cook kitchen. I haven't saw him now for about 2 weeks. But I saw Willis last night and all the fellows were fine and came out good only Jack Junior and his [wound] was only slight for he walked to a dressing station."

McLean's letters often refer to others from Echo Bay and Sault Ste. Marie, including James Swan (754867), with whom he planned to go Edinburgh on leave. On 19 October 1916, he wrote home to clarify a rumour. His letter shows how community connections supported soldiers:

> Well say who on earth ever told that darn lie about Clarence Hurley [754395 of Echo Bay,] he is no more dead than I am. Some people must have darn little sense to tell the like of that. The fellow that died was in the 123 B[attalio]n on the boat behind us. Clarence is here in the same hut as Fred is in his platoon too. They are together. I will write to [M]rs [P]eet and tell her too. Say I got a box of fifty cigarettes from a girl in Toronto last night. She is a cousin to that Lieut Madden that was at the [Echo] Bay and her chum sent Paddy Newhouse a box too and some mcd [MacDonald brand] chewing [tobacco] and he didn't smoke so he gave me his cigarettes and one plug of the tob[acco] so that left me with 100 cigarettes and to-day I got the old chum [brand of chewing tobacco] so I am all right for while now.

In the same letter he regretted the separation from his friends: "Jack Smith is away takeing a course of some kind I dont know where he is he left Bramshott [training camp] the same day we came here and he didn't even know where he was going himself. George Nash [754693] is away too and Neil Munro. Neil is ful corpl. now. I dont know where any of them are."

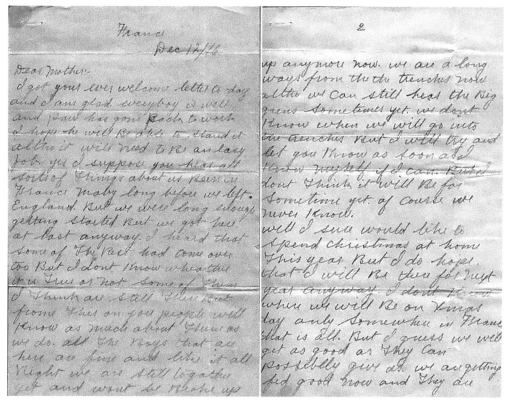

Figure 7.1. Letter from John McLean to his mother, 12 December 1916.
(Courtesy of the Canadian Letters and Images Project)

However, just two days earlier, McLean had reported that "all the lads are fine Jim McBain is in the transports with the mules." The importance of being together appears to have been understood by military leaders, though it is not often noted by historians. However, as more men died or were captured, and replacements filled the ranks, the platoons were increasingly made up of strangers.

Those who were prisoners of war must have felt very alone, far from families at home and the brotherhood that had developed in training and in battle. Sudbury's John James Gutcher (27196), who enlisted 20 September 1914, became a POW between 24 and 29 April 1915 with serious gunshot wounds to thigh, stomach, and left arm. He died on 21 May in a German hospital, perhaps still weak from the influenza in January. His death report states that he "died of wounds while a prisoner-of-war at Oberhausen," in Germany's Rhineland. Carpenter Ernest J. Blackie (16245) from Spring

Bay on Manitoulin, born on 21 November 1891, also died in captivity. He enlisted on 23 September 1914 at Valcartier, and went missing on 24 April 1915. By 9 June, officials knew he was a POW at Bischofswerda, then Giessen, and finally Weidenau by Siegen. Blackie died there "on or around 21 October 1917." The official report does not give a cause of death.

The toll taken on the families at home is starkly brought to light by the letter of condolence from a cousin, Mary Jane McLean, to John McLean's parents after his death in February 1917:

> I saw in the Echo Bay News the account of the death of your noble brave young son. You are again called upon to go through another "Gethsemane". May He who went through his "Gethsemane" sustain you in your hour of deep sorrow. Dear friends you certainly have had your share of sorrow. But remember the words "He whom the Lord loveth he chasteneth." You have been sure tried but the man of sorrows and acquainted with grief understands it all. He will give you that peace that passeth all understanding that the world cannot give and the world cannot take away. From my own experience I can recommend Him I have tested Him and found Him not wanting. For certainly is a grand thing when we can come to God with all our sorrows and burdens. He can make our burdens easy and He can help us to say "Thy will be done."

The empathy and religious fatalism helped with grief.

The mail system reinforced soldiers' ties to home as they faced new and unfamiliar experiences. Many disliked England, with its rainy climate, expensive food and tobacco, more rigid class system, and other differences. On 30 September 1915, while still in training in England, John McLean wrote about army life:

> Well say you may be sure anything from home to eat would be mighty welcome for we have to Buy anything we get over here that is fit to eat and This pay I didnt get any at all we have to have $20 to our credit and they Kept it out of this pay I will only get 2.40 on the 15 of next month and 7.20 at the end of this month so it leaves me pretty hard up But I Borrowed 2 so I guess I can manage. the tobacco is the worst I always smoke cigarettes and it cost an awfull lot but I cant smoke the tobacco at all. tell Jim to send me some chewing tobacco McDonald [brand] for there is times I cant Smoke when I can chew I havent chewed for 2 years now and I hate like the duce to start again But it is pass time and it takes your mind off your long hike and

a Route March when you cant smoke. I am sorry you didnt get the money But I guess no one got it at all yet and it may take quite a while before you do get. you see it has to go from here to the Canadian pay office at London and then to Ottawa …

… I would die on this food it is the same thing all the time. fish or cabbage and I think the fish came down in the Rain the time of the flood and Noah kept them in the ark. they smell like that anyway all the fellows I have Been talking too say They are fed Better over in France but not in the Hospital. So if you ever hear of me been in the Hospital send something to eat right away. well I am cirtanly sick of this country I would not take any money and live here. I Think I have almost crossed the country now and I never saw any place I liked But you Know the climate is differant and They have such a differant way of doing everything … The Farms are differant not laid out the same nor worked the same. everything is dear. well a cup of tea is 1 penny in Canada we got it 2 for 5. Beer is cheaper and that is about all we pay 3 shillings a month for our washing and at Niagara it was 1.25 … I wouldnt trade the Coleman place stones and all for the Best farm I have seen here. of course we may be in a poor part of the country But I dont like The climate …

McLean was writing early in the war, while still in training, but he reveals the profound effect their service was already having on himself and his buddies:

Oliver and Willis is fine But say I can notice an awfull diffrance in all the [Echo] Bay fellows They seem to have Changed all togather since we left there last winter. This trip has been worth a whole lot to all of us we didnt know what home and Friends were till we came over here but we know now and will be able to settle down and take some pleasure out of home when we get Back again.

Nearly two months later, on 22 November 1915, McLean was in France: "I would rather be here then in England anyway." McLean was not alone in his opinion. On 18 July another soldier from New Liskeard, Reuben C. Pettifer (57905), wrote from England to a friend, "This is a very nice country, but I would rather have Canada. I would not live here 'on a bet.'"

Mail allowed families and community groups to fulfill soldiers' practical and emotional needs, as McLean's requests for tobacco and food show. The parcels reminded soldiers that home continued to support them and was waiting for their return. Families sent huge quantities of tobacco over the ocean, as well as socks and photos, raincoats, sweets, and cakes. As chapter 6 has discussed, many groups in Canada, mostly women's leagues, also sent packages to the enlisted men from their region. A group of men still training in southern Ontario wrote a letter of thanks for one package to the *New Liskeard Leader*, which published it on 10 April 1915:

> Dear Editor: Would you please express our extreme thanks for the useful presents or gifts which the boys from New Liskeard received last Tuesday, 6th April? We all appreciate the unity of spirit between those who are not able to join us in this great cause, but lots of work remains to be done at home. Business as usual will help quite a lot ...

> When we get away from here we will write you more fully. There were three or four more parcels than men, but we will distribute them. Below is the list of the men who received the parcels and acknowledge the kindness of the New Liskeard ladies.

The letter identified three corporals from New Liskeard (Vout, Adams, and Plant), then listed the names of all who had received parcels: A.E. Dent, G.E. Martin, A. Johnson, S. Penn, G.S.W. Adams, L. Corp. Molyneaux, C. Lundberg, F. Warner, D. McKenzie, Corp. E. Vout, Corp. C. Plant, Reuben Pettifer, and J. Gemmell. The list suggests that the gifts created a sense of connection and support, even when the giver was not personally known to those who sent the packages. Families and community organizations kept up a steady stream of parcels, to the point that the system of delivery was overwhelmed in 1917. The interaction reinforced ties to home—not only to Canada, but also to soldiers' specific places of origin.

Newspapers provided another tie between fighting men and their home regions. After major battles, newspapers often published letters from local men. For example, after Ypres in April 1915, Tom Weaver wrote a friend who then submitted his letter for publication:

> I see there are other Liskeard boys enlisting. I get some northern papers. We were in some fighting at the Ypres. If anyone thought we did not do much, they would think differently if they saw the casualty list. We were right in the midst of it, and I know it, too. It is a miracle how any of us got through. It just simply rained shells and shrapnel, and bullets were coming by thousands.

When one soldier requested a subscription, the editor returned his money and offered a free subscription to any soldier who asked. On 2 January

1918, the *Porcupine Advance* printed a letter of 16 November from Lieutenant Fred Kenning, an artillery officer in Belgium: "Was sent over here for the time on the 10th of last month, and … I should think it was worse than the Somme. The mud here is simply Hell … Heard about Mike Warnick a few days ago … Have seen Harry Holland, Walter Manley, Battersby (Major soon), Slim Clark, Charlie Pierey, Geo. Insole; in fact lots of boys from the North Country." He gave news of his companions as well as himself: "Came over from England with Tommy Coe and Nick Carter from Cobalt, Yink Thorne, Tartray and Stevens are all O.K … I am in the 7th Canadian Siege Battery and it is big stuff. Guns drawn by tractors." Writers often identified themselves and their companions by place of origin, and their letters, published in the papers, let those on the home front know how soldiers from their community were faring.

Letters also allowed newspapers to supplement official war news with the perspective of an eyewitness account from someone readers knew. For example, Das Dosley of the Porcupine region, "affectionately known as the 'Old Settler'" greeted all Timmins friends in a letter in the *Porcupine Advance* on 13 November 1918, entitled "The Huns Can Sure Run, says Old Settler." Letters from the front were censored while those sent from England went uncontrolled through regular mail. Most of the censored letters tended to be positive, but some described the stark brutality of war, as in this 20 June 1915 letter from Herbert Durand, which was published in the *New Liskeard Leader*:

> In an attack that we made on the Germans, out of 33 in our platoon there were only 11 left, and there were only 320 left out of our Battalion of 800. When we made the attack the bullets were so thick that I thought that it was sure death for me. The three fellows who went ahead of me were killed as soon as they got over, and I had to crawl over them, and wherever I looked some one was falling. It sure was fierce. So many of our officers were killed that there was no one to lead us, so we all just laid in the grass till dark, and then came back. We crawled up close to their trenches as we could without being seen and threw our bombs in, and shot any German who stuck his head out. When it got dark enough I got up and ran, and just then they threw up a flashlight [flare] and about 200 bullets whizzed by me. I thought I was the luckiest man on earth to get back alive. A little fellow who used to wait on table with me was carrying bombs, and a piece of shrapnel hit one of the bombs, causing it to explode, and he was blown to pieces.

While still training in England, Norman Browning acknowledged what awaited them in France. He wrote his aunt on 9 July 1915, "There is awful slaughter going on at the front. I have seen six train loads of wounded go past and the hospitals around here are crowded." The heavy losses left large holes in small, tightly knit communities like Spring Bay and Wikwemikong on Manitoulin, Echo Bay just east of Sault Ste. Marie, and Moose Factory on James Bay.

The soldiers' backgrounds reflected the demographics of the Northeast: prospectors from Cobalt, farmers from Manitoulin, hunters from Moose Factory, and many labourers, sometimes identified by trades such as carpenter or electrician. There were also bank clerks, students, and among the officers a general store manager and engineers. Surprisingly, the number of Canadian-born registered much higher in the nominal rolls (60% to 80%) of northern battalions (119th, 159th, 227th, and 228th) than in the whole contingent, which contained a slight majority of British-born soldiers. That may explain the northerners' strong ties to Canada and to their specific places of origin. Though their length of service varied considerably, surprisingly many of the enlisted from Northeastern Ontario survived the war, partly because of the high proportion in the Forestry Corps and Railway Troops and thus mostly away from the front lines.

Wounded but Working

What happened to the endless number of wounded soldiers? Some had to be demobilized and sent back to Canada. Most received medical treatment for bullet holes or artillery shrapnel, and then returned to the battlefield after recuperating. Some who suffered shell shock went through a long process of institutional rehabilitation. Others never recovered from mental or physical scars that remained unrecognized or were dismissed. Some were given less strenuous jobs away from the front (e.g., Donald Cameron of Sudbury [ch. 3] and John Munroe of Timmins [ch. 6]).

John Major (7999)'s story illustrates the fate of the seriously wounded soldier. A member of the 51st Soo Rifles militia, Major joined the 127 Sault-area volunteers who left for Valcartier on 20 August. He signed his attestation on 23 September 1914 and was found fit to serve. Like many from the Sault, he was assigned to the 2nd Battalion (identified with eastern Ontario). They shipped overseas for more training, and arrived in Belgium in February 1915, where they suffered huge losses at Ypres (fig. 7.2). One year later, in February 1916, he was shot in the head and legs: "Wounded at Walverghem [Belgium] on 9 Feb/16 taken to #2 clearing station at Bailleu for 1 day, #2 Can[adian] Station Boulogne for 17 days. Then Taplow [England] for 5 months. Thence here [Uxbridge]. 1 operation." His progress from clearing station to Uxbridge is typical: the wounded were taken first to medical stations where dressings were applied and cases sorted, and then to hospitals for treatment. Major's wounds included a three-by-three inch gash on his left leg and another above the right knee. They were treated and he received skin grafts. By 15 March the doctor found "improvement," by 20 March there was "less discharge," by the 25 March he was "feeling fine," and on 18 April the doctors reported, "graft taken, a slight discharge." When released he was still in pain, but his physical state was considered "good" and his disability "healed" with "no complications." By 16 August 1916, the army deemed him "recovered," and he was discharged.

Figure 7.2. The chaos of bush, sandbags, trenches, and supplies near Mount Sorrel (east of Ypres) must have made moving around difficult and may have accounted for some of the deaths. (*Canada in the Great World War* [Toronto: United Publishers of Canada, 1919], 3: facing 268.)

Major experienced a steady recovery. His file shows a gap of months, followed by information about his new position: on 4 December 1917 he was reassigned from the 54th District Canadian Forestry Corps to the 51st, at Inverness, Scotland. In March 1918 he was stationed with the 117th forestry company, still at Inverness, and then transferred to the base depot in London, and by April he was serving at the forestry headquarters in Sunningdale, England. He rotated among forestry units, but after May 1918 remained at Ashford where he served as clerk (with more pay than a soldier) until he was transferred to Camp Witley to wait for demobilization. He returned to Canada in March 1919. In sum, this wounded soldier received a desk job fitting his experience as a prewar clerk and helped administer the important timber sector.

A sadder case is that of pipefitter James Hume (455121) of Steelton, who represents one of the many "patch 'em up and put 'em out" approaches to wartime medicine. Hume enlisted on 5 August 1915, left Canada with the 159th Battalion, and was then drafted to the Royal Canadian Regiment on 26 June 1916, headed for France. He served in a field ambulance until he reported sick on 6 January 1917 with a serious tendon problem in his right knee. On 27 January, he returned to field duty after being checked at a medical clearing station. During January and early February 1917, he went through at least nine clearing stations and hospitals. Reassigned to field duty on 6 February, on 21 February he rejoined his unit and died on 9 April 1917: "During an attack at Vimy Ridge he was acting as a stretcher bearer and while searching for wounded in the shell holes, he was shot through the head and instantly killed by a bullet from the rifle of an enemy sniper about noon on April 9th, 1917."[217] For Hume, knee damage merely meant return to duty and death.

Post-traumatic stress created a different kind of wound. On the eve of Remembrance Day 2017, Bruce Wood wrote about his grandfather, Wilfred William Wood (199341), a veteran of World War I.[218] Born in Little Current on 24 December 1894, teamster Wilfred Wood signed his attestation on 26 April 1916, enlisting at Port Arthur. He gave his stepmother, a resident of Massey, as his next of kin. According to his grandson, "Bill" was a "much-changed man" when he returned to Canada in 1919 with shrapnel in his body. He could not hold a steady job or drive, and he frequently became confused. He suffered seizures, which became more frequent and more severe as he aged. Bill's son (Bruce's father) remembered Bill as physically present but emotionally distant, and Bruce's father had no role model to follow as he raised Bruce and his two brothers. The effects of Wood's war experience reverberated through generations.

A friend's death could have as much impact as a physical wound. A conscript from Kagawong, Frederick Matthew Graham (30389720) only arrived in time for the last days on the front at Mons. However, on 5 November 1918 he watched as another Manitoulin conscript, James Percival Merrylees (3037597), was shot. Merrylees died that same day. Graham survived and, like many others, was haunted by the question of why he, and not Merrylees, had survived.

The Many Ways of Dying

World War I created new ways of dying. Lucien Joly (1004191), a woodsman from Blind River who enlisted on 29 December 1915 with the 227th Battalion, was standing on a parade square in Warlus, France, when a German bomber flew overhead, dropped a bomb, and "instantly" killed him and more than thirty others on 24 September 1918 (fig. 7.3). Though he had been transferred to a unit that frequently encountered death in battle, the 3rd Battalion Canadian Machine Gun Corps, he died on parade. Many of the places where soldiers went, fought, and died, have been mentioned in this book. In most cases, how men died is harder to establish. As in all wars, family members wanted to know the circumstances of their relatives' final moments. In letters to the military authorities, they asked for precise information. Sometimes the soldiers' comrades could give details, but sometimes none could be supplied by anyone.

1. NO.	2. RANK OR RATING	3. SURNAME	4. CHRISTIAN NAMES
1004191,	Private,	JOLY,	Lucien,

5. UNIT OR SHIP	6. DATE OF CASUALTY	7. H.Q. FILE NO.	8. RELIGION
3rd Battalion, Canadian Machine Gun Corps.	24-9-18.	649-J-4092.	Roman Catholic.

9. CIRCUMSTANCES OF CASUALTY	10. NAME, RELATIONSHIP AND ADDRESS OF NEXT OF KIN
"Killed in Action." While on parade in No. 1 Camp, Warlus, he was instantly killed by the explosion of a bomb dropped from an enemy aeroplane. 11. LOCATION OF UNIT AT TIME OF CASUALTY	

NOTE:—Items 12, 13 and 14 are not to be completed until grave is permanently located.

12. CEMETERY	13. LOCATION OF CEMETERY	14. GRAVE LOCATION	15. REGISTERED NO. OF GRAVE
Manquetin Communal Cemetery Extension,	6½ miles West of Arras, France.	Grave ____ Plot ____ Row ____	

16. PHOTOGRAPH OF GRAVE TAKEN	17. EXPOSURE NO.	18. PHOTOGRAPH OF GRAVE AND CEMETERY SUPPLIED TO

19. FURTHER PARTICULARS ON REVERSE SIDE OF SHEET.

Figure 7.3. Report on the death of Lucien Joly (1004,191). (*Circumstances of Death Registers*, microform sequence 31, p. 517. Courtesy of Library and Archives Canada)

The *Circumstances of Death Registers* (*CODR*) were kept by the Records Office of the Overseas Ministry, and are available online at the Library and Archives Canada website. The registers came from the military's attempt to keep track of its personnel, and they document the death and place of burial (where known) of Canadian Expeditionary Force personnel between 1914 and 1918, and even into 1919, when some succumbed to their wounds. Often, the records say only "Killed in Action," usually meaning the soldier was killed instantly, or simply disappeared. Some soldiers had no official burial, but at least this record gives an indication of where they died or vanished, and in what battle.[219] The stories below probably do not differ significantly from those of other deceased soldiers, for all shared the chaos of the battlefield. These stories do illustrate the kinds of information families at home would have received, and they reinforce the fact that as the war progressed, Northeastern Ontario soldiers served in many different military units.

Many stories simply end in mystery: a soldier marches into combat and is never heard from again. At Ypres, early in the war, Lance Corporal Thomas Brennan (6774), a North Bay clerk, was killed in action at some point between 22 and 30 April 1915 while fighting with the 1st Battalion. Peter Grant (7970), an electrician from Sault Ste. Marie, was "reported missing, now for official purposes assumed to have died … on or since 22 April," and George Jarrett, a labourer from Steelton, also died "at some point between 22/26 April."[220] More is known about William Adam Irving (27355), former deputy sheriff of Little Current:

> Previously reported Missing, now for official purposes presumed to have Died … On the night of April 23/24 1915, word was received at Brigade Headquarters that a tree had fallen across the road near Fortuin, thereby preventing the ambulances going up for the wounded. Private Irving, who was nearby, volunteered to go out and cut the tree. He took an axe, climbed into one of the ambulances, and started for Fortuin. Shortly afterwards the ambulances were hit by shell fire, and the drivers taken prisoner, but no information has since been received concerning Private Irving.[221]

He was never found.

Similar silence surrounds the fate of many others. John Blair Fraser (409708), a farmer from Gore Bay, died in Belgium serving with the 37th Battalion. The *CODR* indicate that Fraser must have died unnoticed on 19 April 1916: "Previously reported missing, now Killed in Action … The disappearance/death took place near Zillebeke."[222] Wilbert H. Hounsell (7986), a labourer from Steelton, also died at Zillebeke: "Previously reported Missing, believed killed, now Killed in Action … 26 April 1916 … in the explosion of an enemy mine, under our front line trenches at Hill 60" (fig. 7.4).[223] George Edward Baxter (486628), a farmer from Little Current, was killed in action at Zillebeke on 3 June 1916, and his name appears on the Menin Gate Memorial to the Missing.[224] Augustus John Hartung (754837), a farmer from Gore Bay, also went "Missing in Action" on 27 September 1916. Likewise, on 18 November, Henry or Harry Barnhart (177498) of North Bay, a member of the 87th Battalion, went missing in action.

Others simply described as "Killed in Action" include James Henry Hollenbeck (754440) from Iron Bridge, who died 29 June 1917, and Ralph Bolt (754075), a telephone linesman from Richards Landing, who was "for official purposes presumed to have died … on or since 28-8-18."[225] George Lawrence Beatty (754128), a butcher from Manitowaning, went missing near Lens, France, on 3 September 1917 and was later classified as killed in action.[226] Lorne Bradley (406966), a student from Manitowaning, who had enlisted in Sault Ste. Marie, also went missing. According to the *CODR*, Bradley "died 'On or since 2-10-16' … Previously reported Missing, now for official purposes presumed to have died."[227] Many of these men are remembered on the war memorial at Vimy, which lists the names of 11,825 Canadians killed in France, whose bodies were never recovered. They simply vanished in the chaos of battle.

Figure 7.4. Zillebeke, Belgium. (*Canada in the Great World War* [Toronto: United Publishers of Canada, 1919], 3: facing page 266.)

Many other soldiers found graves in France and Belgium, but little else is known about their fates. Thomas Edgar (46573), a steelworker from Steelton, was "Killed in Action" in the "vicinity of Ploegsteert" while serving with the 15th Battalion on 11 January 1916, and lies in Belgium.[228] John Angus (410005), a butcher from North Bay, went missing on 18 November 1916, "fighting with the 38th Battalion near Courcelette." Officially he was "Killed in Action," and the *Circumstances of Death Registers* state that he was buried at Regina Trench Cemetery in France.[229] Reginald Adshead (1006145), a lumberman from North Bay, is buried with six other members of the railway troop; they all died on 4 April 1917. Lance Sergeant Roy James Henley (453580) from North Bay died 26 July 1917 and was buried at Villers Station Military Cemetery in France. Even when the soldier obviously had died, his burial place could remain a mystery. On 16 September 1916, Charles Holmes (121707) from Manitowaning "took part with his Unit [60th Battalion] in the attack on 'Zolleern Graben Trench' near

Courcelette and was killed by a shrapnel from an enemy shell. Body not recovered for burial."[230] In some cases, because of the powerful artillery, there was no body to recover (fig. 7.5).

Figure 7.5. Courcelette, on the Somme. (*Canada in the Great World War* [Toronto: United Publishers of Canada, 1920], 4: facing page 80.)

Passchendaele (31 July to 10 November 1917) cost so many lives that the military bureaucracy often limited itself to the words "Killed in Action." Records with no further explanation include those of James George (754342), a woodsman from Blind River; Pulford Bishop (1004188), a farmer from St. Joseph Island, Orland James Morrow (649387), a bank clerk from Sudbury; and Mattawa-born Russell McIntyre (1003078). The records of Sapper Arthur Duquette (1007104), serving with the Canadian Railway Troops when he was killed in action on 1 November 1917, do not explain whether he died because of enemy bombing behind the lines or because he happened to be at the front line at the wrong moment.[231] "Died at Paschendaele" is all the story these men, and many more, have.

Many, perhaps the most fortunate, died. James Simington Wilcox Ironside (7987), a clerk from Sault Ste. Marie, "was shot through the heart by a bullet and killed while attempting to get over the parados [mound at back of trench]" during the retirement at Ypres (22–26 April 1915). Gordon Cheer (55585), a farmer from Richards Landing on St. Joseph Island, died instantly on 4 April 1916 while on sentry duty near Wytschaete, Belgium. On 19 April 1916, Edgar M. Burritt (409678), a native of Cameron Township near Mattawa but a clerk in North Bay when he enlisted, was "Killed in Action … [while] fighting with the 13th Battalion near Zillebeke."[232]

Those with lethal wounds obviously suffered a worse fate. David George Cooper (7950), a carpenter from Steelton with the 2nd Battalion, "'Died of Wounds' [to his head] at No. 3 Casualty Clearing Station" on 23 April 1915.[233] Martin Brennan (57374), a "tram man" from North Bay, sustained a shrapnel wound in the right femur on 8 April 1916. He "'Died of Wounds'" later that day at "No. 10 Casualty Clearing Station" near Lijasenthoek, Belgium."[234] On 8 June 1916, George Drury Hawkins (193352), a fisherman from Blind River, died "of Wounds when his unit, the 7th Canadian Machine Gun Company, moved through "the trenches at Maple Copse" in Belgium.[235] Sapper Lloyd Boal (648079), a plumber from North Bay, suffered gunshot wounds in the back and legs on 18 May 1917. The wounds led to tetanus. Boal entered a Casualty Station on 30 May and died on 2 June. Another who suffered a lingering death was Corporal David MacGregor Neilson (1003190), a machinist from Sudbury: "Whilst with his Company in the vicinity of Écourt St. Quentin, on the night of 16th September 1918, an enemy shell exploded close to him, and he was severely wounded in the legs and body by shrapnel. He was taken to No. 1 Canadian Clearing Station, where he died two days later."[236] Maurice Archibald Brown (754040), an iron worker from Hilton Head on St. Joseph Island, "suffered from gas poisoning, caused by a gas projector landing in the entrance of the dugout in which he was sleeping, the effect from which he died later at No. 9 Canadian Field Ambulance"[237] on 30 December 1918. William Joseph Danis (755008), an Indigenous paper maker who lived near Sault Ste. Marie, "'Died of wounds' [1 March 1917] at No. 6 Casualty Clearing Station … [and] is buried … [near] Noeux-les-Mines, France."[238] Gunner James Ronald Chapman (318008), a student from Sault Ste. Marie, suffered gunshot wounds on 29 October 1917, and then lingered in agony for two days.

Table 7.1. How soldiers from Northeastern Ontario died in World War I

Official cause	Soldier	Regiment number	Additional details	Date deceased
KILLED IN ACTION	Reginald Adshead	1006145	-	4 April 1917
	Karl John Anderson	755009	Shrapnel	9 September 1918
	John Angus	410005	-	18 November 1916
	Robert John Armitage	438932	-	30 September 1917
	Joseph Atkinson	755186	Gunshot	27 August 1917
	Joseph Aubin	448870	BNR	3 October 1916
	Joseph Alexander Baker	255178	Shell explosion	26 October 1917
	Roy Barr	754115	-	8 August 1918
	George Edward Baxter	486628	-	3 June 1916
	Peter Gordon Beaton	754072	Gunshot to head	25 April 1917
	George Lawrence Beatty	754128	BNR	3 September 1917
	Percy Goudin Beck	184203	-	9 April 1917
	Frank Arthur Bennett	2115702	Shrapnel	29 August 1918
	Pulford Bishop	1004188	Passchendaele	26 October 1917
	Darcie Oliver Borland	658036	-	2 September 1918
	Thomas Brennan	6774	BNR	22–30 April 1915
	Robert Broadford	1003993	Shrapnel	3 September 1918
	William Browne	754051	Sniper bullet	1 October 1917
	George Bulmer	409679	-	15 August 1917
	Edgar M. Burritt	409678	-	19 April 1916
	Dougal Campbell	657123	-	28 September 1917
	John Louis Campbell	3205153	Shrapnel	16 August 1918
	Norman Finley Campbell	3034780	Machine gun	27 September 1918
	Thomas Edgar Campbell	657790	Gun shot	18 September 1917
	Wilbert John Campbell	754184	Wounds	1 October 1917
	William Thomas Carr	754162	-	27 August 1918
	John William Carroll	1003077	-	8 August 1918
	Robert Chalmers	1003425	BNR	8 August 1918
	Charles Gibbon Chambers	452956	-	13 June 1916
	James Ronald Chapman	318008	Gunshot wounds	31 October 1917
	Thomas Charbonneau	85295	-	24 November 1916
	Charles Alfred Cheer	754173	-	28 September 1917
	Gordon Cheer	55585	-	4 April 1916
	Isban Allen Clark	3107207	Shrapnel	6 November 1918
	Roy Clingersmith	55590	Trench mortar	2 July 1916
	George William Collins	486615	-	21–22 October 1916
	Robert George Connelly	178084	Machine gun	30 September 1917
	Edwin Ernest Cook	1003020	Passchendaele	15 November 1917
	Thomas Currie Dallas (Dr.)	755152	Machine gun	29 September 1918
	Guy Dawkins	1003068	Wounds	6 April 1918
	Arthur Deacon	177956	-	21–22 October 1916
	George Howard Dobson	114063	-	14 November 1917
	Hugh Dolan	3033040	-	30 September 1917

Arthur Edward Doxsee	648257	Shrapnel	9 August 1918
Edward Dubroy	648265	Shrapnel	30 August 1917
Arthur Duquette	1007104	Passchendaele	1 November 1917
Wilbert Leonard Durrell	3230999	Shrapnel	13 November 1918
Thomas Edgar	46573	BNR	11 January 1916a
William Samuel Ellery	54203	-	16 September 1918
Sidney George Elms	141902	Gun shot	August–– September 1917
Nicholas England	754285	Wounds	10 August 1918
George Robert Erb	1003176	Passchendaele	14 November 1917
Sidney John Ferguson	754302	Shrapnel	16 August 1918
Hubert Forbes	754926	-	1 March 1917
Michael James Foran	3231476	-	26 August 1918
Joseph Fortin	754303	Gun shot	24 August 1917
John Blair Fraser	409708	BNR	19 April 1916
William Clifford Fyfe	782337	Machine Gun	1 November 1918
Arthur Gagnon	1042060	Shrapnel	2 September 1918
Joseph Charles Gallagher	472167	Artillery fire	3 June 1916
Frederick Rendell Garrison	1003074	Shrapnel	22 July 1918
James Garrow	648341	Machine gun	2 September 1918
Peter Gaudette	407075	BNR	26 September 1916
James George	754342	Passchendaele	22 October 1917
Hugh Milroy Gilchrist	1003034	-	8 August 1918
Albert Giverman	755067		31 October– 1 November 1917
Peter Grant	7970	BNR	22 April 1915
Matthew Green	454376	-	16 September 1916
George Alfred Griffiths	755080	Bomb from aircraft	29 August 1918
James Henry Grimes	1004355	Shrapnel	30 August 1918
Charles Hammond	754419	-	27 August 1918
Mathew J. Hancock	408730	Gunshot wounds	11 April 1917
Cecil Harris	486631	-	19 April 1916
John James Harron	467365	-	28 September 1917
Bernard Harvey	177689	-	21–22 October 1916
Percy Hatten	754383	Shrapnel	10 April 1918
Roy James Henley	453580	-	26 July 1917
Robert Richard Hill	158110	Shrapnel	6 August 1918
Ernest George Hodder	754423	Sniper bullet	30 September 1917
Charles Holbrook	648425	Sniper bullet	15 August 1917
James Henry Hollenbeck	754440	-	29 June 1917
Charles Holmes	121707	Shrapnel, BNR	16 September 1916
Wilford Henry Holmes	486632	Trench warfare	28 July 1916
Harold Victor Hotton	754393	-	4 October 1917
Wilbert H. Hounsell	7986	Mine explosion	26 April 1916
John Simpson Hughson	754439	-	1 March 1917
James Hume	455121	Sniper bullet	9 April 1917
Clifton Alvin Hunter	755002	Shrapnel	5 May 1917
James Simington Wilcox Ironside	7987	Shot	22–26 April 1915

	William Adam Irving	27355	BNR	23–24 April 1915
	John Jenkins	1003825	Wounds	15 April 1918
	Jeremiah Jondreau	754480	Gunshot	3 April 1917
	Frank Lavalley	754529	Shrapnel	2 September 1918
	John Maguire	204684	Wounds	9 September 1917
	Harvey Marshall	486556	Gunshot wounds	11 April 1917
	Russell McIntyre	1003078	Passchendaele	30 October 1917
	Vincent Misinishkotewe	755136	Wounds	14 September 1917
	Thomas William Moore	754670	Wounds	30 August 1918
	Orland James Morrow	649387	Passchendaele	26 October 1917
	Samuel Muirhead	754644	Shrapnel	23 August 1917
	Thomas Niganiwina	754697	Shell explosion	20 August 1918
	Frank Nighswander	754694	-	9 April 1917
	George August Oldenburg	259303	Sniper bullet	27 August 1918
	James Turley Patterson	47921	-	8 August 1918
	Andrew Peltier	754723	Gunshot wounds	7 April 1917
	Percy Edwin Pifer	1003720	Machine gun	8 August 1918
	Franklin Proulx	754718	-	27 August 1918
	Clarence Clyde Rush	3034782	-	30 September 1918
	Leslie Scott	1003299	Passchendaele	17 November 1917
LETHAL WOUNDS	William Joseph Lloyd Boal	648079	Tetanus	2 June 1917
	Samuel Blackburn	755187	Fever	4 December 1917
	Martin Brennan	57374	Shrapnel	8 April 1916
	Maurice Archibald Brown	754040	Gas poisoning	30 December 1917
	David George Cooper	7950	Head wounds	23 April 1915
	William Joseph Danis	755008	Wounds	1 March 1917
	George Drury Hawkins	193352	Wounds	8 June 1916
	David MacGregor Neilson	1003190	Shrapnel	18 September 1918
NEAR FRONT	Oren Crowder	754167	Shell explosion	28 June 1917
	Percy Cameron Hall	1003088	Shell fire	29 August 1918
	James Edward Higgins	754994	Bomb fragment	15 July 1918
	Edgar H. Houldsworth	Lt.	Shell explosion	15 April 1917
	Lucien Joly	1004191	Bomb from aircraft	24 September 1918
MISSING IN ACTION	Henry/Harry Barnhart	177498	BNR	18 November 1916
	Lorne Bradley	408966	BNR	2 October 1916
	Ralph Bolt	754075	BNR	28 August 1918
	Augustus John Hartung	754387	BNR	27 September 1916
	George Jarrett	7989	BNR	22–26 April 1915
CAPTIVITY	Ernest J. Blackie	16245	-	21 October 1917
	James John Gutcher	27196	Wounds	21 May 1915
ACCIDENT	Alfred McDonald Campbell	743	Run over	21 December 1916
	Lawrence Dupuis	648278	Hit by truck	29 January 1918
SUICIDE	Lorne Wallace Rumley	754815	Gunshot	1 November 1918

NOTES: BNR = body not recovered

Table 7.1 lists the official cause of death for some Northeastern Ontario soldiers who died in the war. It appears that most died of shrapnel or gunshot wounds. A soldier's life was always at risk, however. Fighting in battle was deadly, but service near the front could be lethal at any moment. Lieutenant Edgar H. Houldsworth, a telegraph operator from North Bay, who had been with the 97th Algonquin Rifles militia, died on 15 April 1917 "while fighting with the 3rd Pioneer Battalion … Whilst standing outside his tent near La Targette … at 5 p.m.…an enemy shell exploded in close proximity to him and he was killed instantly."[239] Oren Crowder (754167), an engineer from Richards Landing, died "near Lens in France … While returning from a working party on the early morning of June 28th [1917], the enemy were shelling heavily the trenches through which the party had to pass. One of the shells exploding close to Private Crowder, pieces striking him, in the back and groin, instantly killing him."[240] Even guard duty could be lethal. James Edward Higgins (754994), a steelworker from Sault Ste. Marie serving with the 58th Battalion, was killed on 15 July 1918 near Arras in northeastern France: "While standing on duty at his post at Neuville Vitasse in the front line, he was hit by a fragment of an unexploded 'Pineapple' bomb and instantly killed."[241] Percy Cameron Hall (1003088), a moving picture operator from Chapleau, died "instantly" on 29 August 1918 when hit by enemy shell fire as he was "taking horses to water."[242] Very few died of gas; bullets or shrapnel killed most.

Some died in accidents that could have happened in peacetime. Alfred McDonald Campbell (793), a prospector from North Bay, was member of the 4th Divisional Supply Column of the Canadian Army Service Corps. On 21 December 1916, he was pronounced "Dead on arrival at No. 6 Canadian Field Ambulance" after being hit by a truck:

> The Court of Inquiry convened to investigate the cause of death of Private Campbell found that he was accidentally killed while in the performance of his duty and while safeguarding traffic, and that the contributing cause was a defective headlight and that no blame could be attached to the driver of the truck.[243]

Similarly, having survived the battle of Passchendaele, on 29 January 1918, Lawrence Dupuis (648278), a surveyor from Bonfield serving with the 159th Battalion, was hit by a truck as he walked along a highway: "The Court of Enquiry convened to investigate the circumstances of death of Private Dupuis was of the opinion that he was accidentally killed by being struck by a motor lorry, the driver of which was in no way to blame."[244] While modern machinery of war dealt death in large numbers on the battlefield, soldiers also fell victim to what were basically common traffic accidents.

The slaughter continued for four years. Some historians regard Canada's most significant contribution to World War I as the 100 days between the Battle of Amiens on 8 August 1918 and the Armistice of 11 November.[245] Of the 240 deaths investigated here, 88 of them—more than one-third—occurred during those 100 days. Few anticipated the approach of the Armistice, and more soldiers from Northeastern Ontario would die in the last 11 days. On 1 November, William Clifford Fyfe (782337), a farmer from Richards Landing, perished along with his entire unit: "During an attack on Valenciennes on the morning of November 1st, 1918, under heavy machine gun and artillery fire, all members in the section he belonged to became casualties, and no information could be obtained relative to the actual circumstance under which he met his death."[246] Unaware that the horror would end ten days later, Sapper Lorne Wallace Rumley (754815), a farmer from Barrie Island with the 119th, took his own life: "At 6:20 o'clock on the morning of November 1st 1918 he was in a tent with four others North East of BAPAUME, when his comrades were awakened by the sound of a rifle shot. On investigation Sapper Rumley was found lying on his back with the back of his head blown off, and his rifle between his knees covered by his blankets. His death was caused by self-inflicted injuries."[247]

These terse summaries of so many battlefield and battlefield-related deaths make a reader aware that young men born in the 1890s lost in the lottery of life, but so did their countries. These young men would not have children and grandchildren, nor would they return home to contribute their talents to the development of Canada in the 20th century. The cost of earlier conflicts had been mild by comparison. The deceased must have been familiar to almost everyone in Blind River, Gore Bay, Kirkland Lake, Manitowaning, Mattawa, Moose Factory, Richards Landing, or Thessalon.

Even in larger places like North Bay, Sudbury, Sault Ste. Marie, or the Tri-Towns, residents would have been well aware of the unfolding, seemingly endless, tragedy as the casualty figures mounted, week after week.

Notes

Notes

Part 3
Unending War: Memories and Remembrances

Wars do not end when the fighting stops. They are extended by memories and commemorations that can lead to justifications and historical revisionism. No matter what the cause of the war is, its effects are long-lasting. War commemorations persist through time as symbols that draw people together as a country, region, or community, even if the war itself resulted in carnage. Northeastern Ontario took part in the nation-wide commemoration of World War I, creating holidays, events, parks, and monuments in remembrance. Here *remembrance* means all the different ways the past can be memorialized, highlighted, and privately or publicly given lasting attention. Traditionally, military victories have been celebrated by parades, triumphal arches, and too many speeches lauding generals and politicians, and Northeastern Ontario had some of these. But other acts of remembrance immediately acknowledged the sacrifice and contributions of the region's own people.

The twentieth century experienced massive wars and seemingly endless killing, and people repeatedly sought ways to acknowledge their losses, to grieve, and to heal. Before 11 November was officially designated Remembrance Day by the Canadian government in 1931, various peace celebrations occurred. For example, Armistice Day, designated in 1921, coincided with Thanksgiving and emphasized the military victory and the end to conflict; Remembrance Day shifted the focus to honouring all who had fought and died. [248]

Another approach to remembrance involved building monuments, and this became an era of cenotaphs. In Europe, Britain, the Commonwealth countries, and the United States, the countries that had participated in major conflicts—on both sides—built monuments to their victory or to their participation and losses. Many communities sought a physical focal point to commemorate their war losses. The honours that had once been reserved for capital cities or military leaders now acknowledged common soldiers and the places from which they came. Northeastern Ontario was at the forefront of this trend.

CHAPTER 8

Celebrating Peace
and Building Monuments

While the horrors of trench warfare made thousands of combatants want to forget their ordeal, many who fought wanted to acknowledge the end of killing and celebrate the importance of peace. When Timmins unveiled its first World War I memorial in September 1927, the *Porcupine Advance* reported that the main speaker

> Gen. Sir William Furse [of Scotland; one of the war's commanding generals] spoke eloquently and fittingly. He referred to the large percentage of men enlisting from the Porcupine district and the great service they had given to King and country and the Right [meaning the cause]. He referred to the horrors of war and the *senselessness* of it, and expressed the belief that nations could settle their disputes by arbitration.

The general's sentiments were shared by many in Northeastern Ontario who built monuments, commemorated the dead, and celebrated the peace in the years following World War I.

Celebrating Peace in Sudbury and Copper Cliff

The postwar emphasis on peace can be seen in the "Peace Celebration" that took place on 18 and 19 July 1919 in Sudbury (fig 8.1). The festivities began on Friday evening with a performance by the Great War Veterans' Association Orchestra. Speeches by politicians, judges, and religious leaders preceded the dancing, which started at 9:30. Symbolically, the "Peace Waltz" preceded a one-step—then a popular version of the fox trot—named "League of Nations." After 20 more dances and an intermission, the program announced, "At midnight all present will join in singing O CANADA and 1st verse of RULE BRITANNIA."

Figure 8.1. Sudbury Peace Celebration poster, 1919.
(Courtesy of Greater Sudbury Public Library)

Events on the next day opened with a 9:30 a.m. bicycle race from Sudbury to Copper Cliff, followed by stunt-flying displays over both towns. Teams in a Copper Cliff versus Sudbury baseball game competed for the "Peace Cup." After acrobats and vaudeville shows, a Grand Parade included community groups and politicians from both towns. Another competition involved the best decorated residence, commercial block, or store. More baseball, including ladies' teams, was followed by interesting sport competitions: "boxing in barrels, tilting the bucket, kicking the football, throwing the baseball." The winning team of the first round of baseball played off against the British American (mining company) team, an event augmented by more stunt flying. The evening closed with dancing and fireworks, ending with "God Save the King." For this community, peace meant sports competitions and personal enjoyment.[249]

The dove of peace, not the sword of war, dominated the celebration, which focussed on the chance to return to normal summer activities. Marching troops were replaced by parades featuring civic leaders and community groups. Instead of warring armies, sports teams competed for victory. Even the technology that had developed so rapidly provided peacetime pleasure, as aerial combat became stunt flying; a plane ride cost a hefty $10 for 10 minutes. In the immediate postwar era, peace provided more cause for celebration than a costly victorious war. The Armistice Days held to mark victory during the 1920s often ended by applauding peace. After a few years of celebrating peace with such events, however, nearly all Northeastern Ontario communities turned to more permanent ways to remember the conflict and its toll of lives.

Copper Cliff, an Inco company town, built the Copper Cliff Memorial Community Hall in 1936 as a memorial to all the company's deceased. Designed in the style of a half-timbered Elizabethan manor house, it contained a lounge auditorium, gymnasium, and kitchen, emphasizing what a community living in peace could enjoy. A bronze tablet unveiled in 1937 lists "the men of Inco towns who gave up their lives during the Great War 1914–1918." Some of these towns have disappeared or been amalgamated with Sudbury. The full first and last names of 29 from Copper Cliff killed during World War I are listed on the tablet, while fatalities from the other Inco communities are simply numbered: Worthington 2; Bruce Mines 5; Coniston 9; Garson 5; Creighton Mine 7; and Crean Hill 1. The mining company seems to have kept detailed records, undoubtedly reflecting the fact that these were all company-controlled towns. The local legion originally suggested the creation of the hall, which served boy scouts and girl guides as well as company events for decades. The late building of the hall shows that commemorating World War I continued until the next great conflict.

North Bay's Bronze

If asked where the largest bronze statue stood in Canada before 1923, many would probably answer Ottawa or Toronto. In fact, in 1922 North Bay unveiled an eight-foot bronze soldier on a tall pedestal.

The idea of a memorial park dedicated to those who died had been proposed in North Bay in December 1918. In many countries, halls or parks were considered the appropriate places to acknowledge sacrifice and allow gatherings for commemoration. In North Bay, raising money and site planning began by March 1919. During 1920, license fees from the circus and fines from the town went to a Soldiers' Memorial Fund overseen by the Great War Veterans' Association. School children voted on the form of the memorial and, in May 1921, the city purchased park land.[250] On 18 September 1922, large crowds attended as the Lieutenant-Governor of Ontario unveiled the monument. According to *The North Bay Nugget*, the ensemble of base, column, and soldier rose to a height of 26 and a half feet (fig. 8.2). The cost of $15,500 was borne by a population of 10,000. One minute of silence, a roll of drums, the "Last Post," and the presentation of arms preceded the lowering of flags. School children sang "They Shall Sleep in Poppy Land," composed by Mrs. Frank Mackie of North Bay. The ceremony ended with "O Canada," the sounding of "Reveille," and "God Save the King."[251] The combination of martial music and state anthems reinforced the idea of a strengthened community emerging from a shared military enterprise. The resources invested in the monument emphasized

Figure 8.2. North Bay's World War I monument rises more than 26 feet in height.

North Bay's commitment to maintain ties between the deceased and those who survived.

The North Bay monument is similar to many of the time. By using pedestals, nearly all monuments forced viewers to look up to the soldiers, just as previously generals on horses had towered above the common people. Here the bronze soldier holds the symbol of victory, a laurel wreath, in his right hand. He looks down with a contemplative gaze, perhaps suggesting reflection on the great struggle, but certainly he exudes no attitude of triumphant militarism. This cenotaph did not list names, though schools, churches, colleges, and railway stations in North Bay feature plaques with lists of those who served and died in the war.[252] For instance, the artistic Canadian Pacific Railway plaque in North Bay (fig. 8.3) honoured those employees who lost their lives in the war. Those who came together to grieve and commemorate their dead were not just villages, towns, and cities, but also other kinds of communities, such as parishes, workplaces, and schools, seeking remembrance and healing.

Figure 8.3. CPR memorial plaque, North Bay.

Sault Ste. Marie's Week of Discovery (1923) and the New Ontario Soldiers' Reunion

Anticipating many visitors for a large soldiers' reunion planned for 4–8 August, *The Sault Daily Star* speculated on 26 July 1923 that people coming to Week of Discovery (a celebration to honour the founders, discoverers, and contributors to the Sault's early development) would find Sault Ste. Marie "too modern." The paper suggested that locals should reproduce the northern stereotype by wearing "an Indian suit or hunting boots." Visitors, it argued, would want to see an "Indian camp" and "primitiveness," and everyone was reminded not to forget to tell them "how many wolves you killed last year."

By 27 July, the paper had become more serious and invited the public to commemorations and drumhead (religious military) ceremonies. The Great War Veterans' Association band and Scottish Highlanders (of the 48th Battalion, in which many soldiers from the Northeast had served) would arrive on 3 August from Sudbury. Veterans would be participating in the re-creation of a military attack in a specially built trench imitating what they had experienced at the front. The next day, a full page in the paper listed the street carnivals, dancing, and festivities to accompany the more serious events, as well as the unveiling of a series of statues and plaques about the history of the city. The *Star* announced that people had already opened their homes to 1,000 visiting veterans. On opening day, 2,000 visitors were in the city; 200 veterans had arrived from Sudbury. The replica trench (named Snargate after one on the western front) had been constructed. On 6 August, 20,000 spectators watched as 3,500 veterans from the 2nd, 119th Algoma, and 37th battalions, accompanied by local groups, marched in a huge parade for Amiens Day (the date of the last offensive in 1918, though the battle had officially begun on 8 August). The 119th Algoma was the local battalion and many Northeasterners had served in the 2nd Battalion, while the 37th had been raised by local militia leader Colonel Penhorwood. That night, a regatta and a simulated night attack brought an end to the military part of the week.

On the next day, the civic part of the celebration started with the dedication of a plaque to the explorer Étienne Brûlé, the first known European to have seen Lake Superior. The souvenir brochure lists the

11 historical tablets below and their locations, acknowledging the Ojibwa as the first inhabitants of the area (fig. 8.4). On 8 August, an audience of 3,000 watched "Indians stage Hiawatha." The event extensively involved local Indigenous groups. They provided the main actors in all the presentations of Longfellow's play poem, *Hiawatha* (fig. 8.5). Though the play offered a version of the noble savage theme, the brochure dedicated a full page to the actors: "Miss Wabunosa, who plays Minnehaha, is a very good-looking young lady, whose families have been leaders among the Ojibways for generations. Her brother Albert is one of the directors of the play, in which he plays the part of Pau-Pau-Kee-Wis." Longfellow had been inspired by Ojibwa legends, which set the story at Sault Ste. Marie. Symbolically, the brochure cover (fig. 8.6) featured an Ojibwa canoeing, and the play received as much coverage as the war commemorations. The *Star* asserted that the events had drawn 10,000 visitors. This brief outline only touches on the activities of the week.

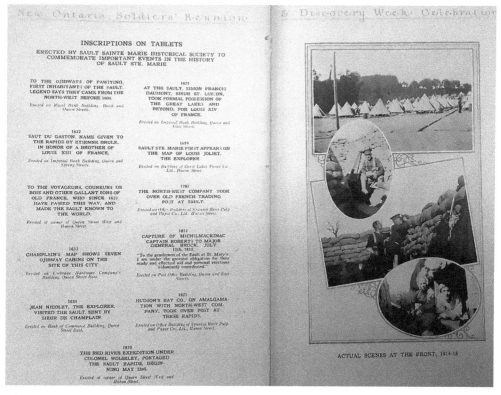

Figure 8.4. Week of Discovery brochure, Sault Ste. Marie, 1923. (Courtesy of Sault Ste. Marie Public Library)

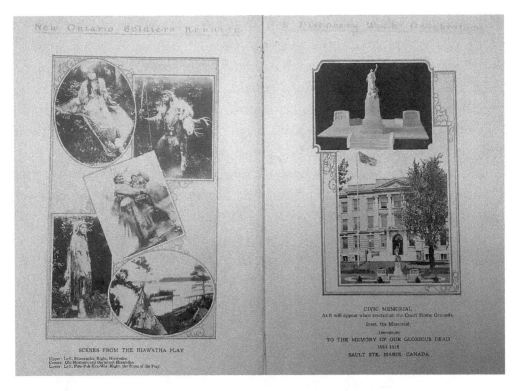

Figure 8.5. *Hiawatha* photographs from Sault Ste. Marie's Week of Discovery brochure. (Courtesy of Sault Ste. Marie Public Library)

Given the size of the city (pop. 22,000), the Week of Discovery was a substantial and well-organized performance of history and remembrance. Looking back, a surprisingly large role had been assigned to Indigenous culture.

During the 1923 Week of Discovery events, a huge granite block served as a temporary memorial. When Sault Ste. Marie built its war monument a year later, it gave the task of design to Alfred Howell, who created several Canadian war memorials during the 1920s (fig. 8.7). He employed allegory and symbols that one commentator found contradictory: "Atop the statue is a woman with oak leaves raised high in her left hand; her right holds a sword pointing down. Under her left foot is a shield under which a male cowers yet his hand is on a German helmet. Is it Civilization triumphing over Barbarism?"[253] The writer continues:

> Two bronze panels on the monument are also by Alfred Howell but point to a very different message from that of the bronze woman and man, one

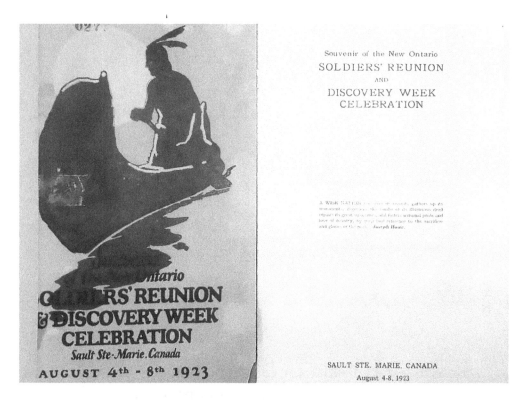

Figure 8.6. Cover image, Sault Ste. Marie's Week of Discovery brochure.
(Courtesy of Sault Ste. Marie Public Library)

that is not at all triumphant. In the first panel, a group of soldiers stand tall, looking resolute, stalwart, and strong. They are bidding farewell to loved ones, a daughter, brother, father, and mother. The scene radiates confidence and well-being … The second panel conveys something else entirely. A group of twelve soldiers … make their way to a front-line dressing station or field hospital. Several of the soldiers are wounded, one on a stretcher, another with his arm in a sling, two more with heads hung low. Even the healthiest-looking appear worn down, emaciated. The juxtaposition of the panels offers a powerful statement about war that is anything but triumphant.

Men go off to war full of robust vigour and enthusiasm, ardent and confident. They are keen to take their role in the Great Game, worried about speculation that it might all be over by Christmas. They have no idea what they are getting into. When reality rears its ugly head, all the eagerness and confidence is gone.[254]

The necessity of peace displacing war could also be read into Howell's Sault monument, in that the contrast of those going to war with those returning proclaims the futility of the effort.

Figure 8.7. Sault Ste. Marie's World War I monument.

For relatively small cities, the communities of Northeastern Ontario produced ambitious monuments, in terms of per capita spending, time allotted, and size, in comparison to monuments built in some of the larger Canadian cities. Like much of English Canada, Northeasterners saw themselves as part of the larger British Empire: the editor of the local newspaper and one of the organizers of the soldiers' reunion in Sault Ste. Marie even asked the imperialist poet Rudyard Kipling to supply a poem for the cenotaph.[255] That poem honoured the dead "from little towns, in a far land" and was inscribed on the front of the cenotaph.

In the smaller centres, the war was commemorated with fewer resources but a similar desire to acknowledge sacrifice and service. Much of the region's reflection on the meaning of the conflict became embedded in stone. Building cenotaphs became almost an industry in the 1920s and 1930s, and much attention was paid to the Vimy monument in France. Thousands of Canadian parents, widows, and politicians attended its unveiling in 1936, and writing about it too has become a mini-industry. Most Canadians are familiar with the image of the Vimy Memorial, which has been reproduced on the current Canadian $20 bill. Yet far fewer Canadians would know how Manitoulin Islanders or those in White River and Wawa or Mattawa and Cochrane commemorated the grim reaping of 1914–18. If Vimy served for nation building, in smaller places monuments also reinforced community identity.

Manitoulin to Moose Factory

The large Manitoulin monument that stands in a park west of Mindemoya began as a simple statue at the centre of the road between Mindemoya and Providence Bay, a place known to many as Monument Corner. Among the earliest Canadian monuments, the 18-foot statue was unveiled in 1921. At the top, a soldier stands at rest, hands folded on top of his lowered rifle, his job completed (fig. 8.8). The soldier's symbolic rest ended when a drunk driver knocked over the monument in September 1959. It was moved just south into the park, and eventually became part of the larger ensemble commemorating later wars as well.

Figure 8.8. Manitoulin's World War I monument. (Courtesy of Tim Laye, Ontario Memorials)

A veteran of World War I, James (Jim) Wilson (1003745) of Gore Bay inspired and directed construction of the original monument. It was dedicated on 15 September 1921 to those who had died during World War I on the battlefield, from battlefield injuries, or as prisoners of war.[256] Both township councils (Carnarvon and Campbell) and individuals contributed money to acknowledge some of those who died. However, the names on the original pillar are a partial list with some from World War II added to the base.

At Little Current, a similar resting soldier stands atop a pillar (fig. 8.9). The names on the side of the monument raise questions about the documentary history of Northeastern Ontario. The stone carver had as much difficulty with the sole French name (fig.8.10) as the military bureaucrats had during the war: James Francis Valliquette's (486659) name also appears variously as Velliquette and Valiquete in his file. Why he is on the monument at all is unclear since he was born in Renfrew and was a member of the 51st Soo Rifles militia when he enlisted with the 37th Battalion at Niagara. Valliquette arrived in England in December 1915, went to France with the 13th Battalion in April 1917, and was killed in action on 5 July. In places like Little Current, New Liskeard, and Moose Factory, the names do not always coincide with those in the official service files. An author who has examined the New Liskeard cairn found: "To my astonishment and disbelief, there were mistakes on the Cenotaph. Several names were misspelled."[257] In New Liskeard, at least, it seems that family members offered the names that were to adorn the cenotaph; given the inconsistencies in service files themselves, it's difficult to say, a century later, what the "right" name is.

Figure 8.9. World War I monument, Little Current

Figure 8.10. Detail of World War I monument, Little Current.

Manitoulin Island takes remembrance seriously. The many plaques, museums, and monuments at Gore Bay, Kagawong, Wikwemikong, and elsewhere offer a formidable tally acknowledging those who served. Given the high numbers who enlisted from these smaller communities, where the losses tore larger holes in the social fabric, monuments became a means of permanently honouring the deceased and offering closure for the living. Nearly every little community built a raised platform, erected a bronze statue, or established a memorial wall or garden. Northeastern Ontario is dotted with war monuments, a fact that seems unknown to those who write about Canadian memorials.[258] The monuments offer a place for reflection and sharing grief. Military wreaths or Christian symbols, especially crosses and crucifixes, frequently adorned the markers, underlining the commonality of suffering.

Echo Bay contributed many men to the Canadian Expeditionary Force in World War I. Afterwards, the small village commemorated its dead with a quite different monument (fig. 8.11). The usual soldier-on-a-pedestal monuments imply that one should look up to those who fought and died. At Echo Bay, the viewer looks up at an angel carved out of white marble. Using an angel creates a more sacred approach, hinting perhaps that the deceased has joined the holy choir. The angel has retained its delightful contours, while the names below are badly weathered. Part of John McCrae's poem *In Flanders Fields* is reproduced in relief on the base.

Figure 8.11. Echo Bay World War I monument. (Courtesy of Lisa J. Buse)

A great contrast to the charming Echo Bay angel is the simpler ensemble at Thessalon, where once again a soldier stands at rest atop a column. The number of names stands witness to the great sacrifices made by small communities. Hundreds attended the mid-1923 unveiling (fig. 8.12). The criteria for inclusion on the monument speak to the ambition that fuelled such acts of remembrance: "In compiling this list of names, it was considered advisable to make the list comprehensive enough to include all the surrounding country of which Thessalon is the natural centre ... The list comprises names of fallen men from Nestorville on the west to Parkinson on the east, the idea being to make it a monument in which the whole country would be interested."[259] A few months later, the Soldiers' Memorial Committee acknowledged that they still had not raised one-third of the $3,000 cost of the monument, despite the help of the Imperial Order of the Daughters of the Empire (which raised $1,000). The debt took years to settle. The monument stands on the west side of the Thessalon River. Seen from the front, the soldier stands in quiet repose. One author, who noted that the Thessalon soldier's statue had hardly weathered and had kept the contours of its design, attributed its survival to the Italian Carrara marble.[260]

Figure 8.12. Unveiling of the Thessalon monument, 1923.
(Courtesy of the Thessalon Public Library)

The public space around cenotaphs can be used in ways that combine remembrance and civic identity. Haileybury's monument was erected in 1925, and like North Bay's, it lists the war's main battles on the sides and the deceased on the front. On Dominion Day (July 1) in 1927, beauty contest winners posed in front of the large obelisk-style monument (fig. 8.13). The combination of war memorial and beauty pageant may at first seem incongruous, but beauty contests are also about identity and civic virtue (Miss Haileybury, Miss Owaissa, Miss Latchford), as the speeches and duties of beauty queens demonstrate. By posing on the monument steps, flanked by guards with rifles at reversed rest, the young women represented their communities, standing with the honoured dead who fought for them.

Figure 8.13. Haileybury's World War I monument, in 1927. (Courtesy Robert Montpetit)

At the northern end of the region, in Moose Factory, a large polished granite block memorializes those who served in both world wars (fig. 8.14). It illustrates a style of monument, angular, with jagged edges, which has come into vogue since the 1990s, as can also be seen at Timmins. Honouring those who served in both wars has become commonplace in remembrance, as a means to update World War I cenotaphs that have weathered badly. Using granite instead of sandstone will provide the permance most family members and communities want.

Figure 8.14. Moose Factory war memorial. (Courtesy Paul Lantz)

The Private Made Public

Sometimes private and public commemoration overlapped. A monument to Private Thomas Henry Bye (754108), a farmer and widower from Goulais River north of the Sault, stands in the Goulais cemetery (fig. 8.15). Born 27 May 1883 in England, Bye willed his possessions and assigned part of his pay to his son as his next of kin. Bye had spent a year in the 97th Algonquin Rifles militia, and on 1 December 1915 he enlisted with the 159th Algonquin Battalion. He went overseas in early 1916 and was sick with mumps before being transferred to France. When he was killed on 4 February 1917, like many from the North, he was serving as a tunneller. Who built the monument is not clear, but it expresses private grief in a public realm.

Figure 8.15.
Monument to Thomas Henry Bye (754108), likely put up by his son. The text reads "Pte T. Henry Bye Killed at Vimy Ridge Feb 4 1917 Aged 34 years."
(Courtesy Phil Miller)

At the Moosenee Community Cemetery, a veteran of World War I who died in 1956 is marked by a gravestone that imitates those used in Canadian military cemeteries in Europe. It honours Private Torguil Gillies (1007089), who enlisted in October 1916 with the Canadian Forestry Corps but ended the war in the 154th Battalion. Again private and public remembrance is intermingled.[261]

One of the earliest monuments mixing private and public remembrance is the large brick building dedicated to Lieutenant Charles Lorne Weller Nicholson of Chapleau, killed in action just a week before the war ended. The only son of the Member of Parliament for East Algoma, George Nicholson, and his wife Charlotte, Lieutenant Nicholson was memorialized with 25 other deceased soldiers from Chapleau. The grieving parents built St. John's Parish (Memorial) House as a kind of shrine (fig. 8.16). It was opened on 19 April 1920, with the Anglican Bishop of Moosenee presiding and Colonel Jones of the 227th Battalion in attendance. Above the entry is a marble plaque commemorating Lorne Nicholson. Nicholson, a "lumberman" (manager) and member of the 51st Soo Rifles militia, enlisted on 18 April 1916 (fig. 8.17). He went overseas in April 1917 with the 227th Men of the North Battalion, and was wounded in January 1918 and again in April while serving with the 4th Canadian Mounted Rifles militia. In late September, he returned to the front, but was killed on 4 November 1918.[262] Eventually the building was sold and later became the Legion hall.

Figure 8.16. St. John's Memorial House, Chapleau. (Courtesy of Shane Evans, Chapleau)

Figure 8.17. St. John's Memorial House, detail of plaque.
Despite the official name given by the bishop, and this plaque's label,
in the community, the building is colloquially known as the memorial hall.
(Courtesy of Joy Heft, Chapleau)

Questions and Puzzles: Mattawa and West Nipissing Cenotaphs

A resting soldier with slightly bowed head stands atop Mattawa's beautiful cenotaph in a fitting location overlooking the Ottawa River (fig. 8.18). However, the monument itself is misleading in several ways and would not have cemented community relations. Erected in the less-than-tolerant aftermath of World War I by the local Women's Institute, its inscriptions appear only in English, despite Mattawa's substantial Francophone population. Further, the list of "Our Honoured Dead" from World War

I names people who, according to their service records, did not have much connection to the area, or did not die overseas or from battle-related events. For example, only two Felix Lacombes exist in the service files: one was a deserter from Montreal; the other Felix (754508), a woodsman from Blind River (where he enlisted), was born in Caledonia Springs near Ottawa. He initially joined the 119th Algoma Battalion, shipped to England in August 1916, and by March 1918 was

Figure 8.18. Mattawa cenotaph.

transferred to the Canadian Forestry Corps working in Scotland. He demobilized in Toronto in July 1919 with the intention of moving to Spanish Station, Ontario, so does not belong on this list of honoured war dead.

Neither does Albert Lalonde because none of the eight Albert Lalondes in the service files of World War I soldiers seems to be from Mattawa. The closest to Mattawa is a farmer (3111063), conscripted from Field, Ontario, in July 1918. He survived the war and returned to Canada in 1919, perhaps because he spent October to December 1918 in prison (the cause is not clear, but he had been arrested and forfeited his pay). Conscript Hilliard John McLeod (3038193), a sailor by trade, at least came from Mattawa, though he survived only one month in action. A sadder case involved a soldier invalided back to Canada with carcinoma (cancer) of the tongue, Eric McConnell (1036032), who died at his home in Mattawa on 1 September 1918.[263]

The names of both of the Verner World War I fatalities also appear on the West Nipissing monument. West Nipissing's bilingual monument is another large polished stone with the names of at least ten Francophones (judging by surnames). However, again for some names no service files could be confirmed. Is Fercol Charbonneau (3329124) from Haileybury, born in Quebec on 3 April 1889, who fought with the 2nd Battalion (Eastern Ontario Regiment), the F. Charbonneau listed on the West Nipissing cenotaph? Albert Lalonde (3111063), who also appears on the Mattawa monument, is more appropriately, listed here. This overlapping commemoration of soldiers testifies to the not uncommon tendency to claim persons who may have had no roots in the community. Was there a desire to celebrate a larger local contribution than may have been true? Or did those creating monuments simply want to recognize anyone connected, however slightly, to the community, as in the Thessalon monument above?[264] Without records describing the criteria for inclusion, little is known about the personal stories or connections that governed the choices that were made. Such puzzles remind us that even monuments in stone do not provide incontrovertible historical evidence.

A Cairn, a Monument, and a Mascot: Wawa, Timmins, and White River

Monuments at Wawa and Timmins provide no names but simply identify the dates of three major wars (World War I, World War II, Korea). Wawa's is but a small, simple cairn, and the one at Timmins gives the dates on a large elongated block of granite.

White River has two monuments. A simple cairn adorned by a maple leaf stands outside the Municipal Building. It identifies only one soldier killed during World War I: T. Monson (186796), a timekeeper born in Sweden who had epilepsy. According to his service file, he died of "confusional insanity" on 10 June 1917, perhaps due to shell shock after three months in the field. The second and more conspicuous monument at White River sits on the south side of Highway 17 and focuses on Winnie-the-Pooh (fig. 8.19). A plaque in the shape of a book, under a banner reading, "Where Harry met Winnie some 100 years ago," recounts the relationship of soldier Harry Colebourn and the bear cub in 1914. War commemoration can take many forms.

Figure 8.19. This memorial at White River commemorates Harry Colebourn, the soldier who brought a bear cub to England, and A.A. Milne's character Winnie-the-Pooh. The familiar profile that illustrator E.H. Shepard gave Pooh in the original books can be seen.

Geographical Commemoration: Changing Names

In the days before "branding" came to mean renaming institutions and places after businesses and business people, soldiers received appropriate attention. In addition to cenotaphs, a popular form of postwar acknowledgement of military service involved changing the names of public places, such as schools, parks, and streets. In Sault Ste. Marie, a school is named after Victoria Cross winner William Merrifield. In North Bay, a street formerly named for a politician became Algonquin Avenue, acknowledging the 159th Algonquin Regiment. "Memorial" parks and buildings appeared in North Bay, Cochrane, and Haileybury, among other places, in honour of those who served in World War I. In Coniston, a street is named for Wesley Tuddenham (142138) who enlisted in 1915 and served with the 4th Battalion. He died at Vimy Ridge. Readers can undoubtedly add local examples.

Maintaining memories of the Great War preoccupied many places during the interwar years. Sault Ste. Marie and Sudbury did not complete their cenotaphs until 1924 and 1927, Cochrane only in June 1935, and Engelhart in September 1938. By then the standard models of cairns, a soldier on a pedestal, or very large granite blocks symbolizing eternity had been established. Only a few places deviated from these norms. What had begun as celebrating peace, erecting the nation's largest monument and combining a soldiers' reunion with historical commemoration, ended by building monuments that resembled traditional war memorials elsewhere. However, the public setting of memory into stone was common across the region.

Private Approaches

Private remembrance takes many forms. The traditional photograph on the mantle has sometimes been supplemented by scrapbooks, shadow boxes, or collections of medals in miniature. Many families saved letters from overseas, often describing the war's difficulties. Increasingly, as the Canadian War Museum collects documentary materials and projects such as Canadian Letters and Images (CLIP) and the Canadian Great War Project make their collections digitally accessible, the number of private letters and photographs saved for a hundred years mounts. The quantity is surprising. These documents emphasize that, for families, signs of life *from* soldiers were as important as the letters and packages sent to them. Mail provided a tangible presence, the hand and mind and voice on paper, though the writer might be gone.

The Canadian Legion of the British Empire Service League

After 1917, veterans' associations emerged in many places to represent the interests of soldiers, especially of the wounded and ill, and the families of veterans. The Great War Veterans' Associations and Veterans' Leagues learned that to fight for pensions, especially for widows, they needed a strong organization. In 1926, the different veterans' groups amalgamated to become the Canadian Legion of the British Empire Service League (fig. 8.20). Among the branches formed across the northeast were Chapleau (Branch 5), Sault Ste. Marie (Branch 25), North Bay (Branch 23), New Liskeard (Branch 33), Haileybury (Branch 54), Sudbury (Branch 76), Timmins (Branch 88), Cochrane (Branch 89), Capreol (Branch 170) and Little Current (Branch 177). As the full name implies, the British connection remained important, until in 1960 the veterans' group became the Royal Canadian Legion.

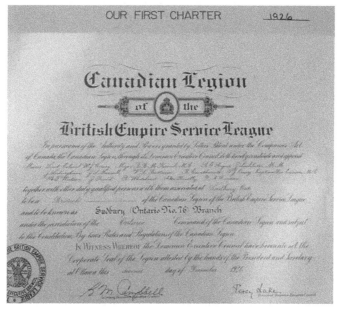

Figure 8.20. Charter for the Sudbury (Ontario No. 76) Branch of the Royal Canadian Legion.

Nearly all legions keep track of their own history and war experience. Since their beginnings, they have insisted on remembrance of their comrades, their experiences, and their postwar difficulties. Sudbury Legion, Branch 76, held Vimy evenings, where veterans of the battle reminisced. Legion halls are filled with mementos: artifacts of war, unit flags, honour rolls, and photos. Among the efforts to maintain their heritage, some have written accounts of their own activities. Branch 76, for example, has created a very thorough history of its organization in two handsome, wood-bound volumes (fig. 8.21). The contents have been placed online (www.sudburylegion.weebly.com), and the branch's activities can be followed over eight decades. From pipe bands to bingos, from sponsored hockey teams to dances, from building halls to holding conventions, from school orientations to selling poppies, the main focus remains support of the fallen and the living comrades.

Figure 8.21. Most legion branches document the history of the branch and its members' participation in Canada's wars.

As a region, Manitoulin may have the largest number of visible signs of commemoration in its monuments, museums, halls, and books. Like many others, its legion halls add to the public display with flag cases, plaques, and collections of military memorabilia. However, of all the Legion halls from Little Current and Gore Bay to Kagawong, from Chapleau to Timmins, from South Porcupine to Cobalt, from North Bay to Sudbury and points in between, the one in Sault Ste. Marie stands out. A small room displays well-identified uniforms and memorabilia. Most impressive are the long walls in the bar and meeting areas dedicated to each of the armed services. Historical photos of battalions, planes, and ships are interspersed with photos of individuals and groups who served in wars from the South African War to Afghanistan. Some heroic individuals receive special recognition. The extensive collection of photos of the region's veterans (fig. 8.22) is particularly informative and the form of display is imaginative. Many war brides and their husbands are depicted, though generally only the men's full names appear.

Figure 8.22. Photograph collection, Sault Ste. Marie Legion.
The collection numbers hundreds of photos, but is easily accessible as they are mounted on the wall in three-by-two-foot frames, which can be swung open to view two pages at a time. The contents are indexed and a binder provides supporting details.

Books of Memories

One form of remembrance popular in Northeastern Ontario takes book form. The format is fairly consistent. For example, the first volume of *Remember Me*, published by the Manitoulin Genealogy Club, tells the stories of both men and women of the Island who served in the wars.[265] Sometimes the relationship to Manitoulin is thin and sometimes the family genealogy is given much more space than the individual being remembered; however, the volumes are valuable summaries demonstrating again the high number who served and their diverse military roles.

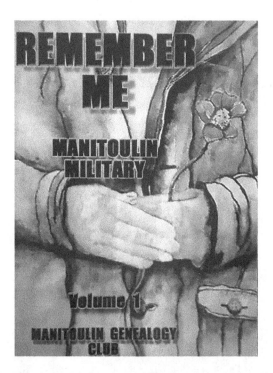

Figure 8.23. Manitoulin's book of memories.

Slightly different as a form of remembrance are local histories that include a section on warfare. One example from Manitoulin is the large volume *Reflections of Howland, Little Current and Vicinity*. Some of the individuals honoured there overlap with those in *Remember Me* because most came from the same military families (fig. 8.23). Similar, is the volume *Tehkumah*, which includes a chapter on local men and women who served and describes the effects of the war on families and the area.[266] In Thessalon, the Legion and women's auxiliary created a multi-volume book of remembrance with a huge photo collection; it is not published but is available in the public library. World War I is represented with attestation papers, clippings, and photographs, illustrating the pride of a small town and showing that it has not forgotten.

Museums and Military Rooms

Museums and archives contain and organize memories. Without them, places are like persons with memory loss: part of their identity disappears. Along with the collections in individual branches of the Royal Canadian Legion, Northeastern Ontario has the Bunker Military Museum at Cobalt, dedicated solely to military matters, and military heritage collections at the Kagawong Old Mill Heritage Centre and the Sault Ste. Marie museum.

The Bunker Military Museum honours military participants from well beyond the District of Temiskaming. World War II veteran Jim Jones moved his personal collection of military memorabilia to a public venue when the Ontario Northland Railway station in Cobalt became available in 1990. In 2012, the museum relocated to its present site, on Prospect Avenue (main street). Pictures, uniforms, and tableaux bring to life the military careers of such people as regional militia leader Donald Cameron of Sudbury. Copies of attestation papers with short biographies help place some soldiers in the context of the war's events. A wide panoramic photo of D Company of the 159th Algonquins Battalion, 1915, such as those often taken when battalions trained or were about to leave for overseas, is explained:

> This picture was probably taken at the end of a Battalion Sports day, won by 'D' Company. This is indicated by the number of trophies on display in front of the Company. Also visible in the photograph are the two mascots of the Algonquins, "Kitchener" the bear and "Bessie" the moose. There is no information available about the fox in the picture but it is most likely a personal pet.

As chapter 6 relates, pets and mascots connected battalions with their regions.

A significant section of Kagawong's Old Mill Heritage Centre pays tribute to the many Canadian soldiers from Manitoulin Island. Chronologically, the displays begin with the Fenian campaign of 1866 and the South African War, and extend to the 21st century's Afghan War. Photographs and biographical information are provided for many, including Kagawong's Oliver Cromwell Hunt (1874–1938), who claimed to have fought in the South African War (but has no service file). The museum displays many photographs from World War I, including panoramic photographs of the Number 13 Platoon D Company, 119th Algoma Overseas Battalion, taken on 28 June 1916. It presents the attestation papers of Hugh Bailey of Mindemoya (754053), born on 19 October 1894, who enlisted on 14 January 1916. Bailey served with the 52nd Battalion in France and Belgium, survived the war, and was demobilized on 23 May 1919. The museum has a collection of the magazine *Through the Years,* devoted to veterans' issues, and examines subjects such as Poppy Day and women who served as nursing sisters.

Other museums also celebrate local war heroes. The Sault Ste. Marie Museum displays photos of William Merrifield, winner of the Victoria Cross. The Chapleau Centennial Museum makes much of the exploits of a local father and son, Henry Charles Byce (409318) and Charles Henry Byce, who fought in World Wars I and II, respectively, and received the same two prestigious citations. The father, Henry C. Byce, was born on 25 July 1886 at Westmeath, Renfrew County, and married Louisa Saylors, a Cree woman from Moose Factory, in Chapleau in 1906. He enlisted at Niagara on 7 September 1915 with the 37th Battalion. On arrival in England, he transferred to the 12th reserve, until in August he was moved to the 23rd Battalion with a signal unit. After training, he was transferred to the 14th Battalion at the end of December 1916, and then saw active service in France as a sniper, advancing to corporal in May 1917. A year later he became a sergeant. At the battle of Amiens, though wounded, he led the charge against a machine gun post. His citation reads: "For conspicuous gallantry and devotion to duty … on 8/9 August 1918 … he, with a few sections, boldly rushed the post … The machine guns were captured, those who offered resistance were killed with the bayonet and thirty one prisoners taken."[267] In the fight Byce was seriously wounded (in the neck, right shoulder, nostril, and chin). For his actions, he received the Distinguished Conduct Medal (DCM) and Military Medal (MM). He returned to Canada in March 1919. This simple chronology hardly touches the difficult situations he faced, since snipers were priority targets for the enemy. Charles Henry Byce, the son, would receive the same medals in World War II.

While the military collections and materials in branches of the Royal Canadian Legion tend to be visible mostly to those who frequent their dances, bingos, bars, and Remembrance Day celebrations, museums generally attract a broader audience. Their mandate to educate usually involves school classes and special exhibitions. Thus they play an important part in preserving, remembering, and disseminating the record of Northeastern Ontario's military past.

Whom and What to Remember?

Edwin Durham, who spent more than three years as a prisoner of war in Germany, reflected on warfare in a Memorial Day speech to American high school students:

> On this day … we pause to remember those who with valour gave so unstintingly of themselves, left all that was life itself to fight for us; because mankind had not yet learned to settle differences by mutual enlightenment but turned in ignorance to war. Let us not become patrons to a self-centered militant patriotism that swells its chest and puffs its feathers on the strains of martial music, but rather let us in all our human relations, personal or international, develop the broader viewpoint: The Brotherhood of Man.[268]

As a veteran of Ypres and a POW, then a militia member and Legionnaire, he offered a message acknowledging sacrifice but also the need for reconciliation. Speaking from the viewpoint of a deceased soldier, he asked if those who survived were taking care of the children, and especially of the mothers, and "those who were robbed of a full life," the wounded, and "those maimed to such a degree that they desire to live out life in seclusion." Durham ended by saying, "God give us Peace!" His message is a reminder that, in the end, to foster peace, remembrance must include all, both enemy and comrade-in-arms.

Northeasterners can be proud of their participation in and contributions to Canadian war efforts. Opinions about the validity of conflict may vary, but the people from northeastern Ontario contributed more than their "bit," whether measured in terms of total volunteers or the way they committed themselves to the struggle. The men and women have received little recognition as a group coming from this region, largely because they were so often transferred to units identified with other places. This account has presented heroes and scoundrels, experiences in the training camps and POW camps, in the trenches and in the hospitals. A number of patterns have become clear: the continuity of military involvement since the formation of the 97th Algonquin Rifles in the late 19th century; the involvement and questionable treatment of the Indigenous recruits; the high number of soldiers and significant work in the forestry corps, railway troops, and tunnellers; the diverse home-front experiences; and the commitment to commemoration and remembrance. Through the many letters, diaries, memoirs, and photographs appearing here, this account illustrates that it is not the specific battles (whether the success of Vimy or the disastrous mud and murder of Passchendaele) that stand out, but the experiences of Northeastern Ontario men and women who found themselves at war in foreign lands. This discovery made them appreciate the climate, the landscape, and especially the people of home. Repeatedly, comments appear to the effect that it might be pretty here (in England, France, or Belgium), yet, they concluded, that nothing matched Northeastern Ontario, "I have almost crossed the country now and I never saw any place I liked"[269]

Much of the story of Northeastern Ontario at war remains untold. This volume has only touched briefly upon such aspects as grief of families, and also the work women took up in the absence of men to keep the country going. The difficulties of postwar adjustment for families in a region of boom-and-bust cycles has not been told, but the fate of the economy in the postwar period is also part of the story of the war. Many stories remain untold.

Notes

Notes

Part 4 : Told Stories
(in Lieu of a Bibliography)

Books help us understand our history and experiences. In lieu of a bibliography, we list here some books, aside from those in the notes that engage with aspects of World War I and Northeastern Ontario, or are important for the basic background.

Six large illustrated volumes of *Canada in the Great World War* (1917–21) are a mine of information presented in clear prose with superb examples and statistics. (They have been digitalized and are available at the Internet Archive, https://archive.org/details/canadaingreatwor06torouoft). All aspects of the war are covered, from financing to industrial organizing, from recruiting to training camps, from volunteers to women's roles, from the chronology of the battles to the technology of warfare. Most instructive are appendices such as "The War in the Air," "The Canadian Forestry Corps," "Canadian Railway Troops," "Canadian Prisoners of War in Germany," "The Alien Enemy in Canada: Internment Operations," and especially "The Canadian Indians and the Great World War." Though these volumes do not glorify warfare, the role of Canadians is generally praised, as might be expected from a wartime publication. In the breadth of social history provided and attitudes toward Indigenous and women's roles, the authors were far ahead of their era. Despite its range, however, the multivolume series illustrates well the usual approach: Northeastern Ontario receives hardly a notice. Similarly, in Kim Beattie's 1932 account of the battalion into which many of the 97th Algonquin Rifles militia enlistees were placed, namely the 48th Highlanders of the 15th Battalion, it was noted that soldiers from Sudbury and Cobalt augmented the Toronto unit. Then they disappear. Kim Beattie's *48th Highlanders of Canada 1891-1928* (Toronto: 48th Highlanders, 1932); it can be accessed at http://15thbattalioncef.ca/wp-content/uploads/2012/08/48th_Hist1.pdf

Writing nearly a hundred years later, Tim Cook has written a thoroughly researched account of Canadian soldiers in World War I. His two volumes, one devoted to 1914–16, *At the Sharp End,* and one covering 1916–18, *Shock Troops,* present the most comprehensive and latest scholarly findings. All scholars are indebted to his informed works. The subtitle of both volumes is *Canadians Fighting the Great War*, with perhaps a narrow definition of *fighting*. He does not consider the Canadian Forestry Corps or the Canadian Railway Troops, two important aspects of the war for men from the Northeast. Miners and sappers, as tunnellers, are noted, but not where they came from. He mentions that some soldiers fought as groups from specific regions and identifies some that way.

A few writers have focused more closely on individual communities. In *They Stepped into Immortality*, André Maheu passionately researches the lives of those listed on the World War I monument in New Liskeard. Through genealogical, archival, and newspaper searches, supplemented by letters and service files, he recreates the lives of some thirty soldiers. In a large, well-illustrated, but repetitious volume he honours their sacrifice. This is the kind of research needed before writing names in stone on cenotaphs. Similar is Michael McMullen and Michael J. Morris, *The Chapleau Boys Go to War,* which recounts the lives of the 32 local men who died in World War I.

Women played more than supporting roles in warfare and often had to fight their own battles while the men were away. The lonely hours, the sole parenting, and family responsibilities required fortitude and endurance. Further, if the soldier was injured or killed, the troubles mounted. Where historians have left the story untold, however, fiction can fill the gap. The novel *Home Fires* (Iguana, 2015), by Susan Johnson Cameron, relates the story of a young woman left in the bush with four children while her husband goes to war. The abnormality of war is matched by the crises at home when the world's seventh largest fire (1916) sweeps through the area from Timmins to Matheson. This very good historical novel takes up many war themes such as VD, trench diseases, and shell shock, but mostly focuses on a woman successfully surviving and coping on the home front.

While other essays and articles about the people of Northeastern Ontario do exist, both on the Web and in conventional publications, the lack of specific focus on the region's military past motivated us to recount some of the untold story in the present volume. The second volume seeks to do the same for the post-1919 era.

Acknowledgements

Karen Bachman (Curator at Timmins Museum, National Exhibition Centre)
Noreen Barbe (Sudbury)
Angela Becks (Manitoulin)
Kristen Bertrand (Greater Sudbury Public Library)
Geoff Bird (History, Royal Roads University)
Marthe Brown (Archivist, Laurentian University)
Judith M. Buse (edited manuscript)
Lisa Buse (edited manuscript, created tables, and photographed monuments)
Leo Doucet (Ottawa)
David Deloye (Laurentian University, Sudbury)
Shane Evans (Chapleau)
Jim Fortin (Sudbury)
Shanna Fraser (Archives of the City of Greater Sudbury)
Amanda Hancox (and Fairlawn United Church, Toronto)
Ellen Heale (Copper Cliff)
Maya Holson (Manitoulin)
Bonnie Lachapelle (Sudbury)
Julie Latimer (Curator at Ron Morel Memorial Museum, Kapuskasing)
Robert Lantz (Toronto)
Tim Laye (Ontario War Memorials)
Anne Marie Mawhinney (Sudbury)
Kevin McCormick (Huntington University, Sudbury)
Kevin Meraglia (Archivist, Sault Ste. Marie Library)
Ric de Meulles (Sudbury)

Phil Miller (Sault Ste. Marie)
Robert Montpetit (Haileybury)
Joan Mount (Victoria)
Rick Nelson (Curator at Old Mill Heritage Centre, Kagawong)
Captain Douglas Newman (RCAF Heritage Officer, North Bay 22 Wing
    Canadian Forces)
Helen Nicholson (Sudbury)
Colleen O'Reilley (Sudbury)
Ontario Genealogical Society, Sudbury Branch
Markus Schwabe (CBC, Morning North)
Jason Turnbull (CBC, Up North)
Petra Wall (*Manitoulin Expositor*)
Staff at public libraries, especially Chapleau, Massey, Sault Ste. Marie, Greater
Sudbury, Thessalon, Timmins, Toronto, and Greater Victoria; at museums in
Cobalt, Kagawong, Kapuskasing, Sault Ste. Marie, and Timmins; at Sudbury
Secondary School library; and at legion halls, especially South Porcupine Branch
287 and Sudbury Branch 76. We have used materials from the Archives of
Ontario (Toronto), Library and Archives Canada (Ottawa), the Canadian War
Museum (Ottawa), and the Archives of Greater Sudbury, and are appreciative
that so much material has become available digitally. Apologies to any of the kind
people who helped, if we inadvertently missed them.

A grant won through Laurentian University's faculty research fund (2016
LURF-R competition) helped with travel and research costs; we remain very
grateful.

Special thanks for making a lengthy manuscript into more readable books go
to publishers Heather Campbell and Laura Stradiotti, plus enthusiastic, devoted
copy editor Lisa LaFramboise.

Notes

1. While recruiting its initial complement of men, the 119th Battalion was often called the "Algoma Overseas" Battalion, but "Overseas" was dropped once the battalion shipped. Henceforth this book follows that practice, dropping "Overseas."

2. *Circumstances of Death Registers, First World War*, microform sequence 60, p. 271, Library and Archives Canada, https://www.bac-lac.gc.ca/eng/discover/mass-digitized-archives/circumstances-death-registers/Pages/circumstances-death-registers.aspx. Hereafter cited as *CODR*.

3. We include the northeastern part of the District of Kenora, Attawapiskat and vicinity, just west of Moosenee, because soldiers from there served alongside Indigenous soldiers from other Indigenous communities along the shores of James Bay.

4. This is almost identical to the region covered in our award-winning guide *Come on Over: Northeastern Ontario A to Z* (Scrivener Press, 2011). While researching that book we became more aware of the lack of consideration of this area in the military and social histories of Canada.

5. See for example, Timothy Winegard, *For King and Kanata: Canadian Indians and the First World War* (Winnipeg: University of Manitoba Press, 2012).

6. Robert Konduros, *World War I: A Monumental History* (Toronto: Start Me Up Publishing, 2014); an exception is Alex MacLeod, *Remembered in Bronze and Stone: Canada's Great War Memorial Statuary* (Victoria: Heritage, 2016), which includes examples from Echo Bay, Sault Ste. Marie, and Thessalon.

7. Though an otherwise excellent account, for instance, Andrew Iarocci's *Shoestring Soldiers: The 1st Canadian Division at War, 1914–1915* (Toronto: University of Toronto Press, 2008) does not note that after training, the 4th Battalion's ranks were filled by men from far beyond its original recruiting area (Brantford to Aurora, Ontario), including many from Northeastern Ontario.

8. Another factor might be that until the past few decades, few professional historians lived in Northeastern Ontario.

9. Officers during World War I received no regimental number but can usually be found through use of name and rank in the Library and Archives Canada website under "Soldiers of the First World War," or at the head of battalion nominal rolls (the lists the military used to keep track of soldiers).

10. See the summary by D. Manitowabi and Alan Corbiere, "Anishinabek and Mushkegowuk," in *Come on Over: Northeastern Ontario, A to Z*, edited by Dieter K. Buse and Graeme S. Mount (Sudbury: Scrivener, 2011), 16–19.

11. See the introduction in "Aboriginal People in the Canadian Military" at www.cmp-cpm.forces.gc.ca, written by a collective that included Indigenous scholars. This is comprehensive, though it does not identify many specific conflicts until the 18th century.

12. Edward H. Capp, *Warriors of the Ojibway Country: 97th Regiment Algonquin Rifles of Canada* (n.p, 1908), 4–6.

13. During the same era, Europeans also practised torture and slavery, and even burned people alive as alleged witches.

14. Kerry Abel, *Changing Places: History, Community and Identity in Northeastern Ontario* (Kingston: McGill-Queen's University Press, 2006). See also "A History of Fort La Cloche," *Culture, Heritage and Tourism* [magazine of the Hudson's Bay Company Archives], 1934, to see how long fur-trade society remained the norm; reprinted at the Willisville website, http://www.willisville.ca/History%20of%20Fort%20La%20Cloche.htm.

15. E.E. Rich, *The History of the Hudson's Bay Company, 1670–1870*, 3 vols. (Toronto: McClelland and Stewart, 1958), 1:213–14.

16. The most detailed summaries of the boundary negotiations are provided by A.L. Burt, *The United States, Great Britain and British North America from the Revolution to the Establishment of Peace after the War of 1812* (Toronto: Ryerson, 1940).

17. For aspects of the War of 1812, George Sheppard, *Plunder, Profit, and Paroles: A Social History of the War of 1812 in Upper Canada* (Montreal: McGill-Queen's University Press, 1994); Alan Taylor, *The Civil War of 1812: American Citizens, British Subjects, Irish Rebels, and Indian Allies* (New York: Vintage, 2010).

18. Mark Zuehlke, *For Honour's Sake: The War of 1812 and the Brokering of an Uneasy Peace* (Toronto: Knopf Canada, 2006), 53–55, 90, 101–102, 153.

19. John Abbott, Graeme S. Mount, and Michael J. Mulloy, *The History of Fort St. Joseph* (Toronto: Dundurn, 2000), 92.

20. Abbott, *History of Fort St. Joseph*, 12–14.

21. For a moving account of the famine, see John O'Rourke, *The Great Irish Famine* (Dublin: Veritas, 1989) and John Kelly, *The Graves Are Walking: The Great Famine and the Saga of the Irish People* (New York: Picador, 2013).

22. A classic on Anglo-American relations during the Civil War is Robin Winks, *Canada and the United States: The Civil War Years* (Baltimore: Johns-Hopkins Press, 1960).

23. For more information on the Fenians, see Leon O'Broin, *Fenian Fever: An Anglo-American Dilemma* (New York: New York University Press, 1971); Peter Edwards, *Delusion: The True Story of Superspy Henri Le Caron* (Toronto: Key Porter, 2008); Hereward Senior, *The Fenians and Canada* (Toronto: Macmillan, 1978).

24. Edward H. Capp, *The Story of Baw-a-ting* (Sault Ste. Marie, ON, 1904), 193. Members of the Canadian Sault Ste. Marie's militia included men with military experience: veterans of the British Army's campaign on the Crimean Peninsula (1853–56); of the Burma frontier; and of forces fighting the Upper Canadian rebels of 1837–38.

25. James Cooke Mills, "The Gateway of the Inland Seas," *Canadian Magazine*, 38 (Nov. 1911): 34-37; see also Abbott, *History of Fort St. Joseph*, 22.

26. David K. Ratz, "Soldiers of the Shield: the 96th 'District of Algoma' Battalion of Rifles, 1886–1896: A Social and Military Institution," MA Thesis, Lakehead University, 1995. Thanks to Phil Miller for this reference.

27. This account omits the Nile Expedition of 1884–85. During the 1880s, European powers divided Africa into spheres of influence. To maintain influence in Sudan and Egypt (the Suez Canal being the direct way to India), British general Charles Gordon as Governor General of Sudan tried to hold the city of Khartoum against the revolting Mahdi. With Khartoum under siege the British sent an expedition under General Wolseley, who brought 400 Canadian so-called Voyageurs to man boats on the Nile River.

28. Carl Berger, *The Sense of Power: Studies in the Ideas of Imperialism, 1867–1914* (Toronto: University of Toronto Press, 1970).

29. C.P. Stacey, *Canada and the Age of Conflict* (Toronto: Macmillan, 1977), 70. Stacey summarizes the politics and military effort of Canada's contribution to the South African War. More thorough is Carman Miller, *Painting the Map Red: Canada and the South African War, 1899–1902* (Montreal: Canadian War Museum, 1993). The service files of Canadians who volunteered in the Anglo-Boer War can be accessed on the Library and Archives Canada website under "South African War."

30. See *Capreol, the First 75 Years, 1918–1993* ([Sudbury: Journal Printing], 1993), 118.

31. His grandson Donald Dennie called him a "liar"; email to Buse, 5 March 2017.

32. The following is extracted from Graeme S. Mount, *Canada's Enemies* (Toronto: Dundurn, 1992).

33. Capp, *Warriors of the Ojibway Country*, 31.

34. Canada, Nominal Rolls and Paylists for the Volunteer Militia, 1857–1922. This source is available at *Ancestry.ca*, which is free at many libraries: http://interactive.ancestrylibrary.com.

35. Livo Ducin, "Labour's Emergent Years and the 1903 Riots," in *100 Years of Labour in Algoma* (Sault Ste. Marie: Algoma University, 1978), 1–18.

36. Douglas Newton, *The Darkest Days: The Truth behind Britain's Rush to War, 1914* (London: Verso, 2014), bases his conclusion on cabinet documents; Christopher Clark, *The Sleepwalkers: How Europe Went to War in 1914* (London: Penguin, 2013) argues that Britain went to war to defend its empire.

37. Precise numbers do not exist because it is not clear if those who joined the British flying corps or other organizations are included, see Desmond Morton, "World War I," in *The Canadian Encyclopedia* (Edmonton: Hurtig, 1988), 4:2343. Compare Desmond Morton and J.L. Granatstein, *Marching to Armageddon: Canadians and the Great War, 1914–1919* (Toronto: Lester and Orpen Dennys, 1989), 1: "One in ten of those [620,000] who joined Canada's wartime army died in its ranks." Canada's population on the eve of war in August 1914 numbered around eight million. Some "430,000 men and women served overseas," says Tim Cook, *At the Sharp End: Canadians Fighting in the Great War, 1914–1916* (Toronto: Viking, 2007), 3. If more than 60,000 were killed, more than twice that many were wounded in battle, "many crippled for life."

38. The statistics vary: the Canadian War Museum in "Tommy Canuck: the Infantry Soldier," indicates that 71% of the first contingent were British born; by war's end only 50%; Chris Sharpe states that more than 60% were British born in the first contingent (Sharpe, "Enlistment in the Canadian Expeditionary Force, 1914–1918," *Canadian Military History* 24, no. 1 (2015): 1–45. Sharpe provides a regional breakdown as well.

39. Rank will be given for all soldiers at the level above private, but in the interests of avoiding repetition, "Private" will be omitted when using soldiers' names.

40. Edwin Durham, Undated speech to school students, Durham collection, TED5, Sault Ste. Marie Public Library Archives.

41. The list included some confusion between regiment (the term used for the militias) and battalion (the term used for the regular troops):
Major Cressey, Sudbury, unattached.
Capt. John Handley, Sudbury, Quartermaster, 5th Royal Highlanders.

Capt. R.R. McKessock, Sudbury, Machine gun officer, 48th Highlanders
Capt. L.S. Robinson, New Liskeard, in command of Canadian Cycling Corps
Capt. Daniels (no first name given), Cobalt, 48th Highlanders
Capt. John Glover, Sudbury, Adjutant, 4th Regiment [Battalion]
Lieut. A.N. Morgan, New Liskeard, 10th Regiment [Battalion]
Lieut. P. Ferguson, Haileybury, 5th Royal Highlanders
Lieut. Norman McKee, Elk Lake, Signaling Officer, 15th Nova Scotia Regiment [Battalion]

42. Matt Bray, "1910–1920," in *Sudbury: Railtown to Regional Capital*, ed. C. Wallace and A. Thomson (Toronto: Dundurn, 1993), 86.

43. Morton and Granatstein, *Marching*, 56. Unlike Australia, Canada did not have its own air force during World War I, and those who flew went with the British, for whom they provided many aces and nearly one-quarter of the pilots; see S.F. Wise, *Canadian Air Men and the First World War* (Toronto: University of Toronto Press, 1980). Gwyn Dyer observes that "Ten of the top twenty-seven aces in the British forces were Canadians, and they included four of the twelve leading aces" (*Canada in the Great Power Game, 1914–2014* [Toronto: Random House, 2014], 107).

44. Andrew Pentland, *Surnames A–B* spreadsheet, available for download at "Royal Flying Corps: People Index," http://www.airhistory.org.uk/rfc/people_index.html.

45. *CODR*, microform sequence 66, p. 965.

46. See, for example, *Porcupine Advance*, "Three Thousand Mechanics for Canadian Air Services," 31 March 2017.

47. Calculations are based upon soldiers' service files, available online at the Library and Archives Canada's "First World War" database (http://www.bac-lac.gc.ca/eng/discover/military-heritage/first-world-war/Pages/introduction.aspx). These files indicate the soldiers' birthplace, residence at time of enlistment, and next of kin with address. For Canadian provincial comparisons see A.F. Duguid, *Official History of the Canadian Forces in the Great War, 1914– 1919* (Ottawa: King's Printer, 1938), vol. 1.

48. See "Recruitment," Great War Centenary Association (of Brantford), http://doingourbit.ca/recruitment, which offers comparative statistics by provinces and Brantford plus Brant County.

49. Michael McMullen lists those recruited to the 227th Battalion, including four from neighbouring Indigenous communities; all were later transferred to 5th Reserve; see *The Chapleau Boys Go to War* (self-published: CreateSpace, 2015), 217–33.

50   15. Richard Plaunt, "Regional Contribution to War 'Way High,'" *Sault This Week*, 8 November 2016. Story based on information provided by local historian Phil Miller.

51. Cook, *Sharp End*, 162. A different account is found in Jonathan F. Vance, *Objects of Concern: Canadian Prisoners of War through the Twentieth Century* (Vancouver: University of British Columbia, 1994), ch. 2, though he does not cite the protective powers' reports and uses no German sources.

52. The Durham Papers are in the Sault Ste. Marie Public Library archives; samples have been made digitally accessible by the Sault Ste. Marie Public Library at "Sault Ste. Marie and World War I: Prisoner of War: POW Recreational Activities," Sault History Online, 2008, www.cityssm.on.ca/library/WW1_POWrec.html.

53. Arthur Corker escaped together with Cameron and described their experiences in a letter of 3 July 1918, available at the Canadian Letters and Images Project website, www.canadianletters.ca (hereafter CLIP) by searching under Corker's name. This is an excellent, indexed online resource.

54. Morton and Granatstein, *Marching*, 63.

55. Colonel G.W.L. Nicholson, *Canadian Expeditionary Force, 1914–1918: Official History of the Canadian Army in the First World War* (Ottawa: Queen's Printer, 1962), 92.

56. Enos Grant's letter is available at CLIP. Many of the letters from the Temiskaming area were printed in *New Liskeard Speaker* during the war and reprinted in André Maheu, *They Stepped into Immortality: The Stories Behind the World War I Veterans Listed on the New Liskeard Cenotaph* (Cobalt: White Mountain, 2016).

57. Available in CLIP; see also Maheu, *They Stepped into Immortality*, 98.

58. Nathan M. Greenfield, *Baptism of Fire: The Second Battle of Ypres and the Forging of Canada, April 1915* (Toronto: HarperCollins, 2007), 341. On the consecutive Battles of Ypres, see Winston Groom, *A Storm in Flanders, The Ypres Salient, 1914–1918: Triumph and Tragedy on the Western Front* (New York: Atlantic Monthly Press, 2002).

59. Nicholson, *Expeditionary*, 64.

60. Ault would be buried by a shell explosion in August 1916 and suffer ear discharges and other complications. He was hospitalized in England and while on leave married Ivy B. from Norfolk on 30 January 1918.

61. Cook, *Sharp End*, 215.

62. Angus McLean, 27 August 1915; available in CLIP.

63. J.B. Lowes, "Just Like Being on 9th Level When Blasting Gang Is Down," *Sudbury Star*, 3 November 1915, reproduced in *Copper Cliff Notes*, https://www.coppercliffnotes.com/recollections-from-the-front.html. *Copper Cliff Notes* website is organized by the Greater Sudbury Public Library. Lowes would be wounded in the right foot in 1918. Rhodes contracted herpes early in 1917, then a knee injury though not from duty; he became a stores guard.

64. Cook, *Sharp End*, 303–22; Nicholson, *Expeditionary*, 114–28.

65. *CODR*, microform sequence 53, p. 233.

66. Cook, *Sharp End*, 324.

67. Cook, *Sharp End*, 42, 324–25.

68. Cook, *Sharp End*, 365.

69. Cook, *Sharp End*, 422.

70. Nicholson, *Expeditionary*, 152.

71. Nicholson, *Expeditionary*, 154.

72. Vincent Crichton, *Pioneering in Northern Ontario* (Belleville: Mika, 1975), chapter on "Men O' The North," 217–23; quotations, 217–19.

73. Crichton, *Pioneering in Northern Ontario*, 217–19.

74. Quoted in Nicholson, *Expeditionary*, 198.

75. Quoted in Nicholson, *Expeditionary*, 198. The official Canadian historian concludes, "At best, the five-month campaign … resulted in a costly stalemate" (200). A leading British historian of the battle, Peter Hart, finds the campaign difficult to judge one way or the other (Hart, *The Somme* [London: Cassell, 2005], 13). John Keegan argues that Haig hoped that the offensive at the Somme would "break the enemy's line," but between 1 July when the campaign began and 19 November when it ended, the line had advanced by a mere 10 kilometres (7 miles); see Keegan, *The First World War* (New York: Vintage, 2000), 298. Keegan considers the Somme effort "the greatest [British] military tragedy of the twentieth century," if not of all time.

76. David Macfarlane, "War Wounds," *Walrus* (July/August 2016), pp. 42–47. For a charming account with much irony about the generals far from the action see Bryan Davies and Andrew Traficante, eds., *A Boy from Botwood: Pte. A. W. Manuel, Royal Newfoundland Regiment, 1914–1919* (Toronto: Dundurn, 2017), ch. 4.

77. Cook, *Sharp End*, 450–51; see also Tim Cook, "The Politics of Surrender. Canadian Soldiers and the Killing of Prisoners in the Great War," *Journal of Military History* 70 (2006): 637–65.

78. *Casualties* refers to both dead and injured. Cook, *Sharp End*, 483. British historians Peter Hart and Hugh Sebag-Montefiore, *Somme: Into the Breach* (London: Viking, 2016) discuss at length battles in which soldiers from Northeastern Ontario lost their lives.

79. Hart and Sebag-Montefiore, *Somme*, 471–73.

80. Cook, *Sharp End*, 502.

81. Nicholson, *Expeditionary*, 160.

82. Pierre Berton, *Vimy* (Toronto: McClelland and Stewart, 1986); Ted Barris, *Victory at Vimy: Canada Comes of Age: April 9–23, 1917* (Toronto: Thomas Allen, 2004).

83. Berton, *Vimy*, 295.

84. Regarding use of gas, see Tim Cook, "'A Proper Slaughter': The March 1917 Gas Raid at Vimy Ridge," *Canadian Military History* 8 (1999): 7–23. Re: the myth of Vimy, see the controversial study by Ian McKay, *The Vimy Trap: or How We learned to Stop Worrying and Love the Great War* (Toronto: Between the Lines, 2016), which analyzes the often repeated myth that Vimy formed Canada as a nation. By contrast, Tim Cook, in *Vimy: The Battle and the Legend* (Toronto: Allen Lane, 2017) and in a new afterword, states, "Vimy did not make the nation, but the nation made Vimy." Cook reviews the military events and many meanings attributed to the battle. At its 100th anniversary, the Bank of Canada placed a stylized image of the monument on the $20 bill, but the image does not do justice to the monument.

85. J.L. Granatstein, *The Greatest Victory: Canada's One Hundred Days* (Toronto: Oxford University Press, 2014), xii. Until 2014, Granatstein chaired the Advisory Board of the Vimy Foundation.

86. Granatstein, *Greatest Victory*, 75.

87. Granatstein, *Greatest Victory*, xiii. For other assessments of the Battle of Vimy Ridge, see Geoffrey Hayes, Andrew Iarocci, Mike Bechtold, eds., *Vimy Ridge: A Canadian Reassessment* (Waterloo: Wilfrid Laurier University Press, 2007).

88. *CODR*, microform sequence 66, p. 479.

89. The sheet music is available from Library and Archives Canada. Harry R. Pearse, *The Men o' the North* (n.p.: C.H.L. Jones, 1916), Library and Archives Canada, https://www.collectionscanada.gc.ca/sheetmusic/028008-3300-e.html.

90. Cook, *Shock Troops*, 145.

91. Cook, *Shock Troops*, 306.

92. Morton and Granatstein, *Marching*, 161.

93. *CODR*, microform sequence 15, p. 11.

94. Nicholson, *Expeditionary*, 299.

95. Cook, *Shock Troops*, 316–18.

96. Nicholson, *Expeditionary*, 329. British historian Philip Warner agrees with the strategic, crass estimate; see *Passchendaele: The Tragic Victory of 1917* (New York: Atheneum, 1988), 235–38.

97. Daniel G. Dancocks, *Legacy of Valour: The Canadians at Passchendaele* (Edmonton: Hurtig, 1986), x.

98. Dancocks, *Legacy*, 231–39.

99. Granatstein, *Greatest Victory*, 82.

100. Keegan, *The First World War*, 368.

101. Nicholson, *Expeditionary*, 333–36.

102. Robert Woollcombe, *The First Tank Battle: Cambrai 1917* (London: Arthur Barker, 1967); his final chapter is called "The Tragedy of Cambrai."

103. See Matt Bray, "1910–1920," in *Sudbury: Rail Town to Regional Capital*, ed. C.M. Wallace and Ashley Thomson (Toronto: Dundurn, 1993), 88–90; for example, du Caillard Street became Howey Drive.

104. Manuscript entitled "World War I: The 227th Battalion 'Men of the North,'" by Jean Lye; in Greater Sudbury Public Library collection (Mary Schantz Room). The information contains gaps and mixes various issues but serves as a useful guide.

105. His memoirs cover part of the war years; see Smylie, Clifford Hugh fonds, Archives of Ontario.

106. The information comes from daughter-in-law Noreen Barbe in a discussion on 23 October 2017; she insisted that he would have wanted the statement recorded as he repeated it frequently. This issue warrants further research.

107. Morton and Granatstein, *Marching*, 161.

108. Granatstein, *Greatest Victory*, xi; he further claims the Battle of Amiens a "sensational success" and "the greatest advance thus far in the war." See also James McWilliams and R. James Steel, *Amiens: Dawn of Victory* (Toronto: Dundurn, 2001).

109. *CODR*, microform sequence 4, p. 601.

110. Nicholson, *Expeditionary*, 459–60.

111. Jim Fortin, former museum curator of Sudbury, provided some notes created by Black in his later years for his family: "Algonquin Rifle Regt. Sudbury detachment in 1910 as a drummer and bugler under Col. Cressey and Col. McKee. Went overseas 1915 to 4th Canadian Infantry Battalion, 1st Brigade, 1st Division. Returned 1919. Had intermittent service with Algonquins, Sault Ste. Marie & Sudbury Regt., Infantry Rifles, then same Regt. as Machine Gun Regt. 69th Survey Regt. RCA and lastly 58th. Sudbury Light Anti Aircraft Regt. RCA ... Was Band officer for two or three years. In 1957 put on retired list of officers with Rank of Major. Total number of years connected with Militia and Active service, about 47 years. Taught hundreds of men while with Armed Forces - Infantry Rifle - Machine Gun" (Private collection).

112. Nicholson, *Expeditionary*, 482.

113. See, for a summary of reasons, Theodore Cox-Dodgson, "A Noble Cause? Allied Intervention in the Russian Civil War," *Historical Journal*, 2 April 2017.

114. Information on both brothers from service files was supplemented by Noreen Barbe (Emil Barbe's daughter-in-law) on 23 October 2017.

115. F.A. Carman provides a very thorough account of the organization of demobilization in his chapter "Demobilization," in *Canada in the Great World War*, vol. 6, *Special Services, Heroic Deeds, etc.* (Toronto: United Publishers of Canada, 1921), 240–69. It has been digitized and is available at the Internet Archive at https://archive.org/details/canadaingreatwor06torouoft.

116. Among them, Charles Beard and Henry Elmer Barnes, American experts on the origins of the war. Tim Cook attributes the rise of Hitler, the French unwillingness to fight in 1940, and the beginning of the end of the British Empire to World War I; see *Shock Troops*, ch. 41, 638. John Keegan agrees that "World War II is inexplicable except in terms of the rancours and instabilities left by the earlier conflict," and that independence from the Austro-Hungarian Empire "brought ... little tranquility to the successor states"; see *First World War*, 423–24.

117. Craig's diary and letters may be found in the Claude C. Craig fonds, MG 30 E 351, Library and Archives Canada; other information in this section comes from census reports, and Ontario marriage and birth registrations.

118. His father, Rufus Craig, swore out a birth certificate in July 1919 that stated that Claude had been born 4 November 1895. Had Claude tried to make himself appear older when enlisting?

119. See his service file under Regimental Number 408060 in the *Personnel Records of the First World War*, Library and Archives Canada, https://www.bac-lac.gc.ca/eng/discover/military-heritage/first-world-war/personnel-records/Pages/search.aspx. He officially enlisted on 12 June 1915 at Niagara.

120. *Sudbury Star*, 7 April 1928, 3.

121. Alfred Baggs, Diary, Canadian War Museum Library and Archives, Textual Records 58A 1 92.1, http://collections.historymuseum.ca/public/objects/common/webmedia.php?irn=5475803.

122. Frederick John Cressey's diary, pay books, and scroll of merit for helping found Legion Branch 76 in 1946 can be found in the Frederick John Cressey papers, Textual Records 58 A 1 1.0. Excerpts from the diary are online at the Canadian War Museum's online catalogue, http://collections.historymuseum.ca/public/objects/common/webmedia.php?irn=5370330.

123. André R. Maheu, *They Stepped into Immortality: The Stories Behind the World War I Veterans Listed on the New Liskeard Cenotaph* (Cobalt: Mountain Publications, 2015), 353–68. We gratefully acknowledge the research Maheu undertook to find Phillips's letters and to make them available.

124. *CODR*, microform sequence 85, p. 143.

125. The identical, official wording is on the plaque honouring Merrifield in front of the commemorative cenotaph in Sault Ste. Marie.

126. *Sudbury Star*, 26 April 1919. The story also erroneously stated that he had been born in Sudbury, Suffix.

127. See the Merrifield file, vertical files, Sault Ste. Marie Public Library.

128. *Sudbury Star*, 19 April 1919.

129. *Canadian Recipients of the Victoria Cross* is an undated brochure published by the Gregg Centre for the Study of War and Society at the University of New Brunswick.

130 14. The headstones are all the same size and style, using the template of headstones in the military cemeteries of France and Belgium.

131. Durham Papers, Sault Ste. Marie Public Library Archives, 992.13; 122–23, the page numbers refer to transcripts of his "memoirs," written during interviews.

132. Durham, Memoirs, 126.

133. Durham, Memoirs, 127.

134. Durham, Memoirs, 132.

135. Durham, Memoirs, 135.

136. Durham, Memoirs, 153.

137. Durham, Memoirs, 143–44.

138. Nathan Greenfield, for example, suggests that Germans starved and mistreated POWs. However, he cites no German sources and uncritically relies on the accounts of former POWs (often anti-German war propaganda published before the war ended). Greenfield presents the case of Frederick Ivey (16907), who had supposedly been starved and on whose face Germans allegedly tattooed an iron cross; see Greenfield, *The Reckoning: Canadian Prisoners of War in the Great War* (Toronto: Harper Collins, 2016), 71. Greenfield provides no reference for Ivey's story. According to Ivey's service file, when repatriated his nutrition level was "good" and no mention was made of any tattoo when scars or notable skin marks were recorded.

139. Heather Jones, *Violence against Prisoners of War in the First World War: Britain, France and Germany, 1914-1921* (Cambridge: Cambridge University Press, 2011). The French and Germans perpetrated the worst abuse.

140. Heather Jones and Uta Hinz, "Prisoners of War (Germany)," *International Encyclopedia of the First World War*, www.encyclopedia,1914-1918-online.net

141. Durham Papers, Sault Ste. Marie Public Library Archives.

142. The following draws on the official report by C.W. Bird and J.B. Davies, *The Canadian Forestry Corps: Its Inception, Development and Achievements* (London: H.M. Stationary Office, 1919).

143. See the summary by Roland H. Hill and H.L. Robertson, "The Canadian Forestry Corps," in *Canada in the Great World War* (Toronto: United Publishers of Canada, 1920), appendix 3, 5:300–308.

144. Charles W. Bishop, *The Canadian Y.M.C.A in the Great War* (Toronto: National Council, 1924), 219–34.

145. Copies of photos, clippings, and letters located at Library and Archives Canada are held in the Sault Ste. Marie Public Library Archives. Selected images can be seen with Penhorwood's story at the library's history website, Sault History Online, http://www.cityssm.on.ca/library/WW1_Penhorwood.html.

146. Colonel J.B. White, Letter to Penhorwood, 11 September 1917, SLP 82, Penhorwood collection, Sault Ste. Marie Public Library Archives.

147. See David Guay, *Tracks to the Trenches: Canadian Railway Troops in the Great War (1914–1919)* (London: Aurum Press, 2014), for a well-illustrated account of the railways and where they were used. He offers less information about the men and their struggles, and little on their origins, so again Northeastern Ontario's contributions are overlooked.

148. Hill and Robertson, "Canadian Railway Troops," 5:319.

149. "Private Bertie Nackogie #1006931, 228th Battalion," *Canadian Expeditionary Force 1914–1919* (blog), 6 December 2011, http://canadianexpeditionaryforce1914-1919.blogspot.com/2011/12/private-bertie-nackogie-1006931-228th.html.

150. An excellent book about tunnelling during World War I is Peter Barton, Peter Doyle, and Johan Vandewalle, *Beneath Flanders Fields: The Tunnellers' War, 1914–1918* (Montreal: McGill-Queen's University Press, 2005). Michael Boire, "The Underground War: Military Mining Operations in Support of the Attack on Vimy Ridge, 9 April 1917," *Canadian Military History* 1 (1992): 15–24, also covers more than the title would suggest.

151. The First Canadian Tunnelling Company's war diary (MIKAN no. 133530) is held in the War Diaries sub-series, Canadian War Office Records (R611-317-7-E), Library and Archives Canada, and can be accessed online: http://collectionscanada.gc.ca/pam_archives/index.php?fuseaction=genitem.displayEcopies&lang=eng&rec_nbr=2004898&title=War%20diaries%20-%201st%20Tunnelling%20Company,%20Canadian%20Engineers%20=%20Journal%20de%20guerre%20-%201re%20Compagnie%20de%20sapeurs-mineurs,%20G%C3%A9nie%20canadien.&ecopy=e001452568.

152. *CODR*, microform sequence 85, p. 697.

153. For context, see Mateusz Borganowicz, "'The White Man's War?'" in *Re-imagining the First World War*, ed. Anna Branach-Kallas and Nelly Strehlau (Newcastle upon Tyne: Cambridge Scholars Press, 2015), 362–78.

154. Thanks to Marthe Brown, archivist, Laurentian University, who brought the undated, handwritten list from the Anglican Diocese of Moosonee archival fonds to our attention. She thinks the list was compiled circa 1930 by the principal of the school, Reverend J.T. Griffin. Brown also supplied biographical information on school attendance by the Indigenous soldiers from the James Bay area, based on the Diocese of Moosonee fonds.

155. Winegard, *For King and Kanata*.

156. The log of the Anglican Diocese of Moosonee reveals the possible influence of teachers and religious leaders in the following entries:

1916 August 7th: Rev & Mrs. Haythornthwaite left for the line [the northern end of the railway line] also a party of recruits for the war.

Oct. 16th Mr Jamieson & a party of recruits left for the line this morning

1917 May 23rd 15 men in 4 canoes left for the line

June 26 - Mr Wilson & Capt. 'Frieskley' [??] left for the line

July 23 - A large party had left for the line

Aug 30 - Bertie Morrison of Rupert House [now Waskaganish] left for the line. The latter is a recruit.

157. Duncan Campbell Scott, "The Canadian Indians and the Great War," *Canada in the Great World War* (Toronto: United Publishers of Canada, 1919), appendix 1, 3:296–97. This appendix gives a detailed appreciation of Indigenous people's contributions.

158. See Scott, "Canadian Indians," 3:318–19.

159. *CODR*, microform sequence 30, p. 67.

160. *CODR*, microform sequence 80, p. 565.

161. Positive comments appear in the CLIP collection (see, for examples, chapter 6) and in letters published in the *Porcupine Advance* (see the discussion of the Forestry Corps above). The Canadian Great War Project (http://www.canadiangreatwarproject.com/searches/gwpSearch.asp) also provides many examples such as the exchanges between Private Reuben Pettifer and the Magladery brothers, Thomas and William, both officers.

162. *Porcupine Advance*, 2 October 1918.

163. Bishop, *Canadian Y.M.C.A*, 227-35.

164. Available in CLIP; the printed version misspells Jim Swan as Him Savin.

165. Bishop, *Canadian Y.M.C.A.*, 234–36, 334–35.

166. The subject of VD is controversial, but when we spoke with those whose relatives had served in the Canadian forces, we had surprising responses. Some responded with the cliché that "boys will be boys." One offered a little grin and comment, "so he played around and had some fun." Yet others suggested, "oh, he was a bit bad," but "a hundred years has passed." We have thus chosen to use soldiers' real names when discussing their medical histories. Prominent military historians, such as Tim Cook, have done the same in writing about World War I.

167. Cook, *Shock Troops*, 176.

168. Donna Blair (granddaughter), email to author, 10 December 2016.

169. Jeffrey A. Keshen, *Saints, Sinners and Soldiers* (Vancouver: UBC Press, 2004), 134–35.

170. Jean Lye, "War Brides 1914-1918 from *Sudbury Star*," unpublished typescript housed in Mary Shantz Room, Sudbury Public Library. Cited hereafter as Lye's list.

171. Lye's list and Hough's service file at Library and Archives Canada (LAC). Since Hough was a Lieutenant, he lacked a regimental number. Unless otherwise specified, subsequent biographies will combine information from the LAC with Lye's findings.

172. Lye's list.

173. John McLean, Letter to his mother, 17 October 1916, CLIP.

174. Bonnie Lachapelle, a granddaughter of James and Lily McBain, kindly shared documentation about her grandparents when we visited her home in Sudbury on 4 August 2017. When James died in 1983, they had two sons, one daughter, eight grandchildren, and eleven great-grandchildren.

175. Bird and Davies, *Canadian Forestry Corps*, 50.

176. References to the team appeared in newspapers, but Captain Doug Newman, RCAF Heritage Officer, 22 Wing North Bay, supplied much information. See his fine summary in "100th Anniversary of North Bay's National Hockey Team," *Bay Today*, 28 November 2016, https://www. baytoday.ca/local-news/100th-anniversary-of-north-bays-national-hockey-team-475538.

177. Robert Gordon Brown entered the following in his diary on 12 April 1917 (from CLIP): "Ammunition is being packed up every day on horses—packs to carry eight rounds are strapped to saddle. Each driver looks after two pack horses—riding when packs are empty and walking when full. The roads are so bad that this is only way to get ammunition to advanced positions of guns. Even so, horses die every day..."

178. Reuben Pettifer, Letter to W. Magladery, 18 July 1915, reprinted in CLIP.

179. Captain Thomas Magladery, letter printed in *New Liskeard Speaker*, 11 February 1916, Canadian Great War Project, http://www.canadiangreatwarproject.com/transcripts/transcriptDisplay. asp?Type=L&Id=447.

180. Buse and Mount, *Come on Over*, 13.

181. *Porcupine Advance*, "159th Battalion's Far-Famed Mascots," 1 September 1932.

182. Durham, Memoirs, Durham collection, Sault Ste. Marie Public Library Archives, pp. 157–60.

183. Jack Munroe, *Mopping Up!* (New York: H.K. Fly, 1918), https://archive.org/details/ moppingup00munrgoog. Wayne McKay wrote a play about Munroe, entitled *With a Strong Arm*; see a review by the *Cape Breton Post*, "The Epic Life of Jack Monroe Makes for Powerful Theatre," 18 February 2010, http://www.capebretonpost.com/opinion/columnists/2010/2/18/the-epic-life-of-jack-monroe-makes-for-p-782388.html. It played twice in Elk Lake. Regarding Munroe's boxing, see *Cape Breton Post*, "Jack Munroe and the 100-round Fight of the Century," 6 January 2012, http://www.capebretonpost.com/news/local/2012/1/6/jack-munroe-and-the-100-round-fight-of-t-2856969.html.

184. Munroe, *Mopping Up!*, 19.

185. Munroe, *Mopping Up!*, 39.

186. Munroe, *Mopping Up!*, 40.

187. Munroe, *Mopping Up!*, 47.

188. Munroe, *Mopping Up!*, 55–56.

189. Munroe, *Mopping Up!*, 58.

190. When Munroe arrived in Timmins, the newspaper exclaimed, on 30 May 1917, "Pte. Jack Munroe Welcomed Back to North Land: Hero of the Princess Pats with the Government Party making Inspection of Land for Returned Soldiers." It described a tumultuous reception attended by hundreds, featuring the Italian band playing patriotic songs. The mayor, board of trade, and other professionals turned out to greet the "pioneer-hero of the north." Munroe noted the city's growth, and told his audience that he favoured conscription as a fairer method to solve the shortage of soldiers at the front. For a while, Munroe worked inspecting land for returnee soldiers, who he thought would help open the North. Soon he would be promoted to lieutenant and become a recruiter. According to the *Porcupine Advance*, on 30 September 1917 Munroe participated actively in the drive to recruit more forestry workers.

191.   Sarah Glassford, "Women's Mobilization for War (Canada)," *1914-1918-online, International Encyclopedia of the First World War*, ed. Ute Daniel, Peter Gatrell, Oliver Janz, Heather Jones, Jennifer Keene, Alan Kramer, and Bill Nasson (Berlin: Freie Universität Berlin, Berlin, 22 April 2015), doi:10.15463/ie1418.10620.

192.   Linda Ambrose's chapter on knitting for the war in *For Home and Country: The Centennial History of the Women's Institutes in Ontario* (Federated Women's Institutes of Canada, 1996) cites the example of a Manitoulin Island branch.

193.   Philip H. Morris, *The Canadian Patriotic Fund: A Record of Its Activities from 1914 to 1919* (n.p., 1919). The figures in the discussion that follows come from this report.

194.   Desmond Morton, in *Fight or Pay: Soldiers' Families in the Great War* (Vancouver: UBC, 2008) provides an overview and some case studies of the fund'use and criteria.

195.   Robert Rutherford, *Hometown Horizons: Local Responses to Canada's Great War* (Vancouver: UBC Press, 2004); the study compares Regina, Guelph, and Trois Rivieres.

196.   Morris, *Canadian Patriotic Fund*, 211.

197.   Sudbury town council minutes, 21 December 1918, accessed at city hall.

198.   Bohdan S. Kordan, in *Prisoners of War: Internment in Canada during the Great War* (Montreal: McGill-Queen's University Press, 2002) focusses mainly on western Canadian camps, though it acknowledges that Kapuskasing amounted to a punishment camp.

199.   Most authors use the number 8,579 from the report of Colonel Otter, Director of Internment Operations. His addition was out by a thousand. His report is reprinted in Lubomyr Luciuk, *In Fear of the Barbed Wire Fence: Canada's First National Internment Operations and the Ukrainian Canadians, 1914–1920* (n.p.: Kastan Press, 2001), 123–44; list on 128.

200.   Under the title "That Never Happened in Sault Ste. Marie," Beaudette gathered a substantial collection of documents from newspapers and archives relating to 1914 and 1915, though the depot did not close until 1918. Her findings served as the basis for placing a trilingual (English, French, Ukrainian) plaque about the internment at the local museum. The city apologized to the local Canadian-Ukrainian community in 2008.

201.   A benign view of the leadership of the camp is offered by a grandchild of Colonel Frederick Clarke, the first commandant of the camp, "A Veteran of the Great War," October 2004, Fairlawn United Church (Toronto), http://www.fairlawnchurch.ca/wp-content/uploads/2014/10/ww1-FFClarke.pdf

202.   Cited in Luciuk, *In Fear of the Barbed Wire Fence*, 132–33.

203.   Robert H. Coats, "The Alien Enemy in Canada: Internment Operations," *Canada in the Great World War* (Toronto: United Publishers of Canada, n.d.), 2:155.

204.   Bohdan S. Kordan, *Canada, the Great War, and the Enemy Alien Experience* (Montreal: McGill-Queen's University Press, 2016), 126.

205.   For example, Alex Ostapchuk and four others from Sturgeon Falls petitioned General Otter for the return of the $368.35 taken from them when they were originally arrested. No restitution was made.

206.   Cited in Luciuk, *In Fear of the Barbed Wire Fence*, 20.

207.   Kordan, *Enemy Alien Experience*, 227, provides further examples.

208.   An odd book which must be used with caution is Dominique Villeneuve's edited collection, *Heritage by Default, 1914–1920: Canada's First National Internment Operations Made Kapuskasing Heir to a Town and an Experimental Farm* (self- publ., 2014) because it mixes historical documents with letters he created for a novel about a part real, part mythical German immigrant family.

209.   Kordan, *Enemy Alien Experience*, 107.

210. Kordan, *Enemy Alien Experience*, 147.

211. Luciuk, *Fear of the Barbed Wire Fence*, 24.

212. Kordan, *Enemy Alien Experience*, 160.

213. Kordan, *Enemy Alien Experience*, 212.

214. Kordan, *Enemy Alien Experience*, 240.

215. This viewpoint is reinforced by some of the same letters reprinted in Maheu, *They Stepped into Immortality*. Maheu thoroughly researched each name, employed the service files, and presented warts as well as heroics.

216. Charlotte Gray, "Letters from the Front," in Mark Reid, ed., *Canada's Great War Album* (Toronto: Harper, 2014).

217. *CODR*, microform sequence 50, p. 1163.

218. Bruce Wood, "The Ripple Effect of Shell Shock," *Globe and Mail*, 10 November 2017, L6.

219. Unfortunately, documentation on soldiers with surnames alphabetically after "Sims" has disappeared, and is not available in the *CODR*.

220. *CODR*, microform sequence 41, 635; microform sequence 53, 327.

221. C*ODR*, microform sequence 52, p. 375.

222. *CODR*, microform sequence 35, p. 1107.

223. *CODR*, microform sequence 50, p. 309.

224. *CODR*, microform sequence 6, p. 979.

225. CODR, microform sequence 49, p. 249; microform sequence 11, p. 491.

226. *CODR*, microform sequence 7, p. 247.

227. *CODR*, microform sequence 13, p. 123.

228. *CODR*, microform sequence 31, p. 345.

229. *CODR*, microform sequence 3, p. 549.

230. *CODR*, microform sequence 49, p. 363. Wilford Henry Holmes and Charles Holmes were probably brothers. Wilford named his mother, Mrs. J.H. Holmes, as next-of-kin. Charles named his father, James Holmes. Both parents lived in Manitowaning when Wilford and Charles enlisted.

231. *CODR*, microform sequence 38, p. 391 (George); microform sequence 10, p. 229 (Bishop); microform sequence 71, p. 767 (Morrow); microform sequence 77, p. 7 (McIntyre); 30, p. 815 (Duquette).

232. *CODR*, microform sequence 16, p. 471.

233. *CODR*, microform sequence 22, p. 535.

234. It is not clear whether Thomas and Martin Brennan were brothers. In his attestation paper, Thomas cited his next-of-kin simply as "Mrs. Brennan"; he was born in Pembroke, Ontario, in 1895. Martin also cited his next-of-kin as his mother but identified her as "Mrs. John Brennan." Martin was born in Sherbrooke, Quebec, in 1893, but the family might have moved from Quebec to Sherbrooke between the two births and before moving to North Bay.

235. *CODR*, microform sequence 46, p. 593.

236. *CODR*, microform sequence 11, p. 309.

237. *CODR*, microform sequence 14, p. 813.

238. *CODR*, microform sequence 26, p. 359.

239. *CODR*, microform sequence 50, p. 281.

240. *CODR*, microform sequence 25, p. 89.

241. *CODR*, microform sequence 48, p. 365.

242. *CODR*, microform sequence 44, p. 149.

243. CODR, microform sequence 17, p. 545.

244. *CODR*, microform sequence 30, p. 801.

245. Granatstein, *The Greatest Victory: Canada's 100 Days* (Toronto: Oxford University Press, 2014).

246. *CODR*, microform sequence 36, p. 555.

247. *CODR*, microform sequence 91, p. 275.

248. "Armistice Day Becomes Remembrance Day: November 11," Canadian War Museum, http://www.warmuseum.ca/cwm/exhibitions/remember/1931remembrance_e.shtml.

249. Official programs can be found in the War Collection, Greater Sudbury Public Library.

250. For the chronology, see "North Bay War Memorial," "We Will Remember": War Monuments in Canada, https://www.cdli.ca/monuments/on/northbay.htm.

251. From the official program in North Bay Public Library archives.

252. Many such plaques and honour rolls contain errors, often caused by the tendency to want to claim persons as having come from the local area (thereby demonstrating how much the community had contributed to the major war). Other errors stem from the difficulties of accessing records, acceptance of relatives' claims, or simply a lack of fact-checking. Building monuments is difficult and costly; and it is tricky to connect individuals to particular places unless clear and consistent criteria are employed.

253. Alan MacLeod, *Remembered in Bronze and Stone: Canada's Great War Memorial Statuary* (Victoria: Heritage House, 2016), 117–21.

254. MacLeod, *Remembered in Bronze*, 120–21.

255. "Remember This? How the Cenotaph Came to Be," *Soo Today.com*, 20 December 2015; based on materials from Sault Ste. Marie Library Archives.

256. See "Manitoulin District Cenotaph," "We Will Remember": War Monuments in Canada, https://www.cdli.ca/monuments/on/manitou.htm.

257. Maheu, *They Stepped into Immortality*, preface.

258. An exception is Tim Laye's "Ontario War Memorials" at https://www.ontariowarmemorials.blogspot.com; over 6,000 war memorials exist in Canada.

259. Letter to Mrs. William Walker, Livingstone Creek, date 14 November 1923; copy in War Collection, Thessalon Public Library.

260. MacLeod, *Remembered in Bronze and Stone*, 117.

261. Paul Lantz, "Moosonee Moments," https://www.paullantz.com/Moosonee/Moosonee-Monuments/i-G35M2NX.

262. *Toronto Star*, Obituary of Lorne Nicholson, 18 November 1918.

263. The monument also misspells as "Rielly" the surname of Irvine Reilly (787615), another sailor who enlisted in December 1915 and died 11 May 1917. He too came from Mattawa, while his father lived in Creighton Mine near Sudbury.

264. See, for instance, the discussion of William Merrifield in chapter 4 of this volume.

265. A second volume is in preparation.

266.	In Sudbury, military heritage is sometimes overlooked. For example, the commemorative volume *Greater Sudbury, 1883–2008* (Sudbury, 2008) includes not one military person among the 100 featured important persons. Perhaps the multicultural nature of the work force of Sudbury compared to the British background of most Manitoulin Islanders and the Inco management in Copper Cliff (who enlisted in high numbers) played a role.

267.	Based on service file with more information on Byce at the website of the Strathroy-Caradoc Lions Club, https://strathroycaradoclions.ca/index.php/byce-henry-charles/

268.	Durham, "Memorial Day," fond TED 5, Durham papers, Sault Ste. Marie Public Library Archives.

269.	CLIP, letter to mother. Similarly R.C. Pettifer wrote to W. Magladery on 18 July 1915, "This is a very nice country, but I would rather have Canada. I would not live here 'on a bet.'"

Index